Social Work Theories In Context

D0057576

Also by Karen Healy:

Social Work Practices: Contemporary Perspectives on Change

Social Work Theories In Context: Creating Frameworks for Practice

Karen Healy

First published 2005 by
PALGRAVE MACMILLAN
Houndmills, Basingstoke, Hampshire RG21 6XS and
175 Fifth Avenue, New York, N.Y. 10010
Companies and representatives throughout the world

PALGRAVE MACMILLAN is the global academic imprint of the Palgrave
Macmillan division of St. Martin's Press LLC and of Palgrave Macmillan Ltd.
Macmillan® is a registered trademark in the United States, United Kingdom
and other countries. Palgrave is a registered trademark in the European
Union and other countries.

ISBN-13: 978 1–4039–1622–8 paperback
ISBN-10: 1–4039–1622–5 paperback

Logging, pulping and manufacturing processes are expected to contorm to
the environmental regulations of the country of origin.

This book is printed on paper suitable for recycling and made from fully
managed and sustained forest sources.

A catalogue record for this book is available from the British Library.

A catalog record for this book is available from the Library of Congress.
Library of Congress Catalog Card Number: 2005041951

10   9   8   7   6   5
14   13   12   11   10   09   08   07

Printed in China

For Dennis

Contents

List of Figures and Tables

Figures

Table

Acknowledgements

One of the privileges of being an author is the opportunity to formally thank the people who have supported one's work. I thank my colleagues at the University of Sydney and, more recently, at the University of Queensland, for their interest in this project and for stimulating conversations along the way. My special thanks to Dr Gabrielle Meagher, from Political Economy at the University of Sydney, for being such a thoughtful, stimulating, and witty research companion and friend. I thank Robert Bland from the University of Tasmania and Fran Conway from Curtin University in Western Australia for their encouragement of this project. I acknowledge Colin Peile who, as my PhD supervisor many years ago, drummed home the importance of logical and grounded argument. In all that I write I appreciate his influence upon me. I want also to acknowledge the social work students and the many practising social workers who attended my 'theory refresher' seminars. Student and practitioner questions and insights were valuable in helping me to clarify my thinking about this project.

I thank my colleagues from the 'real' worlds of social service delivery, especially Anne Hampshire, from Mission Australia, and Karyn Walsh, from Project Micah, for promoting critical thinking about the use and development of knowledge in practice, and my colleagues in Scandinavia, especially Siv Oltedal, Rolv Lyngstad, Lisbeth Lund and Gunn Strand Hutchinson from the University of Bodu in Norway and Synnöve Karvinen from the University of Helsinki in Finland for stimulating discussions about international comparative social work.

Throughout this book, I use practical case studies to illustrate and develop my arguments. I gratefully acknowledge the following social workers for assistance in providing, or developing, these case studies.

- Pauline Coulton and Lyn Krimmer from Cranebrook Child and Family Health Services, Wentworth Area Health Services, Sydney.

- Barbara Squires, Annette Micheaux, Henrietta Foulds and Ally Du Pree of The Benevolent Society, Sydney.

- Sue Green of the Aboriginal Support and Aboriginal Studies Program Centre at The University of New South Wales.

I thank Catherine Gray, commissioning editor for Palgrave, for 'getting' what this project is about. Finally, for friendship and care I thank Julie Conway, Brian, Rachael, and Khloe Healy, and Dennis Longstaff. This book is dedicated to Dennis for his faith, love, and forbearance, particularly in the final days of this work when just about every aspect of our lives seemed to be put on hold. Dedicating a social work book might not be everyone's idea of a loving gesture, but this is what it is.

Preface

I wrote this book to give social work practitioners, students and educators a foothold in the diverse and often perplexing contexts of, and theories for, practice. Throughout my career, first as a student social worker, then as a social work practitioner, and now as a researcher and educator, I have maintained a strong interest in the philosophical foundations of social work practices, particularly how these foundations are expressed and transformed in direct practice. My first book, *Social Work Practices* (Healy, 2000), aimed to expand critical approaches to social work by recognizing the diverse ways social workers go about achieving practice goals associated with empowering and critical practice, such as enhancing service user participation and promoting cooperative action. In short, I argued that there are many ways of being a change agent and that some of the established critical approaches to practice obscured this diversity. In this book, I aim to further my project on the philosophical foundations of social work practices by outlining the key ideas underpinning the contemporary organizations of, and approaches to, practice. If there is a core message to this book, it is this: by understanding the ideas that underpin our institutional contexts and formal theory base we can critically use them and, where necessary, change them to achieve the values and goals to which we are committed.

By introducing you, the reader, to the philosophical foundations and the historical and geographical origins of key practice approaches, I hope to enhance your capacity not only to use theory, but also to contribute to formal theory creation. Despite the persistent gulf between theory and practice, I am convinced that many practitioners also seek to understand and develop theories of professional practice. However, many are alienated by the extent to which social work philosophies and theories are separated from, or even pitted against, the institutional contexts of social work practice. Indeed, this book grows, in part, out the 'theory refresher' seminars that I began conducting for social workers in 2001. The workshops aim to introduce practitioners to formal theories for social work practice. More than one thousand social workers have attended these workshops and have contributed to my thinking about the uses and limits of social work theory in practice, especially in relation to the profound influence of context on shaping social work purpose. Incidentally, the strong interest in these workshops has also strengthened my conviction that social workers do 'do' theory!

In this book, I bring together a critical introduction to both theories of the direct practice and the ideas shaping the institutional contexts of practice. This is because I regard social work as a deeply contextual activity that varies enormously across practice contexts. By integrating analysis of context and theory I aim to contribute to increased opportunities for social workers to develop theories *in situ*. Discussion of social work theories for practice and the contexts of social work practice usually occurs in separate domains, resulting in frustration both for those charged with formal theory building and for practitioners. The difficulties social workers experience in fitting the 'square pegs' of their deeply contextual practice experiences into the 'round holes' of social work theories leads to a view that theory is something done in universities that has little application in the everyday world of practice. Thus a 'secret society of social workers' emerges guided by the credo that one 'throws the theory out of the window once one leaves university'! Not that anyone could blame them for resisting theoretical frameworks that appear irrelevant or unhelpful to the urgent challenges and issues they face in practice. This sense of alienation is deepened when academic commentators use theories as a weapon for chastising workers as insufficiently committed to a particular theoretical ideal or not duly rigorous in their application of formal knowledge. Our theories for practice are the poorer for the stand-off between the world of formal social work theory building and the world of social work practice. One way we can promote dialogue between these two 'worlds' is by recognizing the profound influence of context in the use and development of theories for practice.

I consider that all practising social workers are social work theorists in that each of us constructs understandings that guide us in identifying who and what should be the focus of our practice and how we should proceed. This book aims to open dialogue between social work practitioners and formal social work theory by outlining the philosophical foundations, historical and geographical origins, practical applications, and strengths and limitations of five contemporary theories of practice.

I hope also that this book will help to prepare students for the 'realities' of social work practices by highlighting the interaction between institutional contexts and the formal professional practice base in creating our practice purpose and practice options. Social work education programmes often do a great job of introducing students to the formal professional base of practice. In professional courses students learn much about the value base of practice, basic skills and formal theoretical frameworks for social work practice. But to use this base in practice we must also be able to 'read' our institutional context, particularly its formal and informal goals and practices. Of course, I do not mean that social workers should then simply acquiesce to these organizational dictates, but that to be an effective practitioner and, certainly to be an effective change agent, we should understand the institutional context within which we are working. By merely socializing students into the formal professional practice base, without also linking this to a capacity to read their institutional context, we invite social workers to run 'headlong' into and against their practice context. This is a recipe for burnout and cynicism as practitioners quickly become disillusioned with the formal base of the profession as 'OK in theory' but not much help in practice.

Given that most new social workers graduate to junior positions with limited official organisational power, their capacity to read and work within these organizational constraints (even as they seek to achieve institutional change) is a basic survival skill and, I argue, vital to sustaining and enhancing our capacities for change practices. I speak here from personal experience. My first two years as a graduate social worker were extremely difficult as I was confronted with the complexities of clients' lives and of the organizational contexts of social work. Although I was well trained to critically analyse both my organizational context and the factors, especially structural factors, impacting on service users' lives, my understanding of how to bring these different sets of analyses to bear to inform action in specific situations was weak. In addition, while these institutions professed humane values, I encountered a great deal of hostility, mostly within my organizational contexts but sometimes also from colleagues and clients, about the humanist and contestant ideals that I, in my sincere but naïve approach, was seeking to 'share' or even 'impose'.

Having survived my trial by fire, I became increasingly aware of the uses but also the limits of the formal base of social work for helping me achieve change in practice, at the same time I became more attuned to the extent to which the institutional contexts in which I was working also provided opportunities for, and limits to, the realization of the humanitarian values to which social workers are committed. In becoming more cognizant of the deeply contextual nature of social work practice, I was also surprised to find that a great deal of change work was already going on (often quietly and surreptitiously) within the practice contexts in which I was working. Much of this change work is unrecognized by, and unwritten in, formal social work theory. Perhaps it is not even possible to write it, but, at the very least, we can approach formal theories for practice with an understanding that, probably at best, they provide partial and limited frameworks for practice. Social workers actively construct their frameworks for practice and formal theories provide a thread rather than an entire context for practice.

Social workers practice in a broad range of contexts with people who experience a diversity of concerns and oppressions. Part of social workers' brief is to be agents of change with clients, within our organizational contexts and within society more generally. I hope that this book will further social workers' capacities to understand, and contribute to, the profession's capacity to use its institutional contexts and formal theory base to create change in favour of the vulnerable populations with whom we work. Creating change of this kind should be our primary and unifying concern.

1

Practising Social Work: Why Context Matters

This book is about the ideas that shape the institutional contexts and the practices of social work. Social work is a profession that varies enormously by historical, geographical and institutional contexts. Indeed, within each practice interaction, social workers negotiate their purpose and their practice with others, including clients, employing agencies and society at large. In negotiating our practices, we may draw on our formal practice base, which includes our values and the theories for practice developed within the profession. But this is not enough. Because social work practices are profoundly shaped by our practice environments, it is important, also, that we are able to 'read' the ideas that shape our institutional contexts. This book aims to outline the discourses and theories that shape the ways in which client needs and social workers' practices are constructed in contemporary practice environments. This analysis is intended to extend our capacities to understand how these ideas construct our practices and to use and develop them to realize our values and goals in the diverse contexts of social work practices. In this first chapter, I shall focus on why context matters in practice.

Why Context Matters

Social workers are guided by their practice purpose, which varies considerably across institutional contexts and among practice situations. Many factors contribute to our sense of practice purpose, including the philosophies and ideas shaping our institutional context, our formal professional base, employer and client expectations, and our individual frameworks for practice. Sometimes these different factors 'line up' and social workers experience consistency between their context, their formal professional base and individual framework for practice. Often, however, they do not

1

and, instead, social workers must negotiate conflicts between their formal professional base and various client and employer expectations.

Social workers are well aware of the importance of context in service users' lives. Indeed, understanding, and responding to, the 'person in their environment' is a guiding credo of modern professional social work. However, less attention has been paid to how we might understand and respond to our practice environment, especially the philosophies and ideas underpinning our institutional contexts, as an integral part of direct practice. For example, courses on the institutional contexts of social work, that is the policy and organizational environments, are often taught separately from professional practice. Similarly, theories for professional practice are often written about, and taught, as though the social worker's institutional context were minimally relevant, or even something to overcome, in practising social work. In this book, I argue that our institutional contexts must be understood as integral to how we practise. The main purpose of this book is to provide a comprehensive overview of the key ideas and concepts shaping human service institutions, and what opportunities and challenges these ideas create for realizing the humanistic goals and values to which social workers are committed.

Of course, the meaning and practice of all professional activities – indeed all human activities – varies by context; however, social work is even more variable than most for three reasons. First, it lacks a common knowledge base and agreed ways of building knowledge. This contrasts with established, or élite, professions such as medicine, law and engineering, each of which has a unitary knowledge base grounded in positivist, or scientific, ways of knowing. Thus, for example, professional engineers share many common scientific concepts and knowledge-building methods, grounded in scientific understanding, that are unchanged by institutional and even geographical location. By contrast, social workers are divided over questions about how to create knowledge for practice, with researchers debating the merits and limits of scientific ways of knowing for understanding social work practice (see Chapter 5, this volume). Moreover, many of the concepts social workers use are unique to specific institutional locations. For instance, the knowledge and skills base of a social worker in a statutory child protection authority differs radically from that of a social worker involved in community development work on a public housing estate. Even the way social workers engage practically with common concepts, such as 'social justice', varies markedly by institutional location. Again, the social worker in a child protection authority is likely to have a different interpretation of how this term is expressed from the social worker doing community work on a public housing estate.

Second, in contrast to other human service professions, such as nursing and education, social work does not have a primary institutional base.

So while these other professions may also lack a positivist foundation for their practice, the presence of a primary service context – the hospital or the school – provides a unifying foundation for knowledge development and use. By contrast, social workers cannot be said to have a primary field or organization of practice. For example, social workers work in a wide variety of fields, including mainstream health and welfare services and extending to citizen advocacy services and community development agencies. The social service agencies in which we practise vary in a number of ways, including: size – from no paid employees to institutions with tens of thousands of employees; purpose – including the implementation of statutory law or religious mission to client-directed service provision; management structure – from client-managed to corporate structures. The primary institutions where social workers practise vary a great deal by nation even among the post-industrial countries (see Hutchinson *et al.*, 2001).

Third, the primary task of social work varies by practice context. Across the different practice contexts, the primary task of social work is extremely varied and may include, but is not limited to, any one, or combination of, the following tasks:

- risk management;
- implementation of statutory law;
- support and advocacy;
- therapeutic intervention;
- community education;
- community capacity building;
- research;
- policy development, implementation, and evaluation;
- social service administration.

As we can see from this list, not only do social workers engage in a broad range of activities, also our core task in one context may be incompatible with our primary activity in another. For example, a primary focus on the implementation of statutory law is likely to be incompatible with a community capacity-building role. In addition, while social workers may have some discretion about how they execute their primary task, they cannot usually determine the nature of the task; rather this is determined by the institutional context and, more specifically, by their role description and employer and client rights and expectations. Thus, when constructing our sense of purpose in social work practice we must be mindful of the primary tasks assigned to us within our practice contexts.

The deeply contextual nature of social work differentiates it from other professions. Our professional practice foundations – our knowledge, purpose and skills bases – are substantially constructed in, and through, the environments in which we work. For this reason, enhancing our capacity to understand, analyse and respond to our institutional contexts must be an integral part of our frameworks for professional practice. Through understanding our context, we can both recognize how our practice is shaped by context and how we might act as agents of change both within, and in relation to, our context. As Fook (2002, p. 162) asserts:

> Reframing our practice as contextual ... means we reframe our practice as working *with* environments, rather than working *despite* environments. We see ourselves as part of a context, ourselves responsible for aspects of that context. In this way, we see possibilities for change, for creating *different microclimates within broader contexts*.

In short, we need to take seriously the impact of institutional context for shaping our practice approaches, our knowledge base, our sense of purpose and even of ourselves as social workers. Yet we should also recognize that we are active participants in, and creators of, the contexts and frameworks through which we practise.

Constructing Social Work Purpose: A Dynamic Approach

Like other professionals, social workers are involved in purposeful activities. However, in contrast to other professions, the deeply contextual and varied character of social work practices means that, in each practice encounter, we are involved in constructing and negotiating social work practice. The dynamic model of social work which I have developed (see Figure 1.1) outlines four components through which social work practices are constructed. These are:

● **The institutional context of practice** This refers to the laws, public and organizational policies, and accepted practices shaping the institutions where social workers are located. The institutional context provides the terms of reference for the social work task; that is, what you, as a social worker, are formally employed to do. For instance, a social worker in a mental health authority may be tasked to implement statutory mental health legislation and to build community-based resources, such as housing opportunities and social support networks, to enable people with mental health issues to be supported by the community. Health

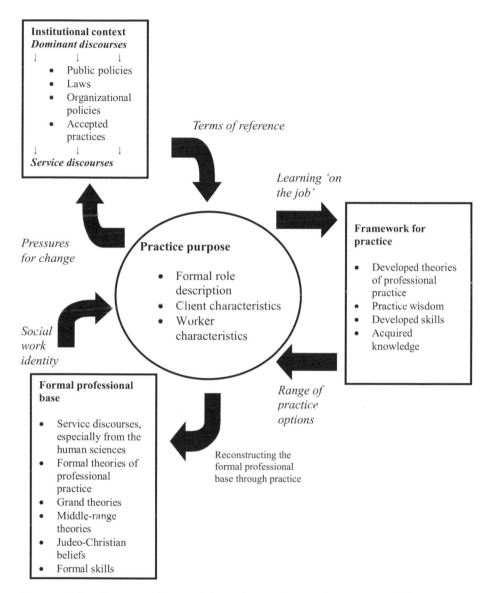

Figure 1.1   Constructing social work practice: a dynamic model

and welfare institutions are sites of competing ideas about the nature of client needs and the optimal ways of assisting service users. In this book I will use a discourse analysis approach to consider competing ideas that shape the institutional contexts of social work practice. We will consider the dominant discourses of biomedicine, neo-classical economics and law, the service discourses associated with the human sciences of psychology and the social sciences, and the alternative service discourses associated with consumer rights discourses and spirituality and religion in social services contexts.

- **The formal professional base of social work** This foundation is developed from a range of philosophical perspectives, theories about and for practice, Judeo-Christian values and beliefs, and the formal skills of social work. It is disseminated through the formal channels of social work education and academic publications. Professional social work education programmes are primarily concerned with introducing and socializing students to the core values, knowledge and skills of the profession. Theories for practice provide a key intellectual component of the professional base of social work. In this book, I will consider five formal theories for practice that are especially relevant to contemporary practice contexts.

- **Our sense of practice purpose** In practice, our formal purpose is shaped by the interactions between our institutional contexts and by our professional base. For example, while a social worker may be employed to provide rehabilitation services to people with physical disabilities, our formal professional base, such as our values and theoretical perspectives, will inform how we construct and carry out this purpose. Moreover, within each specific practice encounter, our sense of practice is further refined by the interaction between the specific activities or tasks we are assigned to undertake within our work team, the clients' characteristics and needs (as they have been expressed and constructed at the specific practice site), and the viewpoints, understandings and capacities we as social workers bring to the practice interaction. As I will highlight in practice and reflection exercises throughout the book, it is especially important that social workers are sensitive to the cultural and linguistic characteristics of the clients with whom they work and that they consider how the various perspectives presented in the book may enhance or limit practice with culturally and linguistically diverse populations.

- **Framework for practice** This refers to the amalgam of formal knowledge and skills and informal 'on-the-job' knowledge and skills developed by social workers in practice. This fusion includes formal theoretical and substantive knowledge as well as tacit, or difficult-to-articulate, knowledge that can be built up through repeated exposure to practice situations. For example, an experienced child protection worker may develop a strong capacity to predict situations of high risk drawing in part on formal risk assessment tools but also through practice-based knowledge of the kinds of situations that are likely to lead to negative outcomes for children.

This dynamic model of social work (Figure 1.1) recognizes that the components of institutional context, formal professional base, purpose and the workers' practice framework influence each other. Let's consider the interaction among these elements. The institutional context, particularly laws and public policies, shapes the key obligations borne by social workers and, in some instances, by service users. Yet, as social workers we can also use our experiences in implementing institutional policies and practices to advocate for change in them. For example, a social worker in mental health services charged with finding suitable accommodation for service users may also work with policy makers and politicians to initiate more effective and humane ways of meeting the housing needs of people with mental health issues.

For many social workers, the formal base of the profession profoundly shapes their sense of purpose in practice. The formal professional base, especially shared values, can also help to forge a common identification among social workers despite the enormous diversity of practice contexts. For example, Banks (2001, p. 37), identifies four first-order principles that are widely endorsed in many national professional codes and in the practice literature. These are: respect for and promotion of individuals' right to self-determination; promotion of welfare or well-being; equality; and distributive justice. However, the formal professional base is not only something that is transmitted to social workers from the formal institutions of social work research and education, but also something that social workers can challenge and transform from their practice experience. The capacity of practising social workers to contribute to the formal base of social work has been limited, in part because of the differences between the relatively informal ways knowledge is built and transmitted in practice and the formal requirements for knowledge production demanded by academic and professional institutions. In recent years, practice research centres and research partnerships between universities and service provider institutions or individual service providers have been established to promote dialogue between the academy and research institutions (where knowledge is further developed), and practice institutions have been established to enable social workers to speak to practice contexts (see McCartt-Hess and Mullen, 1995). Further initiatives of these types are required to promote deep and rich dialogue between the formal professional base and the diverse range of social work practices, and to ensure that our theories of professional practice are relevant and useful for explaining and guiding practice.

The third and central element of the framework is the practice purpose. This is often an area of tension and considerable conflict, for some, in social work practice. Some (lucky) social workers practise in environments where their frameworks and their contexts are consistent. For example, a social worker who is strongly committed to anti-oppressive theory is likely to find that employment in an advocacy agency is consistent with their professional framework, but that employment in a statutory authority presents considerably more challenges for them. Most of us are likely to experience some tension between the sense of purpose constructed by our practice context and our professional base. In part this is because, as I shall show in this book, the sets of ideas dominating most mainstream health and welfare agencies are markedly different from the discourses underpinning human service professions in social work. However, if we can understand these differences, they can be a source of creative tension and inspiration for change in many practice contexts.

The final element of the model is the professional framework for practice. This is the framework that we as social workers use 'on the job' and which we construct from information and directions gained from the other three elements, including our formal professional base, but is not limited to them. As social workers become more advanced in their practice they are often able to draw on a richer framework for practice than is possible for novices. This strong, and to some extent intuitive, understanding of one's practice context allows the advanced professional to handle complex and uncertain situations with confidence and competence (Fook *et al.*, 2000, p. 148). Advanced practitioners can use their unique professional framework to expand their sense of purpose beyond that which might be immediately apparent either from the formal professional knowledge base or from within their organizational context (see *ibid.*).

Discourses of Health and Welfare Institutions

In this book, I use a discursive approach to identify and analyse the key philosophies and ideas that shape social work practices within health and welfare institutions. Parton (1994, p. 13) defines discourses as 'structures of knowledge, claims and practices through we understand, explain and decide things ... they are frameworks or grids of social organisations that make some actions possible whilst precluding others'. From a poststructural view, discourses are the sets of language practices that shape our thoughts, actions and even our identities. In the first half of this book, I will show how a discourse analysis approach can illuminate the assumptions that drive many health and welfare organizations and which are often the sources of considerable tension and conflict within them. I will consider three sets of discourses. These are: the dominant discourses of biomedicine, economics and law, which profoundly shape mainstream institutional contexts of health and welfare; the service discourses drawn from the human sciences, especially psychology and sociology, and on which the formal base of social work depends; and finally, the alternative discourses associated with consumer rights and religion and spirituality which have a (re-)emerging influence on both health and welfare institutions and the formal base of social work practice. I will outline the key concepts in each of these discourses and, in particular, the ways in which they construct client needs and social work practices. Through these analyses, I draw attention to 'the conditional, changeable character of social work. It [discourse analysis] shows that there is nothing fundamental or inevitable about the form of social work' (Rojek *et al.*, 1988, p. 131). A discourse analysis approach urges us to be sceptical about attempts to define social work as a single thing or a unified set of practices; instead it encourages us to recognize the diversity of social work practices.

From a poststructural perspective, I consider that the language practices adopted in our health and welfare institutions actively construct key entities that shape the work of these institutions, including the purposes and practices of social workers working within them. Discourses influence who is regarded as an expert and who is considered to be a client, how client needs are constructed, and what types of intervention are seen as worthy. For example, in many traditional medical contexts, the biomedical discourse will strongly influence who is seen as the expert (e.g. the doctor or health care professional), who is the client (e.g. the 'sick' person), how client needs are constructed (e.g. as a matter of physical pathology), and what interventions are seen as worthy (e.g. biomedical interventions as opposed to, say, social interventions). By contrast, the consumer rights discourse that underpins some contemporary service user advocacy services, particularly in mental health and disability fields, repositions the clients as the expert, encourages the questioning of established 'expert' opinion, and sees society (rather than service users) as the focus of change efforts (see Chapter 4, this volume).

Health and welfare contexts are sites of competing discourses, each of which offers different interpretations about the nature of client needs, expert knowledge, the nature of the social work role and, most specifically, the kinds of 'help' or intervention that will best address the concerns and issues facing service users. In some health and welfare contexts there is very little overt struggle between different discourses. In these contexts, one discourse or set of compatible discourses has gained dominance at least in determining the official practices of the institution. However, in many contexts, considerable tensions exist between different ways of seeing the practice context, particularly in determining the nature of client needs and the social work role.

The relationship between discourses and social work practice is dynamic in the sense that discourses profoundly shape social work practice, yet social workers can also actively use and contest the discourses that influence their practice domains. Of course, to do so requires that we understand them. At a minimum, discourse analysis can help us to understand, and actively use, the concepts that shape our institutional environments and which, in turn, influence our professional purpose. From a discourse perspective it is vital that we, as social workers, understand and use the language practices that dominate our practice contexts if we want to maximize opportunities for our own and clients' perspectives to be recognized in these contexts. For example, in many health care settings, concerns about cost-effectiveness dominate and so, at a purely pragmatic level, it is helpful for us to understand and use this concept in presenting our practices and new initiatives with and on behalf of service users.

Social workers can also use discourse analysis to contest established ways of viewing and responding to client needs. Fook (2002, p. 89) asserts that: '[by] simply choosing not to accept dominant ideas and pointing up contradictions [we] can work to resist, challenge and change these dominant meaning systems'. Through understanding the discourses that construct our practice environments, social workers can be involved in opening these contexts to 'alternative framings of reality' (Parton, 2003, p. 9). By using discourse in this way, social workers can work with key stakeholders to develop different, and more helpful, ways of understanding and responding to client needs. For example, in many fields of health and welfare, social workers have an important role to play in highlighting the social and structural contexts of the issues facing service users and in encouraging service responses that move beyond 'fixing' the individual's problem to addressing the social and structural origins of these issues.

Theories for Social Work Practice

In the second part of this book, I consider the theories for practice that shape our practices as social workers. Social work theories for practice provide guidance for practice as they identify who should be the focus of practice and how social workers should proceed practically. As I will show, these theories draw on service discourses, especially ideas from the disciplines of psychology and sociology, to construct understandings of client needs and to frame practice directions. In short, discourses provide a key foundation for the theories we use in social work practice.

My approach is a postmodern one in that I aim to show that each of these contemporary theories has strengths and limitations depending on one's contexts of practice. While many social workers, and many academics, have a favoured theory of practice, in this book I seek to introduce a range of approaches rather than to push a specific theory for practice. Even as I do this, I am presenting a postmodern view that there are no absolute truth claims and that, rather, the utility of theories should be judged within specific practice contexts. For example, a theory for practice that may assist in realizing our purpose and values in a statutory corrections context is unlikely to be that which will work for us in a community development context.

Unlike the discourses considered in the first part of the book, which shape practice across a broad range of health and welfare services, theories for practice are usually developed within specific practice domains and are meant, at least initially, for practice with specific client groups. For example, the strengths perspective was originally developed for practice in mental health services for people suffering chronic mental health conditions. Yet, as these theories for practice become more widely endorsed within the profession their historical and geographical origins are rarely mentioned even though these foundations are important for us in assessing the uses and limits, and possible adaptations, of theories for our specific practice environment. In this book, I will outline the origins of each practice theory in order that you, as the reader, can assess their utility and potential alteration for your practice context.

Whereas discourses shape the ideas and practices adopted by a broad range of actors within the practice environment, theories for social work practice have a more limited scope of influence. Social work theories for practice have been developed within the social work and human service professions for use by primarily by these professions. Often, in practice, this means we have to explain to colleagues and to service users the perspectives we are using, that is, the thinking behind how we approach a situation. While acknowledging the limited formal influence of the theories for practice within many institutional domains, these theories provide a key intellectual foundation for social work practice. I consider that the formal theories for practice can provide us with insights into the dilemmas facing service users and can also diversify our options for responding to service users beyond that which may seem immediately evident within the practice environment. Theories for practice can challenge and extend our analysis and responses to, and with, service users. At the same time, given the diversity of social work practices, it is important that social workers draw on these theories in informed and cautious ways. I urge social workers to approach theory with the understanding that, at best, theories can provide partial insights into direct practice and that each of us must take an active role in how we use and develop them. It is critical that we understand the specific historical and geographical conditions that give rise to specific theories for practice and take these into account when constructing our frameworks for practice. In short, theories for practice provide *a*, rather than *the*, base for professional practice.

The Structure of the Book: An Overview

The first half of the book is focused on identifying and analysing the discourses shaping the institutional contexts and the formal professional base of social work. In Chapter 2, I identify and analyse the discourses dominating mainstream health and welfare services today and which are separate from the core knowledge base of social work. I use the term 'dominant discourses' to refer to the institutionally powerful discourses of biomedicine, neo-classical economics and law. Of course, many other discourses, such as new public management, are present and, arguably, dominate specific domains of health and welfare services. I have chosen to focus on discourses of biomedicine, economics and law because the power of these discourses transcends specific sectors and domains of service delivery to influence the ways core concepts such as client needs and service responses, including social work practices, are constructed in mainstream health and welfare services. For example, in child protection practice, these discourses profoundly influence the definition of child abuse and neglect in accordance with medical evidence and legal categorizations of these concepts, and shape the sorts of services that will be available to service users.

One of the reasons these discourses are so powerful is that they are consistent with the ideals of the Enlightenment, on which many modern institutions and professions are founded. The Enlightenment refers to an array of intellectual, cultural and political forces that emerged in Western Europe during the eighteenth century (O'Brien and Penna, 1998, p. 9). Enlightenment thinkers promoted ideals of objectivity, rationality and individualism as providing the foundation for progress. Furthermore, progress is understood as linear, rather than something that might happen in a variety of ways. In Chapter 2, we will consider how these Enlightenment ideals are embedded in, and function through, the discourses shaping our practice contexts.

In addition, these discourses are well bounded and their features and operations are identifiable from the substantial literature and research on them. Another unifying feature of these three discourses is that they are external to, or separate from, the formal base of the profession. In other words, while social workers might draw on ideas from biomedicine, economics or law, they are not experts in any of these disciplines.

Social workers are not merely subjects, or users, of discourse; they also endorse and use discourses, particularly those that underpin the formal professional base of social work. In Chapter 3, I examine the human science discourses that the profession has drawn on over the past century to construct its formal professional base. The key human science disciplines on which professional social work depends can be broadly termed 'humanist' in that they place the realization of human potential as their central concern. There is a wide range of human science disciplines that have impacted on social work, including political economy and anthropology. However, in Chapter 3 I will focus on two: the 'psy' disciplines, which draw on ideas from psychiatry and psychology, and also sociology, particularly critical socio-logical perspectives. I focus on these two because of the substantial body of evidence concerning the historical and continuing influence of these two disciplines on social work. I will look at the discourses that arise from these disciplines and, especially, how these discourses shape how social workers construct client needs and develop responses to these needs.

In Chapter 4, I examine a second set of service discourses, which I refer to as 'alternative service discourses', that are (re-)emerging as key ways of understanding and responding to service users' needs and constructing social work practices in many practice contexts. The discourses I consider in this chapter are those associated with consumer rights movements and those linked to religion and spirituality. In very different ways, these discourses contest aspects of both dominant discourses that have shaped many mainstream health and welfare services and also the human science discourses underpinning the formal professional base of social work. For example, both challenge the capacity of the dominant discourses, such as biomedicine, and human science disciplines, such as psychological approaches, to promote holistic responses to service users' needs.

In addition, I have focused on these two sets of discourses because of their increasing influence on the delivery of a range of health and welfare services. As we shall see in Chapter 4, consumer rights movements have grown over the past four decades in some areas of health and welfare provision, particularly disability, women's health and mental health, to underpin consumer-directed alternatives for service provision. The growth of spiritual and religious themes in service provision can be attributed to both agitation from within the profession by social workers who believe that recognition of their own, and service users', spiritual lives is an essential dimension of holistic care, and to the expanding role of religious charities in the provision of non-government social services in many post-industrial societies.

As we shall see, these alternative service discourses can offer social workers options for challenging dominant and human science discourses and for achieving the humanitarian purposes to which the profession of social work is committed. For instance, as we shall see in Chapter 4, social workers can use consumer rights perspectives to challenge dominant ideas about pro-fessional expertise and to advocate for service users' control of the processes for determining and meeting their needs (Campbell and Oliver, 1996). Yet these service discourses can also enact forms of oppression, even of those they claim to liberate (Foucault, 1981a). For this reason, it is vital that social workers engage in ongoing analysis of discursive practices, including the local operations of supposedly empowering ideas (Healy, 2000; Lupton, 1998). I also acknowledge that these discourses do not always serve contestant functions. For example, aspects of the consumer rights discourse have been brought into mainstream policy discourses, and religious discourses underpin some of the major non-government welfare bureaucracies that play an increasingly central role in mainstream welfare provision in many post-industrial countries.

In the second part of the book, from Chapter 5 to Chapter 10, I will concentrate on theories for social work practice. I will discuss debates about theory use in practice and how to assess the relevance of theories in relation to our sense of purpose as social workers. Over the next five chapters, I consider five key contemporary practice theories, including their historical and geographical origins and practice principles. The theories I present are:

- problem solving;
- systems theories;
- the strengths perspective;
- anti-oppressive practice
- postmodern, poststructural, and postcolonial approaches.

Wherever possible, I have used original sources of these practice approaches to remain as faithful as possible to the original intentions of the authors. Drawing on both our sense of purpose, as social workers within specific institutional contexts and practice exercises, we will examine how these theories function in practice and analyse their strengths and weaknesses for achieving our professional purposes.

The book is intended to be used actively by you, the reader. I invite you to think through the perspectives presented here as they apply to your actual or intended contexts of social work practice. Throughout the book, I present exercises and questions that are intended to engage you in different ways in thinking through the material. In each chapter, I present discussion points and practice exercises. The discussion points provide opportunities for you to reflect critically on the material presented in the chapter. Similarly, the practice exercises offer activities to try out in relation to the ideas introduced in the section you will have just read. In each chapter, I will discuss my answers to the practice exercises and discussion points. To assist you to engage critically with the concepts introduced in different parts of each chapter, I strongly recommend that you complete these exercises before you move on to the later material in the chapter. Reflection exercises and summary questions are included at the end of each chapter. The reflection exercises are activities for you to develop and apply the ideas presented; the summary questions will assist you to review key concepts raised.

In many of the activities, I will invite you to consider the implications of the material presented for practice with culturally and linguistically diverse client groups. Traditionally, social work practice with people from non-Anglo-Saxon cultures has tended to be characterized as a specialist area of practice. However, within the profession there is increasing recognition that social workers engage with service users from a range of cultural and linguistic groups. For example, in Australia, the USA and Canada, Indigenous service users are over-represented in many areas of statutory service provision such as child protection and in juvenile and adult detention centres. In addition, globalization has resulted in the mass relocation of populations, especially from Africa, Asia and Eastern Europe, to post-industrial nations, and so social workers, even in 'mainstream' settings, can expect to have contact with service users from diverse cultural and linguistic backgrounds. Culturally sensitive practice requires social workers to develop an understanding of the history and cultural norms of the client groups they work with and to consider the implications of these for practice. It is important therefore that you consider both the cultural and linguistic backgrounds of the client populations with whom you work and the strengths and limits of these different perspectives presented here for practice with these client groups.

Conclusion

Social workers are both active participants in, and subjects of, the practice contexts in which they work. We construct our sense of purpose with service users through negotiation between expectations arising from our institutional context, our formal professional base and our frameworks for practice. In this chapter, we have begun to examine the elements that constitute social work practices while recognizing that our practices are constantly renegotiated in each practice interaction. In this book, we will consider in more detail the discourses and theories for practice through which we, and others, construct social work practices.

Summary Questions

1. What are the components of the dynamic model of social work practice outlined in this chapter?

2. What does the term 'discourse' mean? What discourses shape your actual (or intended) context of practice?

3. What is theory for practice? What are the uses of theories for practice?

Recommended Readings

Adams, R., L. Dominelli and M. Payne (eds). *Social Work: Themes, Issues and Critical Debates*, 2nd edn (Basingstoke: Palgrave, 2002).
This book provides a great introduction to the diversity of social work practice contexts, roles and issues.

Alston, M. and J. McKinnon. *Social Work: Fields of Practice*, 2nd edn (Melbourne: Oxford University Press, 2005).
This book provides a comprehensive introduction to eight fields of social work practice. It is especially useful for readers with limited experience of direct service delivery and can be used to help to ground some of the debates about social service context and practice that will discussed throughout this book.

Banks, S. *Ethics and Values in Social Work*, 2nd edn (Basingstoke: Macmillan, 2001).
This text offers an excellent 'reader-friendly' overview of values and ethics in social work.

Taylor, C. and S. White. *Practising Reflexivity in Health and Welfare: Making Knowledge* (Buckingham: Open University Press, 2000).
This book provides a practical and comprehensive introduction to social constructionist perspectives in health and welfare settings.

Website

The International Federation of Social Workers: http://www.ifsw.org

---

Reflection Exercise

Values and social work

Search this site for information about your national professional association. Examine the International Federation's definition of the ethical principles of professional social work, and consider whether you agree with this statement. How does it fit with your sense of purpose in social work as you have constructed it? What challenges does this code present to social workers working in health and welfare services today?

2

Dominant Discourses in Health and Welfare: Biomedicine, Economics and Law

Social workers often practise in organizations where other professions and various discourses shape the social work role. In this chapter, we will consider three dominant discourses shaping service delivery in health and welfare contexts. These discourses are: biomedicine; neo-classical economics; and law. I refer to these as dominant discourses because in post-industrial countries, these discourses profoundly shape how health and welfare institutions constitute client needs, service provision processes and, more specifically, the formal roles of social workers.

In this chapter and over the next two chapters we will discuss the discourses that shape not only how people think about service delivery in health and welfare services but that also the actual services provided by these agencies. As represented in Figure 2.1, the dominant discourses of biomedicine, economics and law stand apart from, yet also interact with, other sets of knowledges, in particular service discourses. In some contexts, particularly traditional bureaucratic settings, I will show that the dominant discourses, especially those associated with biomedicine, economics and law, shape analysis and response to service user needs. In other contexts, such as 'alternative' services like small consumer-directed services or some religious charities, these dominant ideas are subject to substantially more contest from the alternative framings provided by service discourses, which I discuss in Chapters 3 and 4.

Of course, within specific practice domains, other discourses may also influence the constitution of client needs and service processes. For example, philanthropic discourse shapes practice in the non-profit sector

17

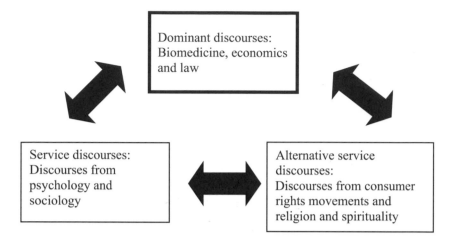

Figure 2.1 Discourses in interaction: highlighting dominant discourses

and educational discourse influences practice in schools. However, the discourses of biomedicine, economics and law transcend these specific sectors and domains to profoundly influence the ways mainstream health and welfare institutions, such as community health services, hospitals, statutory authorities and community services, understand service user needs and construct responses to them.

As I outlined in Chapter 1, dominant discourses are strongly aligned with Enlightenment ideals of objectivity, rationality, individualism and linear notions of progress. In many health and welfare institutions, these discourses profoundly influence what counts as true, right and rational ways of proceeding. In this chapter we shall see that each of these discourses shapes many of the contexts in which social workers practise and, as such, influence how we, and others, construct our purpose and primary practice focus. While these discourses can lead to progressive forms of intervention, I also argue that they can suppress other ways of knowing, thus limiting our options, as well as those of service users, for responding to the issues at hand. For example, when biomedical knowledge is established as offering the true and rational approach to health and social care it prevents us from seeing non-biomedical possibilities for responding to the issues that concern us (see Lupton, 1998; McGrath, 1997).

There is, of course, a broad range of discourses with a dominant influence in mainstream health and welfare institutions. In addition to those I have selected, there also many other discourses, such as evidence-based practice discourse and new public management discourses, influencing these institutions. I have focused on biomedicine, neo-classical economics and law because of the extensive evidence within the social work and the social science literature pointing to the influence of these sets of knowledge on the conceptualization and delivery of health and welfare services, including the ways in which social work is practised in many mainstream institutions. For example, within the social work profession there is a long-standing debate about whether social workers should reflect the medical profession in its professional structures and knowledge use practices. Richmond's (1917) model of social diagnosis is one example of this, some social workers' adoption of a 'bio-psycho-social' model is another. Of course, many social workers are also highly critical of the influence of biomedical discourses (and indeed, the other discourses discussed in this chapter) on health and welfare services. We shall consider some of these criticisms later in the chapter. While within the social work literature the relevance, or otherwise, of key ideas associated with biomedicine, economics and law is often debated, the core assumptions of these discourses are rarely outlined. It is frequently assumed that we all know what these terms mean, even though the speakers and writers themselves may differ in their definition of the terms. In this chapter I aim to remedy this problem by outlining the features and practical implications of these ideas and invite you, the reader, to consider their application to your practice.

While the social work role may be influenced by the dominant discourses discussed here, social workers are not usually considered experts in any of them. Even so, as service providers in health and welfare agencies, social workers need to understand the knowledge claims shaping their practice contexts. At the most basic level, these understandings can help us communicate effectively within our organizations (Opie, 1995). For instance, social workers working in health contexts often develop an extensive understanding of biomedical terminology. But understanding discourses can help us do more than this; this knowledge can also enable us to critically analyse our practice contexts and to identify opportunities, limited as they may be, to use dominant discourses for achieving outcomes for ourselves and service users. For example, in environments where neo-liberal economic perspectives prevail, social workers are more likely to succeed in persuading institutional decision makers by appealing to the values and concepts valued in neo-classical economic discourse, such as cost-effectiveness, rather than referring solely to the humanitarian value base that guides social work.

Of course, understanding dominant discourses is not a 'cure-all' for the problems that social workers face in achieving their practice purposes. Indeed, as we analyse dominant discourses we are also in a position to understand where these discourses *cannot* help us achieve the ends we seek. For example, an analysis of legal discourse may lead us to conclude that the legal concept of justice has limited relevance to achieving social justice in some contexts of social work practice. My point is simply that by understanding the discourses shaping our practice contexts we enhance our capacity to use these discourses purposefully within specific practice sites.

We turn now to an examination of the dominant discourses of bio-medicine, economics and law. I will first consider the features of each of these discourses and their practical effects for social workers and service users. I will then analyse the uses and limitations of each of these discourses for achieving our purposes, as we construct them, within specific sites of social work practice.

The Biomedical Discourse

The biomedical discourse is one of the most powerful discourses shaping practice contexts, particularly in health services such as hospitals, rehabilitation services and mental health services. This discourse is also influential in a wide range of social service contexts, such as child protection practice, where medical experts often play a pivotal role in defining and assessing what counts as evidence of risk of harm and abuse. As a result of biotechnological advances, biomedical discourse is extending further into many areas of socio-legal practice, such as forensic investigations in child protection and criminal assault matters and, of course, into the controversial terrain of genetic testing.

Social workers have a well-established interest in the impact of medical frameworks on social service provision. Mary Richmond's social diagnosis framework (Richmond, 1917) shows the early ambitions of the social work profession to mirror the practices of the medical profession. During the 1970s, radical social workers developed a stinging critique of the medical model of service delivery. They argued that the medical model approach to social work practice, based on the diagnosis of and response to service users' issues, ignored the underlying structural causes of service users' problems (Decker and Redhorse, 1979; Pelton, 1978). In many fields of health and welfare services, social workers continue to argue against a medical model of service delivery on the grounds that this model leads us to focus on 'modifying the person, assuming that any difficulties lie in the individual's deviation from "normal" rather than in the lack of accommodation within the environment' (Quinn, 1998, p. xix).

The term 'biomedicine' is widely used in the biological, medical and social sciences to refer to the dominant contemporary approaches to medicine that derive from the biological sciences. I adopt the term 'biomedical discourse' from the field of medical sociology, where it is used to refer to a specific set of ideas and practices associated with a biological approach to medicine (see Williams, 2003; see also Mishler, 1989). Many elements of the biomedical discourse appear as 'common sense' to people working in the health and welfare fields. They appear so self-evident that we may need to remind ourselves that these perspectives, like all knowledge, offer one way of looking at the world and, further, that this way of seeing things is culturally, historically, and institutionally specific (see Williams, 2003). For example, within a rehabilitation institution it may make sense for service users to seek whatever medical intervention is possible to lead a 'normal life'; by contrast, from a disability rights perspective we would aim to challenge cultural assumptions about the concept of a 'normal life' (see Chapter 4, this volume). Moreover, as we will discuss later on, the biomedical discourse has both uses and limitations for helping us to achieve our professional purposes within specific contexts of practice.

According to Mishler (1989; see also Williams, 2003, p. 12), the key ideas in the biomedical discourse are:

- that diseases and other 'malaises', such as disabilities, are deviations from normal biological functioning. Biomedical assessment and intervention focuses on addressing deviation and correcting it, rather than adapting the environment to accommodate differences;

- the 'doctine of specific aetiology', that is, the notion that diseases are caused by specific biological agents or processes (Kenen, 1996, p. 1545; Mishler, 1989). In the biomedical discourse, biological explanations of diseases are privileged over understanding of the social patterning of diseases, ill health and other phenomena such as disabilities (George and Davis, 1998, p. 151). For instance, a biomedical approach to schizophrenia, a chronic mental illness, would illuminate the genetic causes of the 'disease' while downplaying the role of environment as a significant contributor to the malaise (Turner, 1995);

- the universal nature of diseases regardless of culture, time, and place. For example, from a biomedical perspective we see that 'diseases' such as schizophrenia occur across cultures and have been present throughout history. However, the biomedical discourse fails to acknowledge the enormous cultural and historical variations that affect every aspect of people's experiences of this 'disease', including their understandings and their experiences of it, as well as their responses to it (Jenkins and Barrett, 2004);

- that medicine is a scientifically neutral enterprise. The knowledge prized in the biomedical discourse is that which is, ostensibly, unbiased by the prejudices of the scientist or medical practitioner and which is grounded in evidence obtained by scientific means. The evidence-based tradition in medicine, which has more recently influenced social work, is founded on this ideal.

How does this Discourse Shape Practice?

The biomedical discourse profoundly influences service delivery in many health and welfare contexts. First, this discourse determines who is seen as knowledgeable or expert and who is not. In the biomedical discourse, expertise is associated with knowledge of the biological basis of health and illness. In practice, this confers power on the biomedical experts, particularly medical scientists and practitioners, for defining and leading intervention efforts (George and Davis, 1998). This does not mean, however, that biomedical experts only use biomedical knowledge in their decision making. For example, a doctor in a palliative care unit may encourage the family of a terminally ill patient to resist further biomedical intervention. Rather, I am suggesting that in contexts where the biomedical discourse dominates, a truth status is attached to biomedical knowledge, even though other discourses will also be operating in these environments. Indeed, even in environments where this discourse is strong, such as mainstream hospitals, other discourses, such as economic, legal and religious discourses, can also shape decision making.

One of the practical effects of biomedicine's dominance in many health and welfare environments is that social workers must learn to understand and use biomedical terminology in order to communicate effectively in these practice domains (Opie, 1995). Moreover, we may have a role in translating biomedical terminology for service users as we assist them to negotiate health and welfare systems.

Biomedical discourse determines the focus and nature of assessment and intervention in health and illness. It focuses on the biological, and thus individual, bases of the problems facing service users. For example, illnesses and disabilities are understood primarily as biological conditions that represent deviations from the 'normal'. The purpose of assessment is to understand the nature of the deviation; for example, this discourse leads professionals to focus their efforts on diagnosing the type of illness or disability to which a person is subject and to develop responses targeted at correcting these deviations (George and Davis, 1998).

Advances in genetic research and related technologies have led, also, to the extension of biomedical assessment beyond a focus on existing conditions to incorporate new opportunities for predicting future disease or susceptibility to diseases in foetuses as well as children and adults (Taylor,

2001, p. 4). Information gained via the new genetic technologies is used in a variety of ways, many of which are highly controversial. Genetic information can be used to implement preventive measures to avert or delay disease development (*ibid.*, p. 3). For instance, some women carry a gene that makes them highly susceptible to breast cancer. Armed with this knowledge, these women may choose to seek regular screening for cancer, and reduce their risks through pharmacological and surgical interventions, including prophylactic mastectomy. Genetic information can also help prepare individuals for the onset of diseases for which there is currently no cure. For instance, Huntington's disease, an inherited and fatal brain degeneration condition that does not appear until mid-adulthood, can be predicted but cannot be cured. Individuals may find information about their genetic status useful for decision making in relation to their own lives by, for example, making preparations for the onset of increasing disability.

Predictive genetic testing for foetal 'abnormalities', such as Down's syndrome, is an especially controversial terrain. Advocates of such testing argue that this allows the parents to make an informed choice about whether to continue with, or terminate, a pregnancy involving a foetus with a disease or disabling condition. If parents continue with the pregnancy, though the evidence suggests that few do once an abnormality is detected, they can prepare themselves and their families to care for a baby with a disease or disability. There are many opponents of genetic testing for foetal abnormalities. Many religious groups associate these tests with the denial of the unborn child's right to life. Some disability rights advocates argue that predictive testing extends society's discrimination against people with disabilities to the womb, leading us to focus on the 'problem' of disability, rather than on society's intolerance of differently abled people (for further discussion, see Chapter 4, this volume).

As a result of advances in biomedical technologies, the biomedical discourse has extended further into many areas of health and welfare. This has many implications for social work practice. One implication is that social workers, especially those working in health care contexts, are involved in assisting service users in decision making around an increasing range of biomedical interventions. Social workers have expressed particular concerns about the equity implications of the new biomedical technologies (see Taylor, 1998, 2001). Consistent with the principle of social justice, social workers have raised critical questions about the deployment of these technologies, such as: do service user groups receive fair and equitable access to these technologies; do they receive too little access? Are their rights to self-determination assured? What about confidentiality considerations? The following exercise is intended to assist you to think through some of the dilemmas these new technologies may raise in social work practice. We will discuss these issues further later in the chapter.

Practice Exercise

Genetic testing

Imagine you are a social worker in the Women's Health Service of a large metropolitan hospital. Laura is referred to you by one of the gynaecological specialists at the hospital to assist in her decision making about whether to seek genetic screening for a breast cancer gene. Laura is 35, she is married and has two children under five years. She has a strong family history of breast cancer. Her mother and grandmother died of the disease in their mid-forties and one of Laura's older sisters, who is 41, is being treated for breast cancer. Her eldest sister, who is 43, shows no signs of the disease and does not plan to be tested. Laura is unsure about whether to seek the test or not and she says that she is very afraid of finding out that she carries the gene.

- What do you see as your purpose in this situation?

- What principles and values would be important in working with Laura?

Imagine instead that Laura is considered at risk of Huntington's disease. There is no cure or treatment for this fatal condition and so the primary purpose of genetic testing would be to reveal whether or not Laura will develop the disease, rather than to prevent or treat the condition.

- What do you see as your purpose in this situation?

- In what ways it is similar and different to the previous situation?

- In what ways, if any, would these differences alter your approach to the situation?

Biomedical Discourse: Uses, Issues and Problems

The uses and limitations of the biomedical discourse are the subject of heated debate, particularly within the social sciences and some fields of social work practice (see Taylor, 1998; Williams, 2003). On the positive side, the practical impact of the biomedical discourse on people's lives in post-industrial countries is irrefutable. Biological understanding of the nature of infection and disease has contributed to the development of a range of preventive measures, such as mass vaccinations and screening, that have contributed to substantial declines in illness and death from a range of diseases. For example, the mass introduction of cervical screening has contributed to a sharp decline in the number of deaths from cervical cancer in post-industrial societies.

In addition, advances in biomedical interventions, such as surgical and pharmacological treatments, have contributed to substantial improvements in the management and treatment of a range of illnesses and potentially life-threatening conditions. Kelly and Field (cited in Williams, 2003, p. 20) point out that many modern medical procedures such as coronary artery bypass, renal dialysis, hip replacement and the pharmacology of pain relief, have significantly improved or restored the quality of life of many of those suffering from chronic illnesses. Similarly, proponents of the new genetic technologies argue that these offer opportunities for further advancement in the prevention and treatment of a broad range of conditions. Returning to our first scenario, we can see that genetic technologies can provide Laura with information about her susceptibility to breast cancer. This information could be used to implement strategies for prevention and early intervention, thus enhancing Laura's chances of avoiding or surviving the disease, if she is found to be susceptible. In the second scenario, genetic testing would provide solid evidence on whether or not Laura will develop Huntington's disease. While there is currently no treatment or cure for this disease, Laura could use this information to prepare herself and her family for the onset of the illness.

Much of the time, many of us have no quarrel with biomedical discourse. Faced with a serious illness or injury, most of us would submit to biomedical expertise and we would encourage service users to do the same. Yet, in many practice contexts, we are likely to experience tensions between our formal professional base, particularly our values, and the assumptions and uses of biomedical discourse. One area of concern is the biological reductionism of such discourse. By focusing on the disease or an injured organ, bio-medical discourse is in conflict with the holistic approach to practice often championed by social workers (see McGrath, 1997). A holistic approach seeks to understand the person in their social context and to promote an optimal state of physical, mental and social well-being, not merely the absence of disease (Daly *et al.*, 2001, p. xiii).

In contexts where biomedical discourse dominates, social workers have an important role to play in highlighting service users' interests and needs beyond their medical diagnosis. A holistic approach to assisting Laura in her decision making would not deny the potential benefits of genetic testing but would require us to promote Laura's capacity to be self-determining. One way we could do this is by exploring with Laura her interpretations of the meanings of the family history of cancer, the meanings of the genetic tests for her and by identifying options for care and support whether or not she undergoes the tests (see Darlington and Bland, 1999; see also McGrath, 1997). In short, we would seek to engage with her as a whole person, not primary, in terms of her patient status. In the second scenario, a holistic approach might lead us to question with Laura the relevance of genetic testing for promoting her quality of life. We might probe with her how she would manage a result showing that she carried the gene for Huntington's in the absence of any treatment for the condition (Taylor, 1998).

Another concern is that biomedical discourse, as a dominant discourse, leads to the medicalization of more and more areas of our lives. Hunter *et al.* (1997, p. 1542) assert that 'medicalisation occurs when a behaviour or problem is defined in medical terms and when medical treatments are seen as the appropriate solutions'. Medicalization means that medical explanations are attached to a range of problems or issues that might otherwise be seen as either non-medical in nature, or even as part of the 'normal' range of human behaviour. Medicalization reflects, and contributes to, the increasing dominance of biomedical discourses and institutions in Western societies (Lupton cited in Williams, 2003, p. 16). It also contributes to the devaluing of non-medical responses to problems and issues facing service users. For when a problem is understood in primarily biomedical terms, the only rational response becomes a biomedical one. McGrath (1997) argues that in the field of cancer care this can lead medical experts to encourage patients to do whatever is technologically possible to treat their cancer even when there is little chance of a cure.

Returning to our scenario with Laura, drawing on the principle of self-determination, we could explore what pressure, if any, she feels to undertake the genetic tests, that is, to do what is technologically possible. We could explore with Laura options for resisting the biomedical interventions offered to her. For example, we might explore what pressures she feels from others, such as medical staff or family members, and we could rehearse how she would explain to them a decision not to undergo the tests. Through this exploration we can help to make resistance of the biomedical model a realistic option for her, if she so chooses.

A further concern is the potential for biomedical knowledge to contribute to social oppression. While biomedical knowledge is understood, within the terms of biomedical discourse, to be scientifically neutral, the ends this knowledge can serve are far from impartial. As we discussed earlier, disability rights activists have argued that new genetic technologies can extend disability oppression to the womb (see also Chapter 4, this volume). In addition, genetic information can be used for purposes of discrimination towards individuals identified at risk of illness or disability. Sandberg (1995, p. 1549) warns of the potential for the results of genetic tests to 'help organizations such as employers, insurers, and government bodies, to minimize their future economic risks'.

Returning to our scenario with Laura, consistent with the principle of social justice, we need to be critically aware of the potential for biomedical information, in this instance genetic information, to lead to discrimination towards her. In our practice with Laura we might seek to realize the professional values of equity and self-determination by establishing: (a) whether Laura is required by any external agency to undertake these tests, and (b) the extent to which the test results are confidential and, in particular, if there is any legal requirement for Laura to share adverse findings with an external organization, such as insurance agencies.

Discussion Point

The impact of biomedicine in your practice context

Thinking of your area of practice, or an area of practice that interests you (such as mental health services), discuss how, if at all, biomedical discourse shapes the construction of client needs and social work practices in this context.

Neo-classical Economic Discourse

We turn now to a second dominant discourse, neo-classical economics. At first glance, the discourses of economics can seem irrelevant to social workers. We could respond 'What has economics got to do with me? I'm not interested in money, I'm concerned about people!' Also economics' reputation as the 'dismal science' does little to spark our enthusiasm for the discipline. Yet, as we shall see, economics, particularly neo-classical economic discourse, influences social work practice in a variety of ways.

As a discipline, economics is concerned with the allocation of scarce resources for maximum benefit (Sandler, 2001). Of course, economics is not a single or unified discourse, and economists vary in their views of how their core concerns are to be addressed. Economic discourses span the political spectrum from the right-aligned neo-classical economic discourses through to left-aligned Marxist approaches (Leonard, 1997, p. 112). In this section, we will focus on neo-classical economic discourses. This discourse is also referred to as neo-liberal economics (see Friedman, 1982) or 'economic rationalism'; though, technically, economic rationalism is 'a simplification of a sub-school' of neo-classical economics (L. Edwards, 2002, p. 36). I focus on neo-classical economics because since the mid-1970s this discourse has become the dominant framework in economics and in public policy decision making in many post-industrial countries (Stillwell, 1996).

If social workers are to be active participants in determining how social service resources are to be allocated, it is vital that we also understand the terms of this dominant discourse. By understanding this discourse we can also challenge it on its own terms (L. Edwards, 2002). As we shall see, even neo-classical economists concede that there are limits to this discourse and we can use this knowledge to ensure that these limits are respected in our practice contexts. In this discussion we will, first, consider the key features of this discourse and then analyse the effects of this discourse in social work practice contexts.

Neo-classical Economic Discourse: Key Concepts

In this section, I present the core ideas underpinning neo-classical economics. Whether or not we agree with neo-classical economics (and most social workers do not!), it is important for social workers to understand the key assumptions of this increasingly influential discourse.

The free market occupies a central, even sacred, place in neo-classical economic discourse. Sandler (2001, p. 20), an economist, states that 'markets can be a thing of beauty when they function properly'. According to this discourse, the invisible hand of the market ensures the efficient allocation of resources for the maximum benefit, which, for neo-classical economists, refers to maximum wealth creation. Through the free market, the interests of buyers and sellers are coordinated to ensure the production of goods and services that are valued most by the consumer at the best price. In addition, free markets encourage competition between sellers, which, according to this discourse, also contributes to the efficient allocation of resources. Neo-classical economists argue that free market competition provides a vital mechanism for driving down costs and weeding out ineffective and inappropriate uses of scarce resources.

Across many post-industrial countries, governments have introduced markets to health and social services on the premise that 'the market can deliver better and cheaper services than government' (J. Healy, 1998, p. 32). In the market model, governments become purchasers, rather than primary providers, of these services. Also, in this model, governments purchase services from the non-government sector and these agencies compete with each other for service contracts. The neo-classical economic discourse infers that increased competition among social service providers will ensure that governments, taxpayers and service users receive better value for the welfare dollar.

Markets in social services fields are referred to as 'quasi-markets' because they differ from traditional commercial markets. One of the key differences is that, in the social services, the entity purchasing the service, usually the government or insurance company, is not the entity receiving the service, that is, the service user. In part this is because consumers of social services often have a limited capacity to pay for services. Another difference is that 'consumers' do not necessarily choose the services, such as child protection and corrective services, that are delivered to them. These services are part of the social surveillance role of the state and thus fall outside the usual understanding of consumer goods and services within the neo-classical economic discourse.

The neo-classical economic discourse holds that individuals are self-interested, rational actors. It is assumed that individuals act in ways that reflect and promote their individual self-interest and that, in so doing, contribute to the 'betterment of everyone' (Sandler, 2001, p. 10). Neo-classical economic discourse promotes criticism of all forms of third-party intervention, that is, forms of intervention that the recipient did not request and for which they do not cover the costs. Advocates of this discourse argue that these outside forms of intervention are paternalistic and can interfere with our capacities to act in our own self-interest. Furthermore, because recipients do not pay for third-party intervention, these interventions can lead to the ineffective allocation of resources as goods and services that consumers neither want nor value. Applying these arguments to community care provision, we would assert that individuals choosing their own services will act in their own self-interest to ensure that they get the best service at the best price and, furthermore, if they pay for these services, they will value them more highly than if a third party had met the costs.

Another important concept in this discourse is freedom of choice. Milton Friedman, a winner of the Nobel Prize for economics and key exponent of neo-liberal economic philosophy, contends that

> [At] the heart of the liberal philosophy is a belief in the dignity of the individual, in his freedom to make the most of his capacities and opportunities according to his own rights, subject to the proviso that he not interfere with the freedom of other individuals to do the same. (Friedman, 1982, p. 195)

Neo-classical economists argue that the freedom to choose is a fundamental human right to be protected as long as it doesn't interfere with others' freedom. Proponents of this principle oppose most forms of welfare and social service provision on the grounds that it imposes a tax burden on the others, thus impeding their freedom of choice. In this discourse, freedom of choice is linked also to economic efficiency as, it is asserted, people make rational choices consistent with their individual self-interest. By ensuring that individuals have, wherever possible, the freedom to choose what kinds of goods and services they will consume, we achieve the 'highest possible human welfare out of a finite pot of resources' (Edwards, 2002, p. 39). Returning to our previous illustration of community care, the argument is that when individuals are able to choose their service provider they will choose the most effective and efficient community care services and, in so doing, will weed out operators who lack these qualities.

Neo-classical economists favour minimal government intervention or small government. Proponents of neo-classical economics hold that too much government intervention distorts the operation of free markets, thus inhibiting the efficient allocation of resources (Edwards, 2002, p. 78). For example, the assumption is that if governments provide social services such as community care services they will (a) inhibit the capacity of private providers to compete for this 'business' and (b) limit the development of efficient and effective services because, without the discipline of competition, ineffective and inefficient services will remain. Another reason neo-classical economists call for small government is that they just don't trust the representatives of government to act in the best interests of the community as whole. Consistent with their belief that humans are rational, self-interested actors, they argue that politicians and bureaucrats are likely to act in their own interests at the expense of individual consumers (Sandler, 2001, ch. 5; Edwards, 2002).

In this discourse, the role of government is constrained to three core responsibilities. The first is that government should promote conditions to maximize the free operation of the market. One way governments do this is through legislation to protect private property rights. According to this discourse governments have a responsibility to ensure that non-government service providers can compete for public funding for the provision of health and welfare services (Gibelman and Demone, 2002). A second responsibility of government is to provide public goods, that is goods and services that benefit all citizens but which individuals are unable or unwilling to pay for individually. For neo-classical economists, public goods include items such as national defence systems, anti-terrorist capabilities, protection of the environment and public works (Sandler, 2001). Interestingly, neo-classical economists do not generally regard the provision of health or social services as public goods, but rather as the personal responsibility of service users.

A further responsibility of government is to provide goods and services when the market has failed and where it is established that the involvement of the government would do no further harm to the capacity of the market to respond. As in many countries governments are still experimenting with quasi-markets in human services, policy makers in the fields of health and welfare policy have a responsibility, within this discourse, to monitor the field for market failures and to step in where these occur.

Implications for Social Work

Proponents of neo-classical economics are strongly opposed to the public provision of welfare and social services, viewing this as a contradiction of the fundamental human right – the right to choose. Proponents of neo-classical economic discourse argue against most forms of state welfare and social support to individuals on the grounds that it imposes a burden on the entire community to address the needs of relatively few (see Friedman and Friedman, 1980; Sandler, 2001). In addition, according to Friedman and Friedman (1980, p. 119), the provision of income transfers by the state acts to 'reduce the incentive to work, save, and innovate' and in so doing reduces the freedom of both the taxpayer and the service user. For the most part, neo-classical economic discourse portrays people reliant on state benefits, such as those drawing on unemployment benefits, as unproductive citizens and as a 'fiscal burden' on the state (Leonard, 1997, p. 114). In this discourse, the unproductive citizen has few, if any, rights to make a claim on the state or society for support. In many post-industrial countries, this discourse has been used to justify increasing constraints on welfare provision to disadvantaged individuals.

Similarly, advocates of neo-classical perspectives argue that the provision of social services by a third party is paternalistic and provides perverse incentives for individuals to remain dependent on social service providers (Freidman, 1982, p. 34). One upshot is the view that individuals should be required, wherever possible, to pay part or all of the costs of the services they use. Over the past two decades this concept of user payment has been introduced into a growing range of social services (J. Healy, 1998). In its most extreme form, the concept of 'user pays' means that service users can be required to contribute to the costs of services they did not request and may even resist, such as prison services.

None the less, most neo-classical economists accept, perhaps begrudgingly, that government does have a role in protecting vulnerable citizens and, in very limited instances, to be a social service provider of last resort. These instances include circumstances where the market has been given the opportunity to provide services but has failed to do so. Another circumstance where government involvement may be justified is where the individual whose welfare is at stake is not a 'responsible adult' (Friedman, 1982, p. 195). For example, Friedman (1982) accepts that the state has responsibility towards children at risk of abuse or adults suffering serious psychiatric or intellectual ability that inhibit their capacities for free choice. A further condition for government intervention in welfare provision is where large-scale coordinated action is required to address a problem. For example, government involvement may be required to introduce national policy initiatives such as 'welfare to work' programmes. Even in these circumstances, government intervention is only warranted when such intervention will not do further harm to the market and to the individual right to freedom of choice.

Discussion Point

Neo-classical economics and social work

Working with a partner, identify and discuss what you see as the consistencies and inconsistencies between neo-classical economic ideas and the social work values of promoting self-determination and achieving social justice.

Uses and Limits

Few social work commentators support neo-classical economic discourse. Most consider it to be inconsistent with core social work values particularly social justice (see Leonard, 1997). Yet, as neo-classical economics increasingly dominates many areas of health and welfare provision, some argue that social workers must understand and learn to use its basic concepts (see Gibelman and Demone, 2002). Indeed, Stoez (2000, p. 621), an American social work commentator, argues that our failure to understand the terms of this discourse 'only assures political irrelevance and programmatic decline'.

While it is difficult to think of any consistencies between the core concepts of neo-classical economics and social workers' purposes and values, we can identify some such consistencies in the *effects* of the discourse. One of these is enhanced opportunity for consumer choice in some domains of service provision. One illustration of this is the introduction of direct payments to people with disabilities to enable them to purchase their own care services. For many years, members of consumer rights groups in the disability services sector have agitated for increased consumer control over service provision to them. Ironically, the introduction of neo-classical economic principles of free markets and individual choice into the public policy domain has helped to create an environment favourable to the introduction of direct payments to service users (see Carmichael and Brown, 2002, p. 797). Studies on direct payment programmes have shown that increased consumer choice about service provision and control over payments leads to greater satisfaction than when these services are organized and paid for by others (see Carmichael and Brown, 2002).

Another effect is that neo-classical economic discourse has facilitated an increased role for the non-government sector in the provision of services. One advantage of the expansion of non-government services is that, in some instances, these services provide better value for money than government services. This is because non-government services often bring extra benefits that complement the formal services they provide (Harris *et al.*, 2003). Economists refer to these extra 'unpaid-for' benefits as 'externalities' (J. Healy, 1998, p. 34). For example, non-government services arc often able to draw on public goodwill in the form of donations of time and money. This well of social capital can enable non-government services to offer a fuller range of supports, including informal support, than is usually available through government departments (Scott, 1999). Of course, as d'Abbs (1991, p. 129) has shown, the informal resources of non-government organizations are, at best, a complement to formal service delivery, and cannot provide alternatives to formal services, particularly in situations of high dependence and high risk.

A further effect is that neo-classical economic discourse challenges social workers to evaluate established practices and practice proposals. The principle of freedom of choice encourages us to critically examine paternalism in our practices. Consistent with this principle, we must constantly ask who has determined our involvement in service users' lives and we must also respect their right to choose the focus and form of interventions, as far as possible within the dictates of our practice context. We are also challenged to recognize the economic implications of our practice proposals; this discipline is often missing as, for example, social workers are urged to 'develop provisions for meeting people's needs rather than rationing resources' (Dominelli, 1988, p. 161). Even with a dramatic increase in public funding to health and welfare services, a proposition that seems unlikely in the near future, service provider organizations will have to make decisions about resource allocation. The clear message of neo-classical economics is that there is no magic pudding and that the decision to place resources of time, money and personnel to one end limits *opportunities* to commit these resources to another end. Thus, in presenting our case for resource allocation to one set of ends, such as the establishment of a new youth accommodation programme, we must not only show why this is a useful end in itself, but in addition, why this particular allocation is preferable to the competing possibilities for resource allocation.

Issues and Concerns

Social work and policy commentators have extensively critiqued neo-classical economic discourse. The general thrust of these concerns is that while the principles of neo-classical economics may, or may not, work in traditional commercial contexts, they are entirely inappropriate for social service provision. Key concerns include, first, that neo-classical economic discourse undermines public support for the welfare state. Within this discourse, social services expenditure is represented as a drain on the economy, rather than as a public responsibility and investment in society (Leonard, 1997, p. 113). In this way, the discourse allows governments to distance themselves from their responsibilities to the most disadvantaged citizens.

Critics also argue that service quality, specifically service comprehensiveness and accessibility, is compromised by increased competition in the social services sector. Competition provides incentives for service provider agencies to offer services at the lowest possible costs to the funding body. The incentive to cut corners in service delivery is exacerbated by the fact that service users have little 'buying power' and thus little say in negotiating service contracts. In the social services sector there are few options for cutting service costs, and all these measures compromise service quality. For instance, one way of cutting expenditure is by slicing labour costs. This can be achieved by replacing professional labour with volunteer and non-professional labour, with the consequence that service users have reduced access to professional services. Another way that services maintain their competitive edge is by focusing on service users who are most amenable to fast and demonstrable outcomes (Gibelman and Demone, 2002). J. Healy (1998, p. 38) warns that 'selection inequities are already common in social services, but the profit motive offers yet another incentive for avoiding troublesome consumers'. Furthermore, evidence from the USA suggests that the growth of for-profit enterprises in the social services sector can contribute to the further erosion of service quality. Gibelman and Demone (2002, p. 392) point out that the primary goal of the for-profit agency, maximizing profit to shareholders, is in conflict with quality service delivery.

A further concern is that increased competition, over time, can lead to reduced diversity of service provider agencies. In the short term, privatization leads to an increase in the range of service provider organizations as non-government service providers replace state-run service departments. However, in the longer run, privatization in the social service sector can lead to the replacement of large state bureaucracies with large private monopolies (see Gibelman and Demone, 2002; Healy, 2002). This is because large social service organizations experience significant advantages in a competitive environment. Because of their larger staff and financial base, these organizations can deploy staff specifically to activities such as applying for contracts, networking with funding agencies, and negotiating and administering funding contracts. Smaller organizations and, more specifically, consumer-run organizations, are at a competitive disadvantage because they have much less capacity to dedicate resources to the competitive effort (Healy, 2002).

Finally, the concept of individual choice is not necessarily consistent with self-determination, which is a key social work value. Within the terms of this discourse, the capacity to choose is constrained by one's capacity to pay.

By returning all responsibility to the individual, this discourse obscures the systemic and structural influences on people's 'free choices' as well as the broader impediments to people living a life of their choosing. For example, from a social justice perspective, it is unfair to expect indigenous people who have experienced generations of discrimination and exclusion from economic and social participation to achieve self-determination without the support of key public and private institutions.

Discussion Point

Debating economics in social work

With a partner, debate the following propositions:

1. There is no place for for-profit social services in a just welfare state.

2. Competition among service provider organizations benefits service users.

Legal Discourse

We turn, finally, to legal discourse. In this section, we will consider key impacts of legal discourse on social work practices. We will then turn to an examination of key concepts in legal discourse and the uses of, and concerns about, this discourse as a vehicle for achieving our purpose in social work practice.

Social Work and the Law

Ball (1996, p. 3) defines law as 'the body of rules whereby a civilized society maintains order and regulates its internal affairs as between one individual and another, and between individuals and the state'. Many authors also emphasize the social control dimensions of law. For instance, Austin (cited in Coleman and Leiter, 1999, p. 244) defines law as 'the order of a 'sovereign' backed by the threat of sanction in the event of non-compliance'. There are two main types of law impacting on social work practices. These are:

● Statutory law. A statutory law is one that has been passed by the Parliament; these laws are also known as 'Acts of Parliament' (Brayne *et al.*, 2001). Statutory laws exist in many areas of social services work and shape the role and obligations of social workers in these contexts.

- Case law (or judicial precedent). Case law is law established by previous case reasoning and case findings, it is used to define and refine existing laws and may be used to make new law (Ball, 1996, p. 4). Case law can impact on the way statutory legislation is interpreted and so this can affect our use of statutory law in direct practice.

In addition, as social workers, we may be required to abide by specific codes of practice associated with our institutional contexts (see Ball, 1996, p. 4). These institutional codes are public declarations of what service users can expect from the agency, such as confidential service delivery. Social workers who fail to respect them may be the subject of complaint to a higher authority such as the Ombudsperson or other complaints tribunal and may find that their failure to abide by the code counts against them in court action (Ball, 1996, p. 4).

Law as Discourse

Law, just like biomedicine and economics, is a contested domain; that is, there are many strands of legal thought. In this section, we will focus on the dominant discourse of law, formally known as legal positivism. According to Anleu (2000, p. 6), 'Legal positivists view the law as a formal, logical system of legal rules ... Positivism has been the dominant philosophy of law since the nineteenth century.' The discourse of legal positivism, as the dominant discourse of law, shapes the 'common-sense' understandings widely held by lawyers and the general public about the purpose and processes of law.

The discourse of legal positivism holds that the law is objective. This discourse represents the law as 'impermeable to personal values or individual manipulation' (Anleu, 2000, p. 6; see also Bourdieu, 1987). This commitment to objectivity is expressed in the ways legal processes are described and performed. For example, Bourdieu (1987, p. 830) observes that judicial language 'bears all the marks of a rhetoric of impersonality and neutrality'. Through these language practices, judges and magistrates represent their decision-making as objective, dependent on legal fact and reasoning, rather than on personal views (Anleu, 2000, p. 4). Similarly, this discourse holds that legal actors should distance themselves from the emotional and moral aspects of legal decision making (Coleman and Leiter, 1999, p. 242). In their text on social work and the law, Brayne *et al.* (2001, p. 18) assert that 'One skill a good lawyer should have ... is that of being detached from the client's situation. In other words they will not become "involved".'

The discourse of law asserts that the law is rational. The concept of rationality, in this discourse, means that lawyers use the body of established legal fact as the basis of their reasoning (Anleu, 2000, p. 4; see also Bourdieu,

1987, p. 831). The process of legal reasoning is often confusing to non-lawyers because frequently legal concepts have a different meaning from the common usage of these terms. For example, legal processes for determining just or fair outcomes are 'based upon rigorous deduction from a body of internally coherent rules' (Bourdieu, 1987, p. 820), rather than by reference to, for example, values, social structures and social context.

Also, legal positivism requires that social processes comply with distinct legal categories if they are to be recognized in the formal legal process. These categories construct our identities and actions as static entities which contrast markedly with the fluidity we often experience in our lives (Bourdieu, 1987, p. 832). For example, in legal discourse, one is constructed as either a 'plaintiff' or a 'defendant', 'victim' or 'non-victim', 'guilty' or 'not guilty', 'sane' or 'insane', 'liable' or 'not liable' and so forth (*ibid.*). Yet the realities of clients' lives, and indeed our own, often defy these categorizations. For example, from the available evidence about the childhood experiences of many violent offenders, we know that many people in this population are both perpetrators of abuse and survivors of abuse, especially childhood trauma.

Finally, the discourse of legal positivism assumes that the law is authoritative. The discourse of law is based on the assumption that citizens will recognize the law as the supreme arbiter of truth and thus will comply, whether voluntarily or by coercion, with legal dictates. We can see this assumption in Brayne *et al.*'s (2001, p. 29) assertion that, for social workers, 'good practice must always give way to the requirements of statute, regulations and guidance, if these legal requirements are in conflict'. Put simply, legal discourse holds that our responsibilities before the law should override all other considerations. For example, respecting the client's right to confidentiality is widely seen as a core social work value. Yet in most jurisdictions social workers can by compelled by law to share confidential information in some contexts, such as the courts (Brayne *et al.*, 2001; Swain, 2002b). Consistent with our value of professional integrity, it is vital that we are aware, and that we communicate to service users, how the law may impact on practice relationships.

Discussion Point

The law in social work practice

Identify and discuss how the law impacts on social work practice within your service context or in an area of practice that interests you. In this exercise

Discussion Point (*cont'd*)

think about how the law shapes your current or future role as a social worker, and what opportunities and constraints it places upon service users. If you can, compare your answers with those of someone working in, or interested in, a different practice context.

Legal Discourse in Social Work Practice

Social workers need to understand legal discourse, in part, because the law often defines our key responsibilities to employing agencies and service users. This is particularly evident in statutory contexts where social workers have an explicit responsibility to implement statutory law. Discussing social work practice in these contexts, Brayne *et al.* (2001, p. 1) assert 'Although there is plenty of room for good intentions these do not define your job, the statutes do. The statutes tell you who you have responsibilities towards, and how they should be exercised.' The statutory responsibilities carried by social workers are delegated to them via their employing organization. Social workers are empowered to use statutory law not through their professional training or registration, but rather through their context of employment. This is an important distinction to make as the types of statutory obligations we bear are very much tied to our site of employment, and some social workers do not carry statutory obligations.

Notwithstanding the coercive dimensions of statutory power, this form of law can also have protective and empowering functions. Despite extensive critique of the statutory role of child protection social workers, in some circumstances this legislation can be used to advocate children's right to be free of exploitation and life-threatening abuse (K. Healy, 1998). Indeed, social workers have argued that the *absence* of statutory law in some contexts, such as aged care, limits their capacity to protect some vulnerable service users from abuse and exploitation (Braye and Preston-Shoot, 1997, p. 10).

Also, social workers should have an understanding of the law because it impacts on service users' lives in myriad ways. Many service users' problems and concerns have legal dimensions and, as social workers, we should be able to identify legal concerns and facilitate service users' access to legal representation (Brayne *et al.*, 2001, p. 357; Braye and Preston-Shoot, 1997, ch. 4; Swain, 2002c). This knowledge should include understanding of: statutory laws in your area of practice; human rights and anti-discrimination legislation; operation of the legal system and how to access legal representation in your area of concern; and in some instances, knowledge of case law may be relevant to your area of practice.

Another reason for understanding legal discourse is that we can use it to support and advocate for the protection of service users' rights (Swain, 2002a, p. 266). For example, human rights legislation and anti-discrimination laws are intended to protect all citizens' access to basic human rights such as freedom from discrimination and procedural fairness in administrative matters. Social workers can use this legislation to improve the accountability of social service agencies for providing appropriate and accessible responses to service users (*ibid.*).

Social workers can use the law as a vehicle for social change. One of the ways social workers are involved in the development of law is through research and advocacy about the inadequacies of current laws for protecting groups of vulnerable people. Alongside other interested parties, social workers have contributed to changes in law related to a range of human welfare concerns, including child protection, domestic violence, and the recognition of the human rights of people with disabilities, children and young people. Social workers can contribute to legal reform as part of broader social change campaigns, such as anti-domestic violence or child protection campaigns.

Also, social workers working in policy and legislation, particularly in human service agencies of government, may be involved in the review and development of new legislation, such as child protection legislation. In this role, social workers work alongside legal practitioners and other advisers to design legislation, often in response to political issues and concerns raised within the community about the inadequacy of current legislation.

Practice Exercise

Using the law

Drawing on the previous discussion of the uses of legal discourse in social work practice, identify:

- your legal responsibilities as a social worker in this context;

- legal issues arising in this case study; and

- how you would address these legal concerns.

You are a social worker in a statutory authority delivering services to people with mental illnesses. One of your clients, Jack, is a 42-year-old man with schizophrenia. Jack lives alone in a community housing project flat; he has resided there for about five years. The government funds the community housing project to provide long-term affordable housing to people on low incomes. Jack was recently released from hospital following an acute psychotic episode. Jack spent approximately six weeks in hospital; his stay was extended to enable medical staff to get his symptoms under control. When he returned home, Jack found that the housing project has sent him a notice to quit his residence due to non-payment of rent for the last three months. Jack admits he did not pay his rent and he attributes this to his severe state of illness over the past months. He believes that this notice to quit is the first notice he has been sent by the community housing project regarding his rent arrears. When you contact the community housing project to discuss the matter they state they're unwilling to negotiate Jack's continuing residence in the project. As they see it, Jack has had problems with paying his rent in the past and they have previously given him plenty of support in keeping his payments up to date. For them, his recent lengthy period of non-payment is the 'last straw' and they want him out.

In reflecting on this case study let's first consider our possible legal responsibilities as social workers. As social workers in a statutory authority with responsibility for the implementation of mental health law, we may be required to monitor Jack's mental health. This means that our core, and possibly primary, responsibility is to assess Jack's mental well-being and if necessary refer him for psychiatric care if his health deteriorates to the extent that he presents a danger to himself or others. Other legal issues arising in this case study include, also, concerns about discrimination against Jack on the basis of his mental health status. A pertinent question here is whether Jack is being treated unfavourably because of his mental health status. If this is so, human rights and anti-discrimination legislation is likely to be relevant. A further concern is the possible contravention of tenancy laws by the community housing group for denying Jack opportunities to address rent arrears. Tenancy laws are intended to protect the legal rights of both the landlord, in this case the community housing project, and the tenant, in this case Jack. Tenancy laws usually prescribe processes to be followed prior to the eviction, such as due notification of rent arrears. From the information we have here, we have reason to believe that these laws may have been contravened. Our options for responding to this case study include non-legal options, such as seeking mediation between Jack and the community housing group, and perhaps involving the funding body in determining the respective responsibilities of the housing group and the service user. Our legal options include seeking legal representation for Jack, particularly to address the matters of discrimination and tenancy rights. Given that the matter involves a public-funded entity, we may have recourse to refer the matter to the Ombudsperson to address our concerns about procedural fairness, that is, to raise questions about whether Jack's matter has been dealt with fairly and impartially by the community housing group.

Issues and Concerns

As we have seen, legal discourse shapes social work practice and in some contexts can be used to promote social work values, such as self-determination and social justice. Swain (2002a, p. 267) argues that social workers should 'acknowledge the points at which legal interventions and remedies can prove effective, and to seek to exploit these for the betterment of all'. Yet commentators in the legal and social service fields also raise a number of concerns about legal discourse. Many of these concerns challenge claims that the law is an objective and rational process.

Commentators argue that legal assumptions and processes are value-laden (Bourdieu, 1987, p. 826). Anleu (2000, p. 5) observes that

> Rather than being a mechanical, value-free process, legal reasoning involves interpretation and assessment; ratios decidendi [reasons for deciding] are often ambiguous, amorphous and contradictory, and must be identified or constructed. Reasoning by analogy involves elasticity: judges can interpret precedents expansively or narrowly in order to achieve a particular outcome.

By presenting the law as an objective and neutral process, legal discourse protects legal reasoning from critical scrutiny and contest. Yet such scrutiny is vital for averting the harm that can be caused by the imposition of values that are inappropriate to the matter at hand. Critical analysts argue that what appears as objective reasoning by the judiciary reflects their class, gender and race status, which in turn can make the practices of people from different class, gender and ethnic status appear deviant, abnormal and pathological (Bourdieu, 1987, p. 847). For example, commentators within the field of child protection are concerned that, despite a veneer of objectivity and neutrality, statutory law can be used as a vehicle to impose Eurocentric and middle-class norms on working-class and non-European families (Dung, 1984).

Critical commentators point out that the law can contribute to the production of social inequality. One way the law produces inequality is by limiting access to participation in the legal process to those deemed to be legal experts (Bourdieu, 1987, p. 818). Thus, rather than an instrument for achieving justice, the law is experienced by many service users as 'remote, incomprehensible, expensive or irrelevant' (Swain, 2002a, p. 267). Another way the law contributes to the reproduction of social inequality is by ignoring the social and economic contexts of issues before the law. Anleu (2000, p. 6) observes that judicial decision making focuses on determining individual culpability and on applying the 'correct legal rule or principle to the facts of a particular case, regardless of the consequences. [Thus] Issues of economic inequality or social reform are outside judicial competence and are [viewed as] issues for the legislature.'

Research on the social effects of law has repeatedly demonstrated that the law is an instrument of social control (Anleu, 2000, p. 230; Carrington, 1993). Critical analyses of criminal and welfare laws show that these laws disproportionately affect the most disadvantaged and marginalized groups in society (Bourdieu, 1987, p. 817). When law is understood as a social process, rather than as an objective and rational one, we can see that the law is applied inequitably to different population groups. For example, disadvantaged populations are often subject to much higher levels of legal surveillance and to much poorer access to representation before the law (Carrington, 1993).

The experiences of many service users in relation to the ineffectiveness of law for protecting their basic human rights call into question the authority of the law. For example, in the field of disabilities, significant numbers of service users in community care facilities continue to be denied basic human rights (Clear, 2000). The involvement of government agencies, either as funders or service providers, in the denial of these service users' rights suggests that the law has limited authority in protecting the interests of marginalized groups of service users.

Finally, though the law offers some ways of remedying social concerns, it also limits change possibilities (Bourdieu, 1987, p. 816). Anleu (2000, p. 234) contends: 'The legal arena also constrains social action as it requires social problems and complaints to be translated or transformed into legal concepts and legal remedies.' In this process of translation, structural causes are erased as sites of legal concern because legal action must be directed towards specific parties, such as governments, companies or individuals.

Moreover, complainants are required to use the predetermined categories of legal discourse, rather than express their sense of injustice in their own terms. As we discussed previously, the categories leave little room for recognition of the ambiguities that characterize many social relationships. For example, in crimes of personal violence, such as domestic assault, a person may both love and despise a person who has victimized them, but an adversarial legal process requires the complainant to describe their experience and attitudes towards the defendant in ways that render invisible this ambiguity.

Conclusion

In this chapter we have considered the assumptions and implications of three discourses that have a dominant influence on many practice contexts. Often these discourses coexist and may even compete in defining the role of social workers, and other professionals, as well as the needs and interests of service users. By understanding these discourses, we enhance our capacities to use them, and, where necessary, to challenge their influence on social work practices.

Summary Questions

1. What tensions exist between the social work value of promoting self-determination and the biomedical discourse?

2. What are the uses and limits of neo classical economic discourse for promoting the well-being of service users?

3. What are the core assumptions of the discourse of legal positivism and to what extent can this discourse be used to promote social justice for service users?

Reflection Exercise

The Huong family Case Study

Imagine you work in an emergency department of a children's hospital. The Huong family, a Vietnamese family, have been referred to you because of concerns about the welfare of their child, An, who is eight years old. Thu Huong (29 years) and his wife, Dung (28 years), brought their daughter to the hospital with suspected bronchitis. During the medical examination, the medical staff observed three deep purple bruises on An's arms and back and a welt on her buttocks. An has been referred to the child protection team because of the medical staff's concern about her welfare. She has been placed under a temporary care order and is remaining in the hospital until the care team meets. Thu and Dung are extremely distressed about this. They acknowledge that they have hit An with a belt buckle, but that this is to discipline her. They insist this is the way they were disciplined as children. They state that they deeply love An and would never do anything to hurt her.

Reflection Exercise (*cont'd*)

1. Looking through the lens of the dominant discourses discussed in this chapter, what factors would each of these discourses highlight about this case study?

2. In what ways might these discourses promote or limit culturally sensitive practice with the Huong family?

3. Imagine you have to report a plan of action to the medical team for your work with the Huong family. What would be your plan and how would you justify it using the terms of the dominant discourses operating in this context?

Reflection Exercise

Dominant discourses in your practice environment

With a partner discuss the following questions:

1. Thinking of the area of practice that interests you (or in which you are practising) discuss how one of the discourses introduced in this chapter is likely to impact on your practice.

2. What discourses other than those discussed here exert a dominant influence on your area of practice?

Recommended Readings

Biomedicine

Aldridge, S. *The Thread of Life: The Story of Genes and Genetic Engineering* (Cambridge: Cambridge University Press, 1996).
This book provides a comprehensive and accessible introduction to genetic research and the new genetic technologies. It is especially recommended for readers working, or intending to work in, health care environments.

Williams, S. *Medicine and the Body* (London: Sage, 2003).
In this book, sociologist Simon Williams offers a theoretically sophisticated analysis of contemporary sociological debates about biomedical interventions.

Economics

Edwards, L. *How to Argue with an Economist: Reopening Political Debate in Australia* (Cambridge: Cambridge University Press, 2002).
This book provides a reader-friendly introduction to core concepts in neo-classical economics and the ideology of economic rationalism. Edwards shows how to use economic rational arguments strategically and how to challenge aspects of neo-classical economics in policy making. Edwards uses contemporary policy examples to illustrate her arguments.

Friedman, M. and R. Friedman. *Free to Choose: A Personal Statement* (Melbourne: Macmillan, 1980).
Milton Friedman won the Nobel Prize for economics based on his work on neo-classical economics. In this classic text, Friedman outlines the core concepts of and arguments for neo-classical economics.

Sandler, T. *Economic Concepts for the Social Sciences* (Cambridge: Cambridge University Press, 2001).
This book provides a descriptive overview of neo-classical economic concepts. While the author takes an uncritical view of this discourse, he provides an excellent and detailed description of many core concepts and as such gives the reader a good overview of neo-classical economic discourse.

Law

Anleu, S. *Law and Social Change* (London: Sage, 2000).
This book provides a reader-friendly introduction to the sociology of law. It is strongly recommended for readers interested in developing a sociologically informed analysis of the discourse of law in social service contexts.

Braye, S. and M. Preston-Shoot. *Practising Social Work Law*, 2nd edn (Basingstoke: Macmillan, 1997).
This textbook provides an excellent introduction to the law in social work practice. It examines the uses and limits of law for achieving social work values.

Brayne, H., G. Martin and H. Carr. *Law for Social Workers*, 7th edn (Oxford: Oxford University Press, 2001).
Three lawyers compiled this handbook on social work and the law. The handbook contains detailed information about a very broad range of social welfare laws in Britain and social workers' roles and responsibilities under the law. The book emphasizes social workers' role in statutory law and also in advice and advocacy roles. Although written in a British context, the book is relevant to social workers in Anglo-American legal systems, particularly in Britain, Canada, Australia and New Zealand.

P. Swain. *In the Shadow of the Law: The Legal Context of Social Work Practice* (Annandale, Sydney: The Federation Press, 2002).
This edited collection provides an excellent overview of the impact of the law on a range of domains of social work practice and policy making. The book is primarily

written for Australian and New Zealand audiences but raises issues of concern to social workers in post-industrial countries generally.

Websites

US Department of Energy (2002) Human Genome Project Website: http://www.ornl.
  gov./hgmis
This website provides an overview of history and achievements of the Human Genome Project. The site includes extensive discussion of the biomedical implications of the Project, particularly for predictive testing and gene therapy.

National Cancer Institute (2002): http://cancer.gov
This website carries information on the cancer types, genetic testing for predicting susceptibility to some forms of cancer, and on prevention and treatment of a wide range of cancers.

3

Service Discourses: 'Psy' and Sociological Ideas in Social Work

The formal professional base of social work is heavily reliant on received ideas, especially from the human sciences. While social work has been influenced by a diversity of human science ideas, our focus in this chapter is on discourses drawn from the disciplines of psychology and sociology which have informed the formal professional base of social work and which, in turn, construct how social workers' interpret client needs and their practice responses. Notwithstanding the range of human science ideas that influence social workers, I focus on discourses within the disciplines of psychology and sociology because of the substantial body of evidence pointing to the central influence of these ideas on the formal base of social work practice. Indeed, as we shall see, the struggle between ideas from the disciplines of psychology and sociology has been at the forefront of tensions in the knowledge base of social work, with each discipline playing an influential role at different times in the profession's history, in various practice contexts and in different geographical contexts. Even today, in some contexts, psychological disciplines shape the professional knowledge base, while in others sociology has a fundamental role. This chapter is intended to provide you, the reader, with an understanding of historical and contemporary influences of psychological and sociological discourses on the formal knowledge base of social work.

Service Discourses in Context

In Figure 3.1, I have highlighted the service discourses we will focus on in this chapter and I have positioned them below, but interacting with, the dominant discourses discussed in Chapter 2. This represents the subordinate

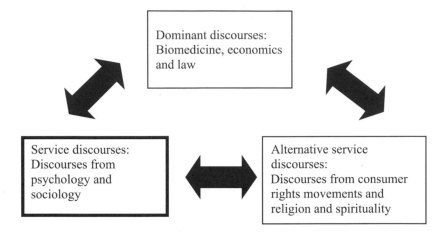

Figure 3.1   Discourses in interaction: highlighting service discourses

position of human science discourses in many practice contexts compared to the dominant ideas discussed previously. While the professional base of social work is primarily constructed through these human science discourses, in practice, social workers also have to understand and actively engage with the dominant discourses which also shape their practice. Sometimes differences in the ways these discourses construct client needs and the social work role contribute to substantial conflict for workers. As we are shaped by, and negotiate, these conflicting perspectives it is important that we are able to reflect critically on the human science discourses underpinning our professional base.

Of course the human science disciplines of psychology and sociology are sites of enormous internal diversity. Social workers have tended to draw on discourses within these disciplines that share a 'humanistic' orientation. This ethos places the realization of human potential, autonomy and self-determination as its central goal (see Johnson, 1994, p. 6). The humanistic orientation of social work, and of the human science discourses on which it draws, has a complex relationship with the Enlightenment ideas of individualism, rationality, objectivity and progress on which the dominant discourses discussed in Chapter 2 depend. On the one hand, many human science disciplines were founded on the recognition of, and have sought to value, the unique worth of the individual. On the other hand, these disciplines have also presented stinging critiques of the limits of Enlightenment ideals, such as individualism for promoting other humanitarian ideas, for example social justice (see Johnson, 1994, ch. 1). In this chapter, I will discuss the historical and contemporary influence of psychological and sociological disciplines on the development of the formal knowledge base of social work. Let's turn first to the influence of psychological discourses.

Social Work and the 'Psy' Disciplines

Historically the social work discipline has been closely aligned with the professions of psychology and psychiatry. In a formative phase of professional social work, from the 1920s to the 1950s, the profession drew heavily on psychodynamic ideas to build a common base of social work practice. Today in the popular imagination, social work continues to be aligned with psychological expertise, even though in practice, the nature and degree of affiliation with the 'psy' knowledge varies by geographical context and fields of practice. While many of the taken-for-granted concepts underpinning direct practice, such as empathy and authenticity, have their origins in 'psy' disciplines, social workers hotly debate the relevance of these ideas for practice.

In this section I will define the term 'psy' knowledge and consider the historical influence of 'psy' ideas on the development of social work and the various ways in which these ideas shape the base of professional practice today. We will consider some of the key debates about the uses and limits of 'psy' ideas for direct social work practice.

A Historical Overview of 'Psy' in Social Work

The term 'psy' was coined by social scientists to refer to 'heterogeneous knowledges' developed from the psychological sciences, such as psychology, psychiatry and the behavioural sciences, that provide practical techniques for understanding, diagnosing and promoting change within the individual (see Rose, 1999, p. vii). According to social workers Parton and O'Byrne (2001, p. 38),

> The 'psy complex' refers to the network of ideas about the nature of human beings, their perfectibility, the reasons for their behaviour and the way they may be classified, selected and controlled. It aimed to manage and improve individuals by manipulation of their qualities and attributes and was dependent upon scientific knowledge and professional interventions and expertise. Human qualities were seen as measurable and calculable and thereby could be changed, improved and rehabilitated.

A core assumption of 'psy' disciplines is that many problems facing service users can be classified and treated at the level of individual psychological processes. Undeniably, 'psy' ideas have had a profound influence on the development of the social work profession. Indeed, many of the concepts widely accepted by professional social workers can be traced to the influence 'psy' disciplines, especially psychoanalytic theory. Yet the profession of social work has an ambivalent relationship to these disciplines and the use of 'psy' ideas varies historically and geographically.

Modern professional social work was founded in the religious charity movements of the late nineteenth century. However, the pioneers of professional education in the first decades of the twentieth century sought to distance the profession from its religious origins and to found a scientific base for social work practice. The first professional social work educators, particularly Mary Richmond (1917), turned to the social sciences, particularly sociology and economics, rather than the 'psy' disciplines as the core knowledge foundation for the profession (Cree, 2000, p. 3; Shoemaker, 1998).

During the 1920s, the social work profession increasingly turned away from socioeconomic theories and towards psychological theories, especially psychodynamic perspectives, as its primary knowledge base for direct practice (Stein, 1958, p. 226; see also Hamilton, 1958, p. 13). In part this was a response to disillusionment with the social sciences, and more specifically to Mary Richmond's social diagnosis approach, which, although strong on analysis of service users' problems, appeared to offer little direction for social casework intervention (Hamilton, 1958, p. 24). Leading social work schools in the USA turned to the 'psy' disciplines, especially the work of Freud, to develop intervention approaches for social casework (*ibid.*). This direction was to have considerable influence on the emerging social work profession.

Over the next three decades, from the 1920s to the 1950s, psychodynamic theory became a dominant and unifying framework in social casework (see Hamilton, 1958, p. 18). In the USA, psychiatric specialities were established in a number of schools of social work, drawing primarily on Freudian psychodynamic theories (see Woods and Hollis, 1990, p. 13; Borden, 2000). In 1946 the Tavistock Clinic was established in London and its training programmes in psychodynamic therapy with children and families had a substantial influence on the scope and focus of professional social work. The Tavistock Clinic drew on ideas from a second generation of psychoanalytic theorists, particularly Donald Winnicott and John Bowlby, whose works focused on child development and maternal attachment. This work provided an intellectual base for social workers to extend their practice domain into psychotherapeutic work with children and families (Rose, 1999, p. 173).

The increasing influence of 'psy' discourses on social work, especially in the post-World War 2 period, can also be attributed to the diversification of the 'psy' sciences themselves. Psychiatrists treating soldiers suffering post-traumatic stress disorders began to question psychoanalytic assumptions about the enduring effects of early personality development and came to support a more dynamic and malleable view of psychological processes (Rose, 1999, p. 21). This changing conception of human personality led psychiatrists to diversify their practice approaches from long-term psychodynamic practice to experiments with brief intervention models. The crisis intervention approach developed by American psychiatrists Caplan and Lindemann was one of the new models to emerge out of this period of experimentation and drew on the view that crises provided opportunities for human growth (Kanel, 2003, pp. 14–15). Crisis intervention was introduced to social work in the 1960s and maintains currency today as a contemporary model of practice. We will consider it further in Chapter 6.

The changing view of the human psychology led also to an increased emphasis on personal growth and preventive intervention. According to Rose (1999, p. 21), in the post-World War 2 period, 'Madness was now thought of in terms of social hygiene. Mental health could be maintained by proper adjustment of the conditions of life and work; poor mental hygiene and stress could promote neurosis in large numbers of people.' In some contexts of practice, social workers' interventions were redirected away from a primary focus on the treatment of chronic conditions towards the prevention of mental health problems and the promotion of personal growth. In the USA, at least this appears to have opened up a niche market for social workers in personal development for, as Woods and Hollis (1990, pp. 4–5) note, 'Probably more than ever, caseworkers concern themselves with the development of conditions and capacities for health rather than only the ameliorization of pathology.' By contrast, in countries such as Australia, New Zealand and the UK, where opportunities for private psycho-therapeutic practice are severely constrained by the lack of third-party funding arrangements for social workers, personal growth therapy has remained a marginal area of professional practice.

The Retreat from Psychodynamic Theory

During the 1950s, social workers' love affair with psychodynamic theories began to cool. Social workers shared many of the concerns raised with psychiatry and psychology about the lack of a scientific base and evidence of effectiveness of psychodynamic therapies. This concern intensified over the next two decades as various experiments on long-term psycho-dynamic casework failed to demonstrate any greater effectiveness than short-term problem-focused interventions (Reid and Shyne, 1969; see also Rose, 1999, p. 237).

But social workers' concerns about 'psy' ideas went beyond a concern with effectiveness to growing discomfort about the retreat from the social dimensions of service users' concerns. From the late 1950s there was a growing interest in putting the 'social' back into social work theory (Stein, 1958, p. 227). Over the next decade the profession threatened to split between those who were aligned to 'psy' perspectives and those who were aligned to the social science disciplines and the new social movements of the period. During the 1960s numerous model were developed to reintegrate 'psy' and social perspectives towards a common base for social work practice. Among the most celebrated and enduring of these is the 'psychosocial' approach to casework developed, initially, by Florence Hollis, an American casework theorist (Wood and Hollis, 1990, p. 14). According to Woods and Hollis (*ibid.* p. 16), psychosocial casework is 'a blend of concepts derived from psychiatry, psychology, and the social sciences, with a substantial body of empirical knowledge derived from within casework itself'. Psychosocial approaches remain popular in social casework today because of their emphasis on understanding and responding to the person in their social environment.

Since the 1960s social workers' critique of the 'psy' foundations of social work has grown substantially, though, of course, many within the profession continue to accept 'psy' discourses. Critical social workers have extensively canvassed their concern about the failure of 'psy'-based approaches to adequately acknowledge, let alone address, the structural challenges facing service users (see Lees, 1972, ch. 1; Leonard, 1966). In response to these criticisms, during the 1980s and 1990s, many critical social work theorists sought to integrate radical and social action perspectives with the 'psy'cho-social model of casework practice. Jan Fook's (1993) model of radical casework, anti-oppressive casework approaches, and various feminist developments of casework practice are illustrations of this movement (Bricker-Jenkins *et al.*, 1991). These initiatives have enabled social workers to integrate analysis of structural and cultural injustices into social casework, which remains a key method of social work practice (see Maidment and Egan, 2004).

'Psy' Ideas Today

Today 'psy' disciplines continue to form a substantial part of the professional base of social work, especially with respect to skills for direct practice with individuals. Many social work education programmes require students to complete core units in psychology and many schools of social work, particularly in the USA, Canada and New Zealand, teach students the DSMIV[1] classifications as part of their professional education. In other countries, such as Australia and in parts of the UK, where, arguably, the social sciences have had a more dominant role in social work education, social workers working outside mental health services are less likely to be familiar with standard psychological diagnostic tools and more aware of the sociological critique of 'psy' knowledge (see Healy, 2001; Dominelli, 1997).

Psychodynamic ideas in social work continue to endure as one set of 'psy' ideas used in medium- and long-term psychotherapeutic work (see Borden,

2000). However, social workers' involvement in psychotherapeutic work of this nature varies substantially by geographical context. For example, in many states of the USA licensed social workers are eligible for third-party reimbursement, and this has given rise to significant opportunities for social workers to provide psychotherapeutic services in private practice contexts (Woods and Hollis, 1990, p. 5; see also Gibelman, 1995, ch. 8). In other countries, such as the UK, Australia and New Zealand, where social workers are primarily employed in government authorities or non-government community services where psychotherapy is not a core social work task, psychodynamic ideas are less central to the professional knowledge base.

Yet, even in contexts where social workers are not involved in psychotherapeutic work, psychodynamic ideas have an implicit, though often unrecognized, influence on the formal base of social work. Indeed, some psychodynamic concepts have become mainstream ideas in social work and an implicit part of the knowledge base of the profession. One illustration of this is the importance most social workers place on the relationship between worker and service user as a vehicle of change *in itself*. This reflects the psychodynamic discourses' emphasis on the importance of 'empathic attunement', self-understanding, strengthening coping capacities and worker/client 'fit' (Borden, 2000, p. 368; see also Woods and Hollis, 1990, p. 25). As we shall see in the second part of this book, the importance of a helping relationship characterized by empathy, authenticity and mutuality is widely accepted as central to effective practice across the vast majority of contemporary models of practice from problem-solving to anti-oppressive approaches (see also Hamilton, 1951, p. 52; Woods and Hollis, 1990, p. 26; Maidment and Egan, 2004).

'Self-knowledge' on the part of the worker is another psychodynamic concept widely endorsed within the formal base of social work. The psycho-dynamic model introduced the notion to social work that 'self-awareness' is an essential component of effective practice (see Hamilton, 1958, p. 34). For example, Hamilton (1951, p. 40), a leading thinker in psychodynamic social work, insisted that 'the worker must first be able to understand himself and his own emotional drives and impulses before he can truly accept the "bad" feelings, aggression, or even love and gratitude in others'. Today, the notion of self-awareness is no longer solely aligned to therapeutic modalities, and instead has become part of a range of practice approaches. Indeed, the anti-oppressive model, which eschews many 'psy' concepts, maintains that workers must understand how their own biography, in this case their membership of various social groupings, affects their capacity to develop an effective working relationship with service users (see Chapter 9, this volume). The emphasis on self-knowledge has come to the fore also in the models of reflective practice that have recently risen to prominence (see Napier and Fook, 2000). These approaches emphasize the importance of reflection on personal biography and personal responses to the client and their situation as an integral part of knowledge use in practice.

For more than two decades now a new set of 'psy' ideas has also gained increasing recognition within the human services and has, to an extent, displaced other 'psy' discourses. This new set of 'psy' ideas, which is central to the contemporary discipline of psychology, is associated with a 'scientific' approach to the management of human problems. Psychological tools associated with categorizing client groups, estimating risk and transforming 'dysfunctional' behaviour are common in professional practice with 'high-risk' client groups, such as families at risk of abuse and neglect, and offenders (Smith and Vanstone, 2002, p. 818; Smith, 2001). Also, cognitive behavioural therapy (CBT) has become a dominant model of intervention in practice settings where social workers are expected to effect rehabilitation of dysfunctional behaviours such as offending behaviour or drug and alcohol use (Smith and Vanstone, 2002, p. 818). Proponents of CBT assert that this approach is consistent with a scientific and evidence-based approach to practice and distant from the more 'emotional' and value-laden approaches to practice that have often characterized social work interventions (see Sheldon, 2000). On the other hand, critics argue that the narrow focus of CBT interventions neglects both the structural factors contributing to phenomena such as offending behaviour and the importance of cultural sensitivities in developing appropriate responses (see Gorman, 2001). Indeed, in their critique of CBT approaches to probation work, Smith and Vanstone (2002, p. 819) argue that 'A standardized, routine one-track approach based on an ideology rooted in the pathologizing of people who offend is likely to sustain structures inimical to social justice.'

Over the past decade, 'psy' discourses have also identified and expanded the role of human service providers in early intervention practices with children considered to be at long-term risk of psychological malaise. For example, recently, governments have supported a range of early intervention initiatives for vulnerable children and families, such as the Sure Start programme in the UK, drawing on brain research demonstrating that children's early psychological development has enduring effects on their long-term well-being (see Perry, 2002).

Discussion Point

What psychological ideas are prevalent in your actual or intended area of practice? How do these concepts extend, or limit, our capacity as social workers to achieve social justice in practice?

Strengths and Limits of the 'Psy' Discourse

Most social workers use 'psy' ideas in social casework practice with service users. Of course, these ideas are not the preserve of the 'psy' professions as they also circulate within the dominant cultures of post-industrial societies (Rose, 1999). Thus 'psy' terminology such as 'self-awareness', the 'unconscious' and 'self-control' are likely to be used in a wide range of organizational contexts and among professional and service users' groups. Even so, commentators remain divided over the relevance of 'psy' ideas to social work practice.

Proponents of 'psy' ideas argue that these concepts provide us with a language and practical strategies for realizing the humanistic values and goals that underpin modern social work (see Borden, 2000). Certainly, 'psy' ideas can reinforce social workers' focus on valuing individual needs and aspirations as the basic guide to intervention. The enduring influence of many 'psy'-based concepts, such as the centrality of the helping relationship, attests to their relevance to the humanistic ethos of contemporary social work.

Some social workers also advocate the use of 'psy'-based risk assessment tools in areas of high-risk social work practice (see Summers, 2003). These risk assessment tools can provide social workers with an overview of the psychological factors associated with elevated risk; many of which may not be immediately apparent in our interactions with service users. While many academic commentators are critical of the increased emphasis on risk management in welfare practice, it is also the case that a comprehensive understanding of risk factors is a professional and legal obligation of social workers in some practice contexts. 'Psy'-based risk assessment tools can make important contributions to the assessment of risk, especially for novice social workers. Contexts in which 'psy'-based risk assessment tools are likely to be helpful include those where there is:

- a significant risk of harm or death for service users, such as child protection and mental health, or to others, as may be the case in work with offenders;

- significant turnover of front-line staff, as is the case in some statutory authorities. In these situations, it is likely that many direct service providers have little direct practice wisdom to draw on that is relevant to assessment especially in high-risk situations;

- an expectation by employer agency or client groups that social workers will be primarily responsible for assessing risk of harm and that, in some circumstances, they may be required to do so 'on the spot', with little assistance from other professionals. For example, a social worker in a statutory health authority is required by law to assess their clients' risk of harm to themselves or others and, in some circumstances, where the client poses a high risk of this nature, the social worker may have to make an immediate decision to schedule the patient for involuntary inpatient mental health care;

● an expectation that the social workers' assessment will contribute to formal decision making where the implications of such decisions may have profound and enduring consequences for service users. For example, some social workers are required by the courts to make decisions about the removal of children from their families and the institutionalization of people suffering severe mental illnesses. It is our ethical responsibility to ensure that these decisions are made from a comprehensive and rigorous knowledge base, and 'psy'-based risk assessment tools can form an important part of this base.

In these situations, it may be unreasonable to expect practitioners to rely on the notions of reflective knowledge building and practice wisdom that have become increasingly popular within the discipline of social work. For example, in practice contexts where there is a high turnover of front-line staff, practitioners do not necessarily have sufficient experience to draw on practice wisdom. Indeed, intuitive knowledge built up from life experience, as opposed to direct practice experience in a specific context, may be especially unreliable in dealing with highly emotive and unusual situations involving high risks to service users (Killen, 1996).

In addition, in high-risk environments the costs of getting our decisions wrong are unacceptably high for clients and so it is our duty to draw on as broad a range of evidence with the lowest risk margins possible. Many of the formal 'psy'-based risk assessment tools have been developed by statistical analysis of risk factors in large numbers of child protection cases and so provide the worker with an understanding of risk factors that may not be apparent in their immediate interactions with service users. For example, in our own practice experience we may have seen a small number of clients deal with heavy drug dependence while managing their parenting responsibilities; yet this practice experience should not blind us to the general association between heavy parental drug use and elevated risk of child abuse and neglect (Semidei *et al.*, 2001). Finally, in formal decision-making contexts, such as courts and biomedical contexts, social workers are often required to demonstrate the principles on which their assessments are made. 'Psy'-based risk assessment tools provide an evidence foundation for decision making that can be used in collaboration with other knowledge sources, such as our relationship with the service user, to develop the comprehensive and defensible assessments in these contexts.

Despite the extensive role of the 'psy' discourse in the formal base of social work, 'psy' ideas are also the subject of extensive critique within the profession. In many practice contexts, the social workers' brief is to work with highly marginalized people, and the adequacy of 'psy' ideas for understanding and responding to clients in their social, political and cultural contexts of oppression is widely questioned. For example, social workers have criticized the rise of cognitive behavioural therapy as the dominant treatment model on the grounds of its failure to acknowledge the broader structural and cultural contexts of service users' needs (Smith and Vanstone, 2002).

Critical sociologists, especially Rose (1999) and Donzelot (1997), have highlighted the role of 'psy' discourses in enabling governments to judge and regulate the behaviour of individuals, children and families. The 'psy' disciplines have established categories for diagnosing and categorizing 'normal' and 'abnormal' child development and family functioning. These categories have been used both to 'treat' and improve individual and family functioning, but, at the same time, have allowed governments and human service experts to wield power at the most intimate levels of service users' lives (Rose, 1999, pp. 133–4).

I am concerned about the potential for 'psy' ideas to do harm to service users when applied to practice contexts divergent from the psychotherapeutic contexts for which they were originally intended (see K. Healy, 1998; see also Smith, 2001). The emphasis on concepts such as empathy and mutuality can be misleading and confusing for service users in contexts where social workers bear statutory responsibilities, such as in child protection, corrections and some mental health roles. Referring to child and family welfare practice, British social work commentator Smith (2001, p. 289) reminds us that

> In their daily work with children and families social workers are constrained by a panoply of regulation, guidance and procedure (Howe, 1992; Garrett, 1999). Their interactions with children, parents and foster carers are governed not by trust, but by formal and often written agreements.

In short, the concept of the 'helping relationship' as the vehicle for change is problematic in contexts where the social work role is not only about helping, as is the case in statutory social work.

A further problem is the potential for the concepts of empathy and mutuality, originally drawn from the 'psy' discourse, to limit workers' capacity to undertake responsibilities associated with decision making in high-risk situations. An empathic approach demands that we put ourselves in the shoes of the other, yet in contexts such as child protection practice it is critical also that workers are able to maintain sufficient emotional distance to enact their protective role (see Killen, 1996). Even in non-statutory contexts 'psy' ideals of empathy and mutuality have the potential to do harm by misleading service users about the nature of social work role. In my own research with young parents, I found that the most marginalized clients were confused and often disappointed by what they understood to be offers of unconditional support and friendship which appeared to be implicit in service providers' emphasis on mutuality (see Healy and Young Mothers for Young Women, 1996). These clients asked not that social workers entirely abandon ideals such as mutuality but that they be more explicit about the boundaries to these ideals in their work with them.

Social Science Discourses

The influence of social science ideas, particularly from sociology, has been no less profound than that of the 'psy' disciplines. Indeed, social work is sometimes described as an applied social science (Rosenman *et al.*, p. 215). Pearman and Stewart (1973, p. 12) describe social science, in its various forms, as the 'attempt to describe the characteristics and products of human behaviour as they occur within social configurations'. In a wide variety of ways, social sciences seek to explain the *social* origins and consequences of human behaviour. In turn, we, as social workers, often use these ideas to explain the phenomena we encounter in practice and to guide our responses to them.

As discussed earlier in this chapter, the first social work education programmes drew mainly on ideas from the social rather than the psychological sciences. In the late nineteenth century, according to Cree (2000, p. 3), the projects of sociology and social work were linked to the 'promise of the "modern age": that through scientific discovery and rational investigation, the "truth" might be uncovered, which would lead to an improvement in the workings of society and in the lives of individuals' (see also Bloom, 2000). During the middle part of the twentieth century, the 'psy' disciplines were the primary source of received ideas for social work, but by the late 1950s the pendulum had swung back towards the social sciences, especially sociology, with a series of ground-breaking publications on this topic, such as Peter Leonard's (1966) widely cited text, *Sociology and Social Work*. The changing political context of this period led to the emergence of a suite of new social and social service programmes including community development, poverty alleviation initiatives and community health services. To be credible and effective in these new settings, social workers had to reorient their knowledge base from an individualistic psychoanalytic frame to perspectives that recognized the social contexts of service users' lives. The following decades saw continued debate within social work about the application of social science ideas to the analysis of the problems facing service users, the social work profession and the organization of social services (see Brewster and Whiteford, 1976; Day, 1987; Pearman, 1973; Sullivan, 1987).

Today, the place of social sciences in social work is not without contest. Indeed, as neo-classical economics ideas and 'psy' discourses have (re)gained prominence, social workers are likely to face increasing pressure to return to a focus on individual responsibility and individual change (Cree, 2000, p. 4). Even so, social science perspectives, particularly sociology, continue to feature in social work educational programmes throughout the post-industrial world (Hutchinson *et al.*, 2001). Furthermore, growing public expectations of quality in service delivery and demands from consumer organizations for more holistic, preventive and democratic approaches to practice make social science perspectives as important as ever for social workers.

It is impossible to do justice here to the enormous and varied contribution of the social sciences to social work, and so we will focus primarily on outlining the contribution of sociological discourse. Even within this more narrow focus we recognize that sociological understanding 'provides a range of perspectives, commentaries and interpretations of social life and experiences' greater than is possible to cover in depth here (Cree, 2000, p. 209). In this section, we will concentrate on the effects of key ideas from sociological discourse on the formal base of social work practice.

Sociological discourse asserts that humans are profoundly social beings. It challenges individualistic explanations of social and personal problems by drawing attention to the social practices and social structures that sustain these problems (Cree, 2000, p. 5; Stein, 2003, p. 106). For example, sociologists Davis and George (1993, p. 22) criticize the biomedical discourse's failure to recognize 'the ways in which disease and health are intimately linked to the social organisation of the population in which they occur'. In other words, sociological discourse suggests that many things that we experience as individuals, such as illness, are also socially organized and produced.

Sociological discourse also highlights the way in which socioeconomic status shapes one's life experiences and life chances. Repeatedly social science research has demonstrated the impact of socioeconomic disadvantage on a range of indicators of health and well-being. This research has established that the most disadvantaged citizens experience significantly higher rates of chronic physical and mental health problems and premature death than more advantaged citizens (McLeod and Bywaters, 2000; AIHW, 2002, pp. 212–14). By exposing the impact of socioeconomic status on our life opportunities, sociological discourses challenge concepts of individual choice and individual responsibility that are central to neo-classical economic discourse (see Chapter 2, this volume).

In addition, sociological discourse draws attention to the social construction of social 'reality' and, in so doing, calls into the question the idea of 'objective reality', on which the dominant discourses, discussed in Chapter 2, depend, and they also question the individualistic orientation of the 'psy' perspectives outlined earlier in this chapter. Critical social science investigations have exposed the historical and cultural variations in common understandings of entities such as health, illness, normality, madness and crime. Moreover, sociological discourse also raises questions about how social reality is determined and whose constructions prevail over those of others. Cree (2000, p. 207) urges us to examine the 'vested interests that seek to forefront specific kinds of meanings, definitions and evidence'.

Finally, sociological sciences focus on professions, like medicine and social work, as well as the health and welfare institutions, as objects of inquiry. In various ways, these research projects have destabilized the 'common-sense' view of professional expertise and health and welfare institutions as caring and benign, showing them to be vehicles for the exercise of oppressive forms of power. In the realm of social work, sociological insight has challenged the occupational self-image of social work as a caring profession by exposing, instead, 'the primacy of its control functions over its caring functions' (Dominelli, 1997, p. 20). These critical investigations can enable social workers to adopt a more self-reflective and critical stance about the purposes and effects of our practice.

Practice Exercise

Comparing 'psy' and sociological discourses: case study

Compare how the 'psy' and sociological discourses discussed in this chapter would assist you to analyse and respond to the following case study. Imagine you are a social worker in a non-government community support organization. A worker from an employment agency referred Michael, a 45-year-old Chinese man, to you for counselling. The worker says Michael is very depressed due to his family situation. The worker says the depression is impacting on Michael's ability to find work.

When you meet Michael you notice he is very neatly dressed and carrying a briefcase as if he is going to work. He speaks quietly and often bows to you.

Michael tells you he has been married for 20 years and has a 15-year-old son and a 12-year-old daughter. He says it was an arranged marriage. Their family are all overseas. Michael says he is an accountant and used to have his own successful business.

Michael says that about ten years ago his wife began acting aggressively towards him, physically and emotionally abusing him. He says she harassed and abused his clients, making it very difficult for his business to continue.

Practice Exercise (*cont'd*)

Michael says her aggression has been a lot worse over the last few months. He describes her following him in the street, abusing him, physically attacking him when he is asleep and threatening him with knives. Michael says his son is also starting to verbally abuse and threaten him at home. He says his business failed and he is now reliant on welfare payments as his primary income.

Michael wonders if his wife has a mental illness but she refuses to see her doctor. He says that his mother-in-law has hinted at mental health problems when his wife was a teenager. Michael says he once contacted the mental health crisis team after she had been very violent but they stated they could do nothing unless his wife was willing to see them.

Michael says his Buddhist beliefs tell him he must have done something wrong to cause his wife to be upset, but he is unable to work out what this is. He wonders if he is being punished for something he did in a previous life. Michael says he must stay with his wife and children as that is his duty. He says he feels ashamed that his family are so unhappy and says he is not worthy to be called a man.

Michael is unwilling to talk to the family doctor, as it will expose the family's shame.

He says he is unable to sleep, is tense, anxious, depressed and unable to concentrate on his work.

Michael says he feels helpless, and fearful for himself and his family, and sees no positive solutions.

Michael wants to work so he can pay the mortgage and support his family. He would like help to regain some self-confidence and to develop strategies to help him cope with his family situation.

To guide your thoughts, it may be useful to consider:

1. What information and issues would the 'psy' discourses highlight from this case study.

2. What information and issues would the sociological discourses highlight in this case study.

Responding to the Case Study

Both the 'psy' and sociological discourses on which social workers draw are humanist in their orientation and so would lead us, as social workers, to seek to understand Michael's view of his situation and to promote his self-determination. The case study also raises issues about Michael's safety and that of his wife, given the issue of use of knives to threaten Michael. Our legal obligations under mental health and criminal code legislation to report matters of this nature to the relevant authorities may cut across both our use of the 'psy' and sociological discourses to analyse and respond to this case study. None the less, these discourses would lead us to approach the case study in quite different ways.

Looking through a 'psy' lens, we would be likely to focus on:

- investigation of both Michael's and his wife's psychological conditions with a view to diagnosis. The information we have here is suggestive of possible psychological disorder. For example, Michael is showing some symptoms of depression and possibly also other psychological disorders such as anxiety. His description of his wife also suggests that she may be suffering a severe psychiatric disorder;

- assessment of psychological risk factors. The information presented in the case study suggests that Michael may face serious risk either to himself, as a person possibly suffering from a depressive illness, or from his wife, especially in relation to his assertion that she has threatened him with knives;

- sources of resilience. The case study also indicates that Michael has faced some considerable challenges in his life – migration and adaptation to a foreign culture and more recently through the loss of status associated with his failed business. From a 'psy' perspective we would explore sources of resilience that Michael has used in facing these challenges.

From this analysis, a likely course of action is referral of Michael and his wife to mental health specialists for psychiatric assessment and possible psychiatric intervention, such as pharmacological interventions. 'Psy' professionals may also offer treatments such as cognitive behavioural therapy which have been found to be useful for alleviating depression. Using insights from the 'psy' discourses, the social worker could also continue to offer supportive casework intervention to help Michael overcome his feelings of helplessness and isolation while he undergoes psychiatric assessment.

By contrast, using a sociological approach we would highlight:

- the social organization of family life and gender roles. For example, we might examine the cultural expectations, such as the expectation that, as a husband and father, Michael should be in a breadwinner role and consider, with him, the ways in which these expectations contribute to his depression;

- cultural constructions of mental health and illness. From a sociological perspective we may question the referring worker's construction of

Michael's problem as one of 'depression' as a way of categorizing his concerns. We might seek to understand Michael's response as less one of individual psychopathology, as the label of 'depression' implies, and instead view it as a response to conditions of structural injustice. We would also explore Michael's view of his experiences with his wife to discover a broad range of explanations, not only the one of mental illness hinted at in the case study. Another possible explanation we could explore is whether Michael is a victim of domestic violence and, if so, how we can provide the appropriate supports and options for him to escape the situation;

- a focus on structural and social injustices. A sociological lens would encourage us to see Michael's problem in structural and social contexts. In many post-industrial societies, there is a growing body of middle-aged men in white-collar occupations facing unemployment partly as a result of globalization and changing technologies in the workplace. Michael's situation is not simply one of his 'depression' impacting on his ability to find work, but also one where as a middle-aged white-collar worker he is structurally disadvantaged in the marketplace. It is also possible that, as a member of a cultural minority, Michael faces racial and cultural discrimination in his attempts to find employment. From a sociological perspective, we would explore these structural and social concerns with him.

From this analysis our likely course of action would be, first, to reduce Michael's sense of 'helplessness' by identifying the broader conditions that contribute to his situation and assisting him to focus on these rather than the personal explanation of his situation. We would encourage him to reflect critically on the social expectations that he carries about being in paid work in order to be a 'man'. We would aim to build social support that may enable him to achieve socially and culturally meaningful roles. For example, we may focus on how he can use his accounting and business knowledge within his own community to, for example, support Chinese agencies or help young people develop skills in this field.

Practice Reflection

Now that we've considered the key themes of social science discourses and their application to a case study, discuss what you see as the key strengths and limitations of sociological discourse in an area of social work practice that interests you.

The Uses and Limits of Social Science Discourse for Social Work

Sociological discourse has much to offer social work practitioners. The social sciences, particularly sociology, offer theoretical and research perspectives that enable us to understand service users' problems within their social contexts (Stein, 2003, p. 105). Many social work texts draw explicitly on sociological concepts, such as socioeconomic disadvantage, status and stigma, in analysing problems facing service users and in developing social work and social policy responses (see Cree, 2000; Dominelli, 1997; McLeod and Bywaters, 2000). Cree (2000, p. 5) asserts that, without this critical understanding of social context, social workers are likely to pathologize and blame individuals and families for the problems they face and, in so doing, 'perpetuate the oppression and discrimination which characterize the lives of users of social work services'.

Sociological analysis can also help us to think critically about our own practices and the health and welfare institutions in which we work. For instance, a sociological approach can enable us to critically examine how social service practices and institutions contradict our values, such as respect and self-determination, and our practice goals, such as empowerment (McLeod and Bywaters, 2000, p. 12). Critical analysis can lead to the development of new kinds of responses to consumer needs, such as consumer-led institutions (*ibid.*; see also Crossley and Crossley, 2001). For example, in the case study with Michael, a sociological approach would lead us to question 'psy' labels such as depression and focus instead on assisting Michael to achieve socially and culturally meaningful roles in his cultural community.

Despite the uses of sociological discourse for contemporary social work practice, it also has many issues and limitations. First, significant tensions exist between the core purpose and focus of the social sciences, that is, to systemically build knowledge about society, and the primary action orientation of social work (Bloom, 2000). Davies (cited in Cree, 2000, p. 6) asserts that 'sociologists ask questions; social workers must act as though they have answers'. The different scale of the problems typically dealt with by social workers and sociologists further exacerbates these tensions. In particular, when approaching welfare concerns many sociological analyses seek systematically to analyse whole social systems, such as the organization of prisons, child welfare systems or even whole societies, such as post-industrial societies. By contrast, social work intervention is typically on a much smaller scale, focusing on individuals, families, groups or communities. The vastly different foci of social science investigations, particularly sociological studies, and social work intervention demands caution in the transfer of ideas from one field to the other, lest the complexities inherent to each context are overlooked (Leonard, 1966, p. 97). For example, it is one thing for a sociologist to analyse the social origins of delinquency; it is quite another to work, as a social worker, with a young person in trouble with the law and to face with him/her the consequences of his/her actions for family, peers and, in some instances, victims.

Also, social workers and social scientists often adopt different processes of knowledge development and application. The action orientation of social work leads social workers to focus on social science knowledge that is directly useful for practice, such as 'facts' and theories concerning the particular phenomena – mental illness, child abuse and so on – with which they work. This material is often disconnected from the wider gestalt of social science research from which it was originally produced. Thus, according to Leonard (1966, p. 97), the action orientation of the social worker may lead him/her to 'endow [social science] knowledge with greater certainty and with greater simplicity, than would the sociologist'.

Furthermore, despite a long history of association between social work and social science, the relationship between these disciplines is often characterized by a lack of mutual respect and exchange. For example, some social workers criticize social scientists for their lack of practical *nous*, while some social scientists stand in judgement of social workers for a perceived lack of theoretical sophistication or for the failure to live up to social science ideals even though these ideals are rarely developed in social service contexts. The mutual hostility generated by caricaturing each 'side' of the social worker/social scientist divide has been most unhelpful to a thorough exploration of the uses and limits of social science discourses in social work.

Finally, the truths of sociological discourse, like those of all discourses, can be used to devalue other perspectives. In some sociological analyses, the truths of other discourses, such as biomedicine, are critiqued as social constructions and 'mere territorializations' of social life (Williams, 2003, pp. 16–19). Yet these other constructions, such as biomedical perspectives, can also offer useful ways for understanding and responding to client concerns. For example, in our case study, sociological discourse, on its own, may lead us to overlook the possible contribution of biology to Michael's depression and the relevance of biomedical response to his condition. Social workers work in environments where there are often competing definitions of problems and where service users' problems demand complex responses that may, in many instances, require us to draw on the resources of these competing discourses. For instance, Michael may be assisted by a combination of biomedical and social interventions. Thus, in social work, we cannot afford to privilege social science discourse over other discourses present within the practice context. As Leonard (1966, p. 98) warns, 'Sociological propositions similarly need to be treated with caution, to be questioned as to the evidence which supports them, and to be placed within a framework that takes into account the whole man, biological, psychological, and social.'

Conclusion

The formal base of social work draws on a range of received ideas. As the profession has emerged over the course of the twentieth century, it has drawn most strongly on human science discourses drawn from the disciplines of psychology and sociology. Today there remains considerable contest among these discourses, and the extent to which they construct modern professional social work varies a great deal by geographical and practice contexts. Given the foundational role these discourses play in constructing us as social workers and our practice purposes, it is important that we are able to reflect critically on their uses and limitations for achieving our goals and values within our specific contexts of social work practice.

Summary Questions

1. What ideas from psychoanalytic discourse continue to influence social work practice today?

2. How might knowledge from 'psy' discourses assist or limit social workers capacity to promote the self-determination of service users?

3. What are the strengths and limits of sociological discourse for helping social workers to realize the value of social justice in practice?

Recommended Reading

'Psy' Discourse

Borden, W. 'The relational paradigm in contemporary psychoanalysis: Toward a psychodynamically informed social work perspective', *The Social Service Review*, 74(33) (2000), 352–79.
This article offers a historical overview of the impact of psychodynamic thought on interpersonal social work practice. Borden is sympathetic to psychodynamic ideas and argues for the reintegration of these ideas into a broad range of contemporary social work practices.

Rose, N. *Governing the Soul: The Shaping of the Private Self*, 2nd edn. (London: Free Association Books, 1999).
This widely cited work provides a sociological history of the rise and impact of psychological sciences. It includes well-researched material on the influence of 'psy' ideas in the social sciences. The book is highly critical of the role of 'psy' sciences in the government of individuals and takes a strongly critical position towards social workers and other human service professionals' engagement with these ideas.

Woods, M.E. and F. Hollis. *Casework: A Psychosocial Therapy*, 4th edn. (New York: McGraw-Hill, 1990).
Now in its fourth edition, this classic text provides an excellent introduction to the psychosocial model of practice, which attempts to integrate psychodynamic and ecosystems perspectives into social casework.

Sociological Discourses

Cree, V. *Sociology for Social Workers and Probation Officers* (London: Routledge, 2000).
This book provides a reader-friendly introduction to sociological perspectives and their application to a variety of social service contexts.

Note

1. DSMIV refers to the Diagnostic and Statistical Manual Disorders of the American Psychiatric Association. It is the standard classification of mental dysfunction developed primarily by the 'psy' professions of psychiatry and psychology.

4

Alternative Service Discourses: Consumer Rights, and Religion and Spirituality

In this chapter, we turn to another set of service discourses that have a (re-)emerging influence in many contemporary practice contexts. The discourses we consider in this chapter are consumer rights and discourses associated with religion and spirituality. I refer to these as alternative service discourses because, like the human science discourses discussed in the previous chapter, these discourses are concerned with providing holistic responses to human need, but dispute aspects of the human science discourses that social workers have relied upon in constructing their knowledge base for practice. While I realize that these alternative service discourses offer much more than ways of constituting health and welfare services, my focus in this chapter is on how these discourses construct core

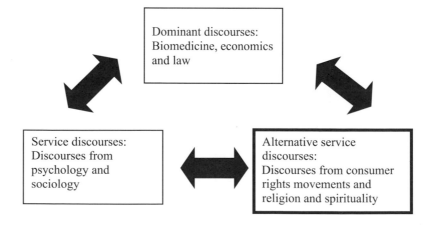

Figure 4.1 Discourses in interaction: highlighting alternative service discourses

68

concepts, such as client needs and capacities, and the provision of health and welfare services, including the role of the social worker in service delivery. Figure 4.1 highlights the discourses we will focus on this chapter.

Alternative Service Discourses in Context

In Figure 4.1, I have positioned alternative service discourses below the dominant discourses to demonstrate that, like the human science discourses I outlined in Chapter 3, these alternative service discourses are also subordinate to the dominant discourses of biomedicine, economics and law that shape modern health and welfare institutions. I have positioned the alternative service discourses across from the human science discourses, from which the formal knowledge base of social work has historically drawn, to show the strong interaction between the two sets of discourses.

Of course, many discourses from outside the human sciences shape how client needs and social work practices are constituted. Other relevant discourses, such as human rights and communitarian discourses, also inform some aspects of the reformation and critique of service provision and social work practice. I have chosen to focus on consumer rights and discourses associated with religion and spirituality as alternative service discourses because of their growing influence in determining client needs and service provision processes in mainstream health and welfare contexts, such as hospitals, statutory authorities and large non-government community service organizations.

For more than four decades now consumer rights movements in a range of health and welfare domains have challenged the dominant constructions of service users as passive recipients, to promote, instead, recognition of service users as active participants in determining their own service needs and responses to those needs. Also, for at least two decades, religious and spiritual discourses have re-emerged as powerful practices in health and welfare services. This influence can be attributed, largely, to the privatization of service delivery and the growing role of religious organizations as key providers of non-government health and welfare services. In addition, the growing influence of spiritual discourses in health and welfare services can be attributed to agitation from service providers and service users who have argued that recognition of spiritual needs is critical to holistic and culturally sensitive health and welfare service delivery.

These alternative service discourses offer profound contests to the ways in which both the dominant discourses, outlined in Chapter 2, and the human science discourses, discussed in Chapter 3, constitute client needs and health and welfare provision. In different ways, this alternative set of service discourses contests the notions of individualism, rationality, objectivity and linear notions of progress underpinning the dominant discourses of bio-medicine, neo-classical economics and law. For instance, the consumer rights movements have challenged the status of biomedical interventions as progressive, showing that these interventions can also serve to deny service users other options for achieving their own welfare and well-being. The alternative service discourses also contest the human science discourses on which human service professions, like social work, have historically relied. For example, discourses associated with spirituality can challenge the humanist ethos, central to modern social work, that focuses on humans as the agents of achieving personal and social change and, in so doing, has denied the place of spiritual authority and meaning in some service users' lives.

As I will demonstrate in this chapter, the relationship between the two sets of service discourses is an interaction characterized by both complementarities and tensions. For while the alternative service discourses challenge core assumptions of the human service discourses on which social work depends, they also rely on some of these discourses. For example, the consumer rights discourse draws on ideas from critical sociology, such as recognition of the conflicting interests of different groups within institutions, to construct practice approaches. In addition, while the alternative service discourses challenge the formal base of social work, they can also offer new opportunities for achieving the kinds of values such as the promotion of self-determination and social justice to which social workers are committed. For example, discourses of religion and spirituality can be drawn on to expand the ways in which service providers constitute service users' needs.

In this chapter, I will urge you, the reader, to approach these discourses critically and cautiously. I will argue that while they may offer useful alternative constructions of client needs and service roles, they can also limit our, and service users', opportunities to achieve the sorts of humanistic values and goals to which social workers are committed. Within the social work literature there is an emerging critique of the growing influence of religious themes in some areas of service practice and we will consider these critiques as well as criticisms of consumer rights discourse in health and welfare service provision. In short, I will argue that social workers must adopt a critical stance toward these discourses, recognizing their limitations for achieving the emancipatory ends often claimed by their advocates. Let's turn now to an analysis of the features and influence of consumer rights discourse in health and welfare services.

Consumer Rights Discourse

Consumer rights discourse presents service users as rights-bearing citizens who have the right and the capacities to fully participate in determining their health and welfare needs. This construction of the rights-bearing citizen is contrasted with the tendency of dominant and human science discourses to constitute service users as passive objects of health and welfare interventions (see Crossley and Crossley, 2001). Consumer rights discourse aims to deconstruct dominant constructions of the 'normal' and 'abnormal' and in so doing create opportunities for those formerly deemed 'abnormal' to gain increased opportunities to live full and productive lives of their choosing. We are 'different' but 'equal' is the guiding credo of many of the consumer rights movements from which this discourse has emerged.

The consumer rights discourse is associated with consumer rights movements in health and welfare that are also referred to as patients' rights and citizens' rights movements. Today consumer rights movements have emerged across the spectrum of health and welfare fields and cover a wide range of concerns, including: breast cancer; sexual health; HIV/AIDS; organ donation; and ageing. Over the past decade, in particular, there has been a substantial growth in research on, and practice in, disability politics across the fields of psychiatric, intellectual and physical disabilities, so it is these fields of practice that will be our primary focus in this section.

Consumer Rights Movements in Health and Welfare

The new social movements in the fields of health and welfare first emerged during the 1970s (Campbell and Oliver, 1996, p. 49; Crossley and Crossley, 2001). Although members of these new consumer rights movements acknowledge earlier forms of resistance and action among members of health and welfare minorities, they link their approach to the various civil rights movements that developed in the 1960s and 1970s (see Campbell and Oliver, 1996, p. 46). Members of these new social movements seek to challenge the pathologizing labels often ascribed to them by health and welfare professionals on the grounds that these labels denigrate the lived experiences and capacities of service users. For example, the term 'differently abled' is preferable to 'disabled' on the grounds that the former recognizes the capacities gained through disability.

Consumer rights movements are often associated with the development of communities of people with specific lived experiences and capacities. One aim of these communities is to build alternative services through which the capacities and life choices of the consumer can be recognized and enhanced. For example, some Deaf Communities have established alternative schools in which the social and cultural needs as well as the academic interests of deaf children are served. Another aim of the consumer rights movements is to build critical consciousness within their communities of the ways in which specific groups of service users, such as women, people with disabilities, young parents, and so on, are poorly served and, in some instances, oppressed by mainstream health and welfare systems and by society more generally (Barnes, 1996, p. 109).

Members of consumer rights movements aim to develop services that are empowering and appropriate to service users' specific needs. In contrast to dominant modes of health and welfare delivery which rely on professional experts, these services seek to engage service users in decision making at all levels of service delivery from consultation about direct provision through to participation in manager decision making. The key strategies used by consumer rights movements to empower service users include questioning of professional expertise and the revaluation of service user knowledge, and increased focus on peer and mutual support processes for meeting service users' needs. In the process of developing collective support, consumer groups often participate in developing new understandings of themselves, to, in effect, reinvent themselves not as victims or service users but as survivors and rights-bearing citizens (Crossley and Crossley, 2001).

Often, consumer rights advocates view the law as a vehicle for promoting and protecting service users' rights (see Barnes, 1996). In particular, the United Nations Declaration of the Rights of Disabled Persons (1975) is widely seen, within disability rights movements, as a turning point in affirming the social participation rights of people with disabilities (Campbell and Oliver, 1996, p. 19). Using a human rights framework, consumer rights groups have reconceptualized some of the apparently personal decisions affecting oppressed health and welfare minorities as human rights issues. For example, some consumer rights advocates argue that apparently personal issues such as the management of contraception and menstruation for young women with severe intellectual disabilities should be understood as human rights issues, rather than as personal decisions for family members and care-givers (for discussion see Brady, 1998; Carlson and Wilson, 1998).

As in other civil rights movements, some members of consumer rights groups have used public protest to achieve social change. For example, people with disabilities have demonstrated against the public transport and building authorities for failing to ensure disability access to these public utilities (Campbell and Oliver, 1996, pp. 152–3; Golfus and Simpson, 1994). Not only have these actions achieved practical change, such as improved access to public spaces; these public campaigns have also challenged cultural stereotypes by showing that people with disabilities can be active agents of change.

Key Themes in Consumer Rights Discourse

Consumer rights movements in health and welfare are diverse. In this discussion of themes we will focus on consumer rights discourse that is associated with new social movements. These movements draw on critical social science theories and the progressive political values and stances, such as collectivism and redistributive justice, broadly associated with the political Left (see Campbell and Oliver, 1996, pp. 100–101; Oliver, 2001).

A core theme of the consumer rights discourse is a focus on the social structures and cultural problems as the original causes of the problems and barriers facing service users. Tom Shakespeare (2003, p. 199), a disability studies scholar, argues that 'Clearly, the problem of disability is more to do with social and cultural processes than it is to do with biology' (see also Barnes, 1996, p. 109). Members of consumer rights movements in many fields of disability are highly critical of the focus on individual biology and personal pathology that dominates health and welfare institutions' construction of client needs and the service provision process. In contrast to the biomedical discourse which focuses on diagnosis and amelioration of biological pathology, consumer rights discourse presents a social model of health and wellness which focuses on 'the removal or amelioration of social and environmental barriers to full social, physical, career, and religious participation' (Quinn, 1998, p. xix; see also Campbell and Oliver, 1996; Oliver, 2001; Shakespeare, 2003). This construction of client need from one of personal change to change in society has led to the formation of alternative services for, and the opening up of mainstream services to, differently able people.

Another theme is that of equality in the context of difference. Consumer rights discourse challenges the opposition between 'normal' and 'abnormal' that dominates many health and welfare discourses, such as 'psy' and 'biomedical' discourses, to argue that the needs of differently abled people should be recognized as part of the broad spectrum of human experiences and capacities. This discourse challenges health and welfare institutions to open themselves to the diversity of client needs rather than to treat specific client groups, such as survivors of mental illnesses, as 'special' cases who place an extra burden on these institutions.

The consumer rights discourse presents the needs of service users as the need for 'community' rather than for 'cure'. Consumer rights discourse shows that many 'advances', particularly medical practices, and helping practices, such as supportive casework and welfare provision, do little to promote the social inclusion of service users. What is needed, according to this discourse, is support for alternative communities in which the services users' needs can be recognized in dialogue with service users and responded to in a holistic, rather than fragmented and individualistic, fashion. Indeed, some members of consumer rights movements have pointed out that the 'helping' practices of health and welfare professions actually further the oppression of service users by failing to recognize and support socially inclusive responses to the service users' concerns (Crossley and Crossley, 2001, p. 1484; Oliver, 2001, p. 158). For example, some members of the Deaf

Community argue that new technologies that offer 'hope' of hearing are indicative of the profound intolerance of the hearing society towards deaf people (Hyde and Power, 2000).

Consumer rights discourse associated with the new social movements draws on a conflict theory perspective to challenge the centrality of professional experts in service provision and to reconfigure the relationship between service providers and service users to become one based on equality and, in particular, recognition of the expertise gained through the lived experience of service users. This discourse highlights the ways in which service users' interests are constructed through powerful professional groups within these institutions and, from this position, argues that in order to meet their own needs, service user groups must first take decision-making power from powerful groups within these institutions. As Oliver (2001, p. 158) asserts, the 'Independent Living [movement] is nothing more or less than rescuing the [disabled] body from the hands of medics, other professionals and welfare administrators'. Through processes of recovering and valuing their lived knowledge as members of oppressed communities, members of consumer rights movements assert their expertise in their own lives and, more specifically, in defining their health and welfare needs. Consumer rights discourse also calls into question professionals' claim to knowledge that is objective, rational and true (Crossley and Crossley, 2001, p. 1484; Oliver, 2001, p. 158). Instead, the accounts of professional experts become *a* truth, rather than *the* truth, about service users' lives.

Finally, according to consumer rights discourse, a key need of service users is to develop a critical self-awareness of their oppression before they can act in their own best interests. For some members of disability rights movements this process of critical self-awareness involves challenging the dominant cultural narrative of disability as personal tragedy to recognize, instead, the structural and cultural bases of the difficulties facing people with disabilities. In addition, the development of collective identification is vital to overcoming oppression. For example, one is no longer primarily a person with schizophrenia; instead, one becomes a member of an oppressed health minority, in this case, those labelled as mentally ill. This process is described by Crossley and Crossley (2001, p. 1484), who, in their review of consumer rights movements in mental health services, observe that '[the] use of collective pronouns such as "we" and "us" alongside such typifications as "survivor" or user, is highly significant ... No longer are they purely individual experiences of a solitary ego. They are the experiences of a group; collective and shared experiences.'

Let's turn now to consider a practice example of how consumer rights discourse might conflict with a dominant construction of client need and service provision.

Practice Exercise

Getting inside the cochlear ear implant

Imagine you work in a paediatric hospital. The paediatric surgeon has referred Dawn, 25 years, and John, 32 years, to you to assist them in their decision making. Dawn and Joe are uncertain about whether to seek a cochlear ear implant for their 18-month-old daughter, Zoe, who is profoundly deaf. Dawn is also profoundly deaf and she is an active member of the Deaf Community. John is not deaf but is a strong ally of the Deaf Community. Both Dawn and John believe that deaf people are members of a linguistic minority within an oralist culture.

Dawn and John are confused about what to do. While both recognize that the surgery is pathologically unnecessary, that is, Zoe's wellness does not depend on the surgery, they want to make the best decision for Zoe's quality of life. Dawn says that she feels very happy with her life as a deaf person, but she is not sure whether the new technology may offer Zoe important opportunities in life that might otherwise be unavailable to her as a deaf person. Dawn says that her uncertainty has increased after recent discussions with the paediatric ear, nose and throat specialist, who outlined progress in the cochlear ear implant that will dramatically improve Zoe's chances of living her life as a hearing person. John is strongly of the view that Zoe should not have the implant, yet, respects Dawn's ambivalence about the surgery. From his perspective, not only is the operation pathologically unnecessary, but that to agree to this operation would be to impose an oralist culture on Zoe; that is, in effect, it would deny her the opportunity to participate in deaf culture.

As a social worker in this area you are aware of the debate within the deaf community and among health professionals about the pros and cons of the cochlear implant. Health professionals involved in cochlear ear implantation argue that:

- the cochlear implant considerably enhances the capacity of profoundly and totally deaf people to participate in mainstream society, including, for example, increased access to educational, social and economic opportunities;

- the younger the child at the time of implant, the more successful the outcome. Infancy is widely regarded by medical and development specialists as a neurologically critical period for the development of spoken language. In other words, if the operation is left until Zoe is older, it is unlikely to lead to the substantial improvements in her hearing capacity that is possible to achieve now.

Practice Exercise (*cont'd*)

Opponents of the cochlear ear implant argue that:

- being deaf is not an illness; it does not need to be 'conquered'. Deaf people can and do lead rich and fulfilling lives, particularly when they have access to opportunities to achieve social and economic participation;

- while the surgery is most effective for young children, they are unable to provide informed consent to the procedure. The requirement of early implantation of the cochlear device effectively denies them the choice to participate in deaf culture;

- all surgery carries risk, and this surgery, although widely presented by the medical community as safe, carries some potentially negative effects, including disturbance of taste, dizziness and constant ringing in the ears.

- What do you see as the key issues in this case study from your perspective as a social worker?

- What principles would inform your practice here?

- How would you assist this couple in their decision making?

This case study illuminates some of the conflicts between the ways consumer rights discourse constructs client needs and service responses and the ways these concepts are constituted in other discourses, such as, in this case, the biomedical discourse. These different constructions can create conflict for social workers and service users as we seek to negotiate our purpose and course of action. For example, in the case study, as social workers we would probably want to promote the 'best interests of the child'. Yet we can see that consumer rights discourse constitutes best interests in a different way to biomedical discourse. We can see that health professionals, and those working in contexts where biomedical discourse is privileged, are likely to view cochlear implantation surgery as 'obviously' in Zoe's best interests. This view is likely to have public support as well, for as Hyde and Power observe (2000, p. 117), 'Most lay observers find it hard to believe that there should be any opposition to what is presented as a benefit to deaf children and their parents.' On the other hand, from a consumer rights perspective, we recognize that by 'giving' Zoe the 'opportunity' for a cochlear implant, we open opportunities in one culture, the oralist culture, but deny her access to another, the deaf culture. At the very least, an awareness of consumer rights discourse should alert us to the possibility that advances in health and welfare may 'take away' and oppress, in the same moment as they offer opportunities.

In this situation the principle of informed consent is probably more useful than that of best interests for guiding our decision making, given that the concept of best interests is constructed in irreconcilable ways between the two discourses of biomedicine and consumer rights. The principle of informed decision making means that individuals involved in decision-making 'should not be hindered in his or her understanding, reasoning or decision making and should be able to make a decision in a context free from constraint or undue influence' (Hyde and Power, 2000, p. 120). Zoe's age poses a clear barrier to informed consent and medical opinion suggests that to defer the decision until Zoe can effectively consent would be to deny her some of the 'benefits' of the technology. We can, however, ensure that Dawn and John are given opportunities to access information about the benefits and risks associated with each of the decisions available to them. According to Hyde and Power (2000, p. 123), this benefit and risk analysis 'should be broadened to include the social, linguistic and culture characteristics associated with being Deaf; namely that, in contrast to the perception that there is a disadvantage in being deaf, the "viable Deaf life" alternative' should be explored. We could recognize Dawn's expertise by inviting her to reflect with us on the 'personal, social, cultural, and linguisitic context' of her life as a deaf person and what that could offer Zoe.

Consistent with the principle of informed decision making, we should be sensitive to how our location, in a hospital context, might constrain Dawn and John. In this setting, we would need to make sure that the information offered by health professionals, who are likely to hold a privileged expert status, is balanced with other views on the situation. Indeed, the case-study material suggests that Dawn is already experiencing some pressure from biomedical experts to adopt a particular course of action. To ensure that these pressures are reduced, we might also involve Dawn and John in gathering information about the procedure from a range of perspectives, including the views of: parents who have consented to and those who have refused the procedure for their children; people who have had the procedure and those who have refused it; and members of the Deaf Community. In order to build a facilitative environment, we could meet with Dawn and John in a more neutral context than the paediatric hospital, such as their home.

Consistent with the social work value of promoting client welfare and well-being, we might want also to consider with Dawn and John how either decision will affect the quality of their family life now and in the future. An important consideration here would be the language spoken at home and in their network of friends. If a sign language is used at home and among their friends, consideration might be given to how the implantation of the cochlear ear might impact on this language use and the family dynamics and what implications either decision will have for Zoe's integra-tion into the Deaf Community of which her parents are a part.

Critical Analysis of Consumer Rights Discourse

Consumer rights discourse is highly consistent with some of the key values asserted in social work and human services fields. Consumer rights discourse is built on themes of empowerment, self-determination and social justice, and offers practical strategies for consumers to insist on their rights to participate in determining their needs and choosing how these needs will be met. In many contexts of practice, the growing influence of consumer rights discourse can make it easier for us, as social workers, to support client decisions that run counter to dominant discourses within mainstream health and welfare settings. Partly as a result of consumer rights initiatives in policy making, many mainstream health and welfare institutions are required by policy and sometimes by statute to involve service users in decision making. Consumer rights initiatives have also led to broader public awareness of consumer-directed alternatives in many areas of service provision. As social workers we can use these changing policy practices and levels of public awareness to support consumer self-determination. For example, in the context of the increasing influence of consumer rights discourse in health and welfare services, our wish to support Dawn and Joe in exploring a range of options, including non-intervention, is likely to be recognized by other health team members as a basic client right, but without this discourse, we are in a far weaker position to support clients' rights to choose, especially to choose non-intervention.

In a myriad of ways, consumer rights discourse has returned power to the hands of the people oppressed within modern health and welfare systems. It has helped to break down the isolation, self-blame and stigma experienced by many service users of health and welfare systems, especially those with chronic illnesses or disabilities. According to the testimonials of members of consumer rights movements (see Campbell and Oliver, 1996; Crossley and Crossley, 2001), the processes of support, critical awareness raising, skill development and collective action have, in themselves, energized many members and enabled them to achieve substantial improvements in their quality of life on their own terms. By challenging service provider groups to recognize the broad range of needs of service users, other than 'cure' of a condition, consumer rights discourse has facilitated the creation of services that expand the opportunities for service users to live a quality of life of their choosing. These initiatives move beyond a focus on addressing 'health' or 'welfare' needs to promote the social, cultural, and economic well-being of the service user. For example, the Deaf Community has created deaf choirs that help build pride in and community recognition of deaf culture.

Consumer rights discourse has contributed to the substantial expansion of consumer-led services in many fields of health and welfare provision, especially among people with disabilities (Campbell and Oliver, 1996).

These services break down professional domination of service delivery processes in health and welfare and diversify the range and form of services available to oppressed service user groups. Consumer-led services usually move beyond direct service provision to health and welfare minorities to supporting the capacity of service users to participate in organizational governance and broader social change activities. Consumer rights discourse has focused on ensuring that service user groups have a voice in 'relevant political and economic fora throughout the world' (Campbell and Oliver, 1996, p. 169). Again, the consumer rights discourse moves beyond a narrow construction of client needs to a more expansive recognition of needs and interests with the aim of promoting social inclusion and celebrating social diversity.

Despite the many strengths of consumer rights discourse, there is currently much debate, within and outside consumer rights movements, about the limits of this discourse for promoting service users' interests and well-being (see Corker and Shakespeare, 2002). One area of contention is the reliance of modern consumer rights discourse on fixed identities forged around social categories of gender, race, class, wellness and ability, and so on. Of course, these identity categories can be extremely useful and politically necessary (Thornton, 2000, p. 19). However, the reliance on a fixed identity, for example, the definition of oneself as a 'a person with a disability', 'queer' or 'a breast cancer survivor' disregards the 'temporal and fluid character' of identity (*ibid.*, p. 21). In other words, a focus on fixed identity overlooks the extent to which one's identities may vary over time as, for example, one's condition may alter, and the meaning of each identity often changes through time, circumstance and context. For example, a person with a mental illness may find that their mental health status is not always the most salient aspect of their identity, especially during periods of wellness.

In constructing the consumer identity around specified characteristics, 'a differently abled person' or 'a mental health survivor', the consumer rights discourse can rely on the suppression of differences and conflicts among members of the community. While this may be politically necessary for a period, a reliance on a fixed collective identity can become oppressive when it involves the suppression of differences, such as differences of political perspectives, interests and identifications (Humphrey, 1999, p. 182). For example, women with disabilities and women of colour have raised concerns about the extent to which the concerns of white, middle-class and able-bodied women have dominated feminist politics. Similarly, some members of HIV/AIDS consumer movements have challenged the dominance of health initiatives around the needs of gay men on the grounds that the interests of other groups, such as HIV-positive women and lesbians, are marginalized (Humphrey, 1999, pp. 177–8).

Furthermore, when specific identities and interests dominate an identity group, members of that collective will face pressure to conform to group norms. Humphrey (1999, p. 183) warns that 'all communities engender their own norms which will consolidate over time; and a community grounded upon a particular identity is likely to essentialize that identity and to enforce homogeneity, to a greater or lesser extent'. Hence individuals who choose not to conform to claims made on behalf of the collective face the threat of sanction and, possibly, exclusion (for discussion, see Campbell and Oliver, 1996, pp. 78–80). This has particular implications for social workers as we seek to promote clients' capacity for self-determination. For example, in working with Dawn and Joe in their decision making about Zoe's hearing status we might explore the pressures they face not only from the biomedical system but also from their peers and how they will free themselves from these pressures in order to make an informed decision for Zoe and their family.

Another set of concerns relates to the conflict perspective on which some forms of consumer rights discourse are based. While this perspective exposes macro-processes of power, such as the power of men over women and able-bodied and disabled, it can also render invisible the complexities of power relations at the levels of interpersonal and institutional practice. For example, care-givers, such as professionals and family members, are often involved in difficult decisions with, or on behalf of, people with disabilities. Such decisions may be whether or not to consent to family members with disabilities undergoing surgical procedures aimed at improving hearing or managing menstruation and contraception. Using a human rights discourse, advocates have exposed some areas of human rights abuse such as the sterilization of young children (see Brady, 1998). Yet, when this discourse is invoked as the primary framework for decision making, it fails to honour the difficult interpersonal dimensions of these decision-making processes, particularly when the decision bears significantly on the care workload carried by other 'stakeholders', such as family members. This is especially so in situations where the person's circumstance or condition means that they have a limited capacity to consent to or refuse intervention, and where family members bear significant personal responsibility for ongoing care and thus have a stake in decision making about the family member with a disability. For example, in seeking to assist Dawn and Joe in their decision making it is more helpful to prioritize the principle of informed decision making about what will work best for Zoe's and her family's interest now and in the future, rather than to characterize this decision as primarily a human rights issue.

A second problem is that an oppositional approach to power and identity can give rise to what Nietzsche, the German philosopher, has referred to as the politics of 'ressentiment' (Healy, 2000, p. 53; Thornton, 2000, p. 19).

In the process of consciousness raising associated with consumer rights discourse, consumers comes to understand themselves as survivors who bear 'witness to the hidden injuries done to them by others – or by fate' (Rose, 1999, p. 268). On the one hand, this can be experienced as liberating when one comes to challenge negative stereotypes about the self as issues not of personal deficit but of structural oppression for which others are entirely responsible. Yet, on the other hand, this can limit one's capacity for power by placing responsibility for change in the hands of the other, more powerful person/group and by limiting one's identity as the stigmatized self. Rose (1999, p. 269) points out that, in the politics of ressentiment, one's identity 'is organised around the ideas of suffering, of demanding recompense, of making amends, of holding to account – a way of making sense of stigma by reversing it and attaching oneself to it as the very mark of one's virtue'. If the aim of consumer rights discourse is to diversify consumers' opportunities for choice, constructing our identities in terms of consumer or group membership can again close down these choices.

In the politics of ressentiment, consumers hold other more powerful groups directly responsible for their oppression (Thornton, 2000, p. 19). For example, in some contexts, consumer rights discourse goes beyond a critique of powerful health and welfare institutions to criticize the power wielded by their professionals. In this interpretation, professional service providers are caricatured as self-interested and oppressive (Healy, 2000, pp. 111–13; see Golfus and Simpson, 1994). Such an approach prevents us from recognizing the differences within the powerful group and from using these to achieve change within the group. For example, if we label all care professionals as 'self-interested', we have no way of differentiating between those who are potential allies, nor do we have any way of recognizing the forms of constraint to which even powerful allies are subject (Healy, 2000, p. 113).

A related concern is the potential for oppositional politics to alienate possible sources of support within the general community and among the powerful groups within the institutions of health and welfare. For example, many members of the Deaf Community want the medical professionals and medical scientists engaged in developing cochlear ear technology to understand that deaf people can lead full and productive lives and that cochlear ear implants can limit their opportunity to participate in deaf culture. While there are powerful medical and economic interests involved in the development of this technology, careful consideration needs to be given to how to engage key stakeholders such as surgeons and product development companies in recognizing consumer interests. Confrontative approaches such as picketing surgeons' conferences and labelling them as the new 'Butchers of Belsen', as some consumer rights advocates have done (Hyde and Power, 2000, p. 119), may be counterproductive for promoting public and service provider interests in recognizing consumer-based alternatives to this technology. These confrontative actions deny the diversity of views even within consumer rights groups about the uses and limits of new technology for furthering their interests and among the professional groups developing and applying this technology. A great danger is that rather than building interest in alternative service discourses, these approaches can close down options for a dialogue between 'powerful' groups, such as scientists and surgeons and service user communities.

Finally, consumer rights economic discourse can, perhaps inadvertently, reinforce some dimensions of neo-classical economic discourse, particularly the drive to achieve greater economic efficiency in service delivery. Care must be taken lest the demand of consumer rights movements for increased control over service delivery and reduced professional involvement be used by governments and other funding bodies to justify a reduction in social services funding.

Religious and Spiritual Discourses

We move now to a consideration of how discourses associated with religion and spirituality construct service users' needs and service provision, including social work practice, in health and welfare institutions. Although most social workers view the profession as a secular one, we shall see that health and welfare contexts and the social work profession are strongly shaped by religious and spiritual beliefs and ideas. I begin this section by differentiating between spirituality and religion and by outlining key themes in these discourses. I will then discuss how these discourses impact on social work contexts and service delivery. I will also consider the uses and issues concerning the operations of religious and spiritual discourses in social work practice contexts.

What are Religious and Spiritual Discourses?

In the secular world, the terms spirituality and religion are often used interchangeably. Yet for many scholars, practitioners, and service users, there are important differences between these two terms. Lindsay (2002, p. 48) defines religion as 'a systematic body of beliefs and practices related to a spiritual search'. These beliefs and practices vary and can include prayer sessions and meditations through to radical social action. In addition, as Hutchison (1998, p. 58) asserts, 'religion also refers to a communal expression of some form of mutual aid and some communal compassionate concern for people and the environment in which they live'. In short, religious discourses usually produce forms of organized service activity in addition to supporting individual spiritual search.

By contrast, spirituality refers to the search for meaning and purpose in life and an understanding of one's place in the universe (Lindsay, 2002, p. 32). According to Hutchison (1998, p. 58), 'Its [spirituality's] primary focus is on the individual and the psychological processes by which he/she organizes some type of world view and consciously relates to that world.' Unlike religion, spirituality does not necessarily involve organized practices and institutions for the expression of faith. Yet this does not mean that religion and spirituality are necessarily separated from one another; only that the search for spiritual meaning can occur in the absence of an organized and institutionalized base for that search. Furthermore, many groups not formally associated with religious faiths or institutions, such as some feminist and environmental groups, are strongly committed to spiritual activities as part of a broad change mission (Lindsay, 2002, p. 35).

Key Themes in Religious and Spiritual Discourses

Despite the considerable diversity of religious and spiritual discourses, we can detect at least four common themes. First, religious and spiritual discourses draw attention to a non-material world. This belief in, and focus on, a non-material world is in sharp contrast to the focus of Enlightenment thinking on the rational, observable world. The non-material world may include one's internal world, such as one's beliefs and values. Many religious discourses also focus on a non-material world beyond our earthly existence, such as the after-life.

Second, religious and spiritual discourses focus on our relationship to a divine or mysterious power. Notions of the divine vary dramatically across religious and cultural groups as does the individual's relationship with the divine. For example, Christian and Jewish religions imagine God as a higher being. By contrast, some forms of Indigenous spirituality see spirituality as embedded in the natural environment. Thus Indigenous spiritual practices may focus on one's relationship with the land and one's ancestors, sometimes referred to in the Aboriginal context as 'The Dreaming' (see Tripcony, 1996). Furthermore, many non-Western religious traditions do not separate people from 'the divine'; for example, Hindus believe that the divine is within (Nigosian, cited in Crompton, 1998, p. 33).

Third, a primary purpose of religious and spiritually oriented activities is to promote spiritual well-being. In most religious and spiritual belief systems, good works in the world are a likely outcome of this quest for spiritual well-being, but they are not the primary purpose of these works.

Instead the central purpose of good works is to build one's relationship with God. Yet for other spiritual groups, one's spiritual well-being is entwined with action in the material world. For example, liberation theologists assert that one's personal relationship with the divine should be expressed through revolutionary action aimed at freeing people from social and structural oppression (Lindsay, 2002, p. 27).

Fourth, religious and spiritual discourses produce moral frameworks grounded in religious and spiritual belief systems (Hutchison, 1998, p. 59; see also Kissman and Maurer, 2002). Despite the enormous diversity of religious and spiritual belief systems, most advocate value systems that can be broadly defined as promoting human well-being and care and compassion for others (see Hutchison, 1998). The moral frameworks emerging from diverse religious and spiritual belief systems offer profound challenges to the key ideas underpinning dominant discourses. For example, religious and spiritual discourses can challenge biomedical principles around the preservation of life, as, for example, an individual may refuse potentially life-saving intervention on the grounds that it contravenes their religious belief systems and thus compromises their relationship with God. Similarly, notions of compassion and care can also challenge the emphasis on rationality and economic efficiency found in neo-classical economic discourse.

Spiritual and Religious Discourses in Social Work Practices

While most post-industrial societies are becoming increasingly secular (Levine, 1998, p. 118; Lyons, 2001, p. 58), religious and spiritual discourses profoundly shape social service delivery and social work practices in many service contexts, especially in the non-government sector. Here we will consider key ways in which these discourses shape contemporary social work practices.

Professional social work was founded in religious organizations (for discussion, see Levine, 1998; Lindsay, 2002). In most post-industrial societies, including the Australia and New Zealand, the Nordic countries and the UK, charities based on mainstream Catholic and Protestant religions were the forerunners of modern social work. In the USA, Christian and Jewish faiths provided the basis for American social work (Levine, 1998, p. 119). As a result of its origins in religious charities, professional social work shares a common value base with some mainstream religious faiths, particularly Christian and Jewish faiths. Recognizing this commonality, some social workers see the profession as a vocation that is consistent with their religious or spiritual commitment to the service of others. For example, in her study of 30 social workers committed to either Christian or Buddhist belief systems, Lindsay found that all of them asserted that 'the common emphasis on social justice and empowering people to live full, authentic lives linked social work to their spiritual beliefs' (Lindsay, 2002, p. 77).

Another way religious and spiritual discourses impact on social work practice is that, sometimes, social workers are called upon to respond to the religious or spiritual needs of service users. In some areas of social work, the spiritual issues facing clients are quite apparent, such as social work in palliative care. Yet in many other areas of practice, service users may raise spiritual and religious issues. According to Speck (cited in Lyall, 2001, p. 48), the kinds of situations in which spiritual and religious issues are likely to come to the fore include: loss of meaning, such as the breakdown of an important personal relationship or the loss of employment; intense suffering, such as that associated with a serious mental illness or a drug addiction; a sense of guilt or shame, which may be raised for parents of children who are abused; a concern about the ethical issues involved in various forms of professional intervention, such as the decision whether to embark on *in-vitro* fertilization treatment; a lack of the sense of God or anger towards God, that could arise, for example, from the death of a loved one.

Service users may turn to social workers to work on religious or spiritual issues precisely because they see the profession as a secular one. Service users may see the profession's lack of alignment with a specific religious or spiritual base as providing a safe environment in which to discuss spiritual concerns, such as anger at God or a loss of belief. Some commentators argue that understanding the religious and spiritual needs of service users is a key dimension of holistic care for service users, inseparable from attending to material and emotional needs (Edwards, 2002, p. 83; Kissman and Maurer, 2002, p. 35). Arguably, then, practitioners should be comfortable talking about spirituality if they are to respond holistically to service users' needs, even if this response is limited to referral to others to deal with spiritual issues in depth.

A further way religious discourses shape social work is through the growing influence of religious organizations in social service delivery. Across the post-industrial world, the trend towards privatization of social services has led to an expanding role for religious organizations in the delivery of services (Harris *et al.*, 2003). Privatization involves the transfer of responsibility for service delivery from governments to the non-government sector (J. Healy, 1998, p. 10) and many of the medium to large established non-government social services organizations in post-industrial societies have a religious base (see Industry Commission, 1995; Hutchison, 1998, p. 63). Moreover, many of these agencies are founded on the mainstream religious traditions of post-industrial countries, particularly Christianity and Judaism (see Hutchison, 1998, pp. 63–4; Harris *et al.*, 2003). Consequently, social work graduates will increasingly work in religiously affiliated organizations.

Similarly, clients will be increasingly served by organizations with dual religious and service missions.

Just as religiously affiliated organizations have a well-established role in the provision of social services, so too debate about the appropriate scope of such services is of long standing. As the following discussion point exercise demonstrates, these debates are gaining renewed attention with the expanding role of religiously affiliated services in social service delivery.

Discussion Point

Religious freedom or discrimination?

As governments in many post-industrial countries have privatized large areas of health and welfare services, religiously based agencies have re-emerged as key providers of these services. Many of these organizations assert their rights to religious freedom and the rights of their organizations to insist that employees act according to the values the community expects of specific religious denominations (Shanahan, 2000). So, for example, if a religion professes opposition to homosexuality, then its service provider organizations are within their rights to refuse to provide safe sex information to gay and lesbian people to whom they deliver other services, such as accommodation or counselling. Some religious organizations insist on their rights to demand that staff, especially those in leadership positions, demonstrate a commitment to the religious belief system of the organization. For example, if the organization is a Christian charity, recruits may be required to make a written statement of religious belief and provide a reference from a minister of religion as part of the employment selection process.

What is your view?
In what circumstances, if at all, should religiously affiliated organizations be allowed to require employees to demonstrate commitment to the religious belief system of the organization? In what circumstances, if at all, should such a requirement be outlawed?

Critical Analysis of Religious and Spiritual Discourses

In this section, we will consider how religious and spiritual discourses may support and extend or limit social work practices and social service delivery. First, many religious and spiritual discourses, including Buddhism, Christianity, Islam and Judaism, are aligned with, and offer support for, the humanitarian value base of social work (Canda, 1988; Lindsay, 2002). Thus, in some practice contexts, the religious mission of the organization and the social work service mission are compatible. For example, Hutchison

(1998, p. 57) argues that 'In the Judaic–Christian tradition ... church-related agencies are well situated to play a major role in providing compassionate care for vulnerable and poor populations and in advocating on their behalf for policies that make services more affordable and accessible.'

One benefit of religious discourses is that services constituted thereby may offer more holistic responses to service users than are typically available through many secular welfare services. In particular, service providers in religiously affiliated services are likely to see spiritual needs as part of a range of service users' needs and, in some contexts, this may be very important to service users. Also, religiously affiliated organizations tend to construct response to need as not only the preserve of service professions but the responsibility of the whole faith community. From this perspective, these agencies are able to draw on members of their faith community to provide support and care outside the official service contract between the funding body and religious organization (Harris *et al.*, 2003). For example, a religiously affiliated employment service may be able to involve business people within their community to provide employment opportunities for service users, or a religiously affiliated mental health service may be able to involve community members in general social support of people living with mental illness. In this way, services based in religious communities may, in some instances, offer more comprehensive and cost-efficient services than secular organizations (*ibid.*, p. 95).

Despite these benefits, many social workers and social commentators raise concerns about the religious and spiritual discourse in social service provision. These concerns include that religious institutions have, historically, played a role in the oppression and dispossession of some groups of service users. For example, in countries such as Australia and Canada, mainstream churches are charged with historical involvement in the colonization of Indigenous peoples through missionary activities that failed to recognize indigenous spiritual belief systems and sought, instead, to impose Christian beliefs systems on such peoples. Also, as historical and recent investigations have shown, religiously based child welfare institutions were both sites of great care, but also sites of horrific abuse for children in their care and protection. Thus some groups of service users, such as the adult survivors of child welfare institutions, may be reluctant to accept services from religious organizations.

A further criticism is that religious discourses are incompatible with the human science discourses through which professional social work is constituted. Some hold the view that religious and spiritual ideas are incompatible with the image of a modern profession as founded on rational and objective knowledge (P. Edwards, 2002).

Another area of conflict is that religious and secular community services construct their primary purpose in different and quite often conflicting ways. Members of religious communities, as well as secular commentators, question whether religious organizations should be involved in non-religious service provision. Some members of faith-based services are concerned that government funding will dilute the religious mission and value base of their services (Levine, 1998, p. 123). The autonomy of religious organizations is severely constrained by dependence on government funding as, for example, programmes are shaped by funding criteria and by the requirements of the service contract. This can constrain the activities of religiously affiliated service providers. For example, religiously based services may have a core mission to advocate for the poor and the oppressed, yet their service contract may also require them to refrain from public critique of government policy.

Some commentators raise concerns about the potential inaccessibility and inappropriateness of faith-based services to non-religious service users and service providers. As Levine (1998, p. 133) points out, 'Clearly, sectarian agencies were established to serve the needs of distinctive clienteles or promulgate specific goals.' These goals may conflict with social service provision. For example, youth and family support agencies often provide services, such as referral to family planning services or information on safe sex practices, that may conflict with the belief systems of some religiously affiliated organizations. Similarly, some service providers may be reluctant to access services with links to specific religious groups, even if these links are primarily historical associations. For instance, a Muslim family may be reluctant to use the services of an organization with a Christian title. Similarly, a gay or lesbian person may be reluctant to access counselling and support services from a service affiliated to a church that is fundamentally opposed to gay and lesbian sexuality.

Further concerns are raised about the potential for religious discrimination against service providers and other personnel involved in the administration and delivery of social services. Most religious organizations have a core mission to spread the word and the love of God and see it as essential that organizational members, including service providers, share this mission. In many countries, faith-based organizations in receipt of government funds must comply with equal opportunities legislation associated with freedom of religion (see Levine, 1998, p. 128). Yet discrimination against people of other faiths, or of no faith, may occur in quite subtle ways. For example, Hutchison (1998, p. 68) concedes that religious organizations 'enunciate a spiritual interpretation of reality that views persons as members of communities that provide the type of support and interaction that leads to health growth and development. They try to recruit board and staff who share similar values.' This emphasis on similarity of values can also lead to the marginalization of groups who do not identify with these mainstream Christian or religious traditions, such as people of Indigenous faiths,

Buddhists, Hindus, Sikhs or Muslims. Other forms of religious differentia-tion are less subtle. For instance, faith-based community service organiza-tions often require employers to declare acceptance of the religious mission of the organization. This can take the form of a worker's statement of willingness to work in sympathy with the value stance through to much more constrictive practices such as requiring employees to sign a statement of faith or to show evidence of church attendance as a condition of employment (Levine, 1998, p. 128).

Conclusion

In this chapter we have considered the ways in which alternative service discourses construct client needs and service missions. We have considered how consumer rights discourse and those associated with religion and spiri-tuality can extend our capacities to achieve our practice purposes and, in particular, how these ideas challenge the dominant discourses shaping many contemporary practice contexts. Yet, as we have shown, these discourses, like all discourses carry within them truth claims that can silence other ways of knowing and responding to the needs of service users and of doing social work practice.

Reflection Exercise

Imagine you are a social worker at a haematology oncology (blood cancer) unit of a paediatric hospital. The children who are inpatients in this unit often face extremely painful treatments and a substantial minority of thom die from their cancers. Many families attending the unit have complained to you that, while they are very happy with the standard of medical and nursing interventions, they do not believe that their spiritual needs are being ade-quately acknowledged at this critical time. Concerns have been raised by families from a range of religious dominations, though those of non-Christian faiths appear to have experienced least recognition of their spiritual practices. In particular, families of non-Christian faiths have stated that hospital staff members have usually ignored their requests for recognition of their spiritual practices such as blessing of their child's room before the child's initial entry into it, or opportunities for prayer time with the child before major medical interventions. A family of Islamic faith told you that they were ordered by hospital staff to remove the prayer mat they had placed near their child's bed. How would you, as a social worker, go about promoting greater recognition of religious and spiritual need and diversity in this practice context?

Summary Questions

1. Thinking about your area of social work practice, or an area that you intend to work in, identify what you see as the strengths and limits of consumer rights discourse for achieving social justice with and for service users in this context.

2. How do religious discourses shape social work practices today?

3. Some social workers and service users argue that social workers should respond to the client's spiritual needs as an essential dimension of holistic practice. What is your view?

Recommended Readings

Consumer Rights

Campbell, J. and M. Oliver. *Disability Politics: Understanding Our Past, Changing Our Future* (London: Routledge, 1996).
This book offers a fascinating review of key stages in the development of consumer rights movements among people with disabilities in the UK.

Clear, M. (ed.) *Promises, Promises: Disability and Terms of Inclusion* (Sydney: Federation Press, 2000).
This edited collection offers a series of personal insights into consumer rights activism among disabled people in Australia.

Corker, M. and T. Shakespeare (eds) *Disability/Postmodernity: Embodying Disability Theory* (London: Continuum, 2002).
This book offers a theoretically sophisticated analysis of contemporary disability politics.

Religion and Spirituality

Lindsay, R. *Recognising Spirituality: The Interface between Faith and Social Work.* (Nedlands, Western Australia: University of Western Australia Press, 2002).
This book examines the history of religious organizations in the development of professional social work. It also reports on a study of social workers' and service users' experiences of religious and spiritual themes in social work practices. This book is useful for all interested in this topic, but is especially recommended for Australian readers.

Orchard, H. (ed.) *Spirituality in Health Care Contexts* (London: Jessica Kingsley Publishers, 2001).
This edited collection examines issues of spirituality in health care from a range of religious perspectives including Christianity, Judaism and Islam.

Website

United Nations: www.un.org/esa/socdev/enable
The United Nations Enable website is dedicated to disability issues. At this website you will find information on the Declaration of the Human Rights of People with Disabilities and other information about the United Nations' support for the social and economic participation of people with disabilities.

Consumer Rights Videos

Golfus, B. and D.E. Simpson. 'When Billy Broke His Head: Life After Brain Damage'. National Disability Awareness Project, USA, 1994 Video cassette.
'When Billy Broke His Head and Other Tales of Wonder'. Written and directed by Billy, a 49-year-old man with an acquired brain injury. The video presents the oppressions experienced by people with disabilities and reviews some of the political campaigns undertaken by people with disabilities in the United States to liberate themselves from a disablist society.

5

Theories for Social Work Practice: Approaches to Knowledge Development and Use

In the preceding chapters, I have presented the discourses shaping the institutional contexts, and the formal professional base, of social work practice. We turn now to focus on theories of social work practice. Consistent with other social work theorists (Howe, 1987, p. 16; Payne, 1997, p. 35; Thompson, 1995, p. 20), I use the term 'theories for professional practice', also known as social work theories, to refer to formal theories that are intended to guide and explain social work practices. Returning to the dynamic model for constructing social work practice discussed in Chapter 1 (Figure 1.1), we see that formal theories are integral to the formal professional base of social work. These theories substantially shape our purpose in social work practice because they define who or what should be the subject of social work intervention and the practical approaches social workers should use to achieve their purposes as presented in these theories.

In this chapter, I first outline the relationship between discourses, discussed in earlier chapters, and theories for practice and then I discuss how social workers use and build theories in practice. We will consider three dominant ways of using and developing theories for practice. These are: evidence-based practice; reflective practice; and reflexive practice. Finally, I will introduce the theories that will be analysed in this second part of the book and suggest how you, the reader, might evaluate them from the different perspectives on theory use in practice presented in the chapter.

Discourses and Theories for Practice

Figure 5.1 illustrates the hierarchical relationship between the discourses discussed in previous chapters, especially the service discourses outlined in

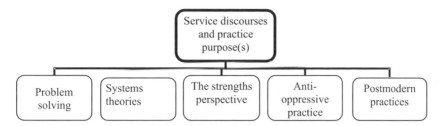

Figure 5.1 Service discourses, practice purpose and theories for practice

Chapters 3 and 4, and theories for social work practice. Social work is a profession based on received ideas, that is, our theories for practice draw
substantially on discourses drawn from other disciplines and fields of service
activity. For example, anti-oppressive practice (Chapter 9) draws on ideas
from sociological discourse and also from consumer rights discourse. I have
characterized the relationship between service discourses and theories for
practice as hierarchical, for although these discourses influence the social
work theories for practice, the practices of social work do not, in turn, substantially shape the service discourses from which they are drawn. It is important to recognize that none of the service discourses on which social work
theory relies is primarily developed in or intended for social work practices.
For this reason, it is necessary for social workers to approach these discourses
critically and cautiously, rather than to look to them for the 'truth' of practice.

In the process of creating theories for practice, social workers transform
ideas from service discourses for practice in specific contexts of social work
practice. Theories for social work practice are usually developed within actual,
or intended, contexts of practice. Thus in the process of theory development, ideas from service discourses are combined with social workers' specific
purposes and experiences within particular practice contexts. For example,
the problem-solving approaches were originally developed for interpersonal
practice with service users experiencing problems of adjustment in daily
living. In understanding and actively using social work theories it is vital that
we understand the historical, geographical and institutional origins of these
theories. Such an understanding can assist us to adapt and transform
these theories for practice within our specific institutional contexts and with
reference to the unique characteristics of every practice interaction. In this
active approach to theory use, we recognize social workers not only as users
of theory but also as active participants in theory in creation.

Barriers to Theory Use in Practice

Although social workers often make theory in practice, the relationship
between formal theory and practice in social work is a vexed one. Social

workers often express an ambivalent, if not hostile, attitude towards theory (Howe, 1987, p. 15). For many social workers theory is, at best, a luxury to think about when the 'real' work of social work is done, at worst it is rejected as authoritarian and irrelevant to practice (Healy, 2000, p. 1).

The commonly encountered criticisms of formalized theories of professional practice in social work can be attributed, in part, to the processes of theory development. Traditional forms of theory building have separated theory development from its application. Often social workers have been reluctant to engage with theories developed in the ivory towers of academia, far away from the complexities – and the mundane aspects – of social work practices. In addition, some social work researchers have treated social workers and service users as objects of study, rather than as co-participants in knowledge development. Again the separation of researcher and researcher roles, as well as those of theorist and practitioner, has created barriers to social workers' use of theory in practice. The recent movement towards research/practice partnerships in social work provides an important pathway for overcoming this separation (see McCarrt-Hess and Mullen, 1995).

In addition, practising social workers have objected to the kinds of theory developed through traditional research methods. Munro (1998, p. 2) observes that

> There have been long-standing debates about how to integrate theory and practice, to use heart and head, and to combine clear, logical reasoning and a caring and humane style ... The dominant scientific model, until recently, has been a behavioural/positivist one which, to many, has seemed irreconcilable with their existing wisdom.

The reflexive approach to theory use and development we adopt in this book (see Chapter 1) asserts that a conflict between theory and practice does not exist when it is recognized that as social workers use theory, *we are also creating theory* in practice. In this way, we do not simply apply formal theory, such as the theories we will consider over the next five chapters, but we can use them as a basis for making knowledge in practice.

The changing organization of social work also leads some social workers to question the role of theory of practice. Theories of professional practice are intended to enable social workers to enact practice as a thoughtful, analytic and creative activity. In the changing contexts of social work practice, in which practice is becoming increasingly fragmented, the opportunities for practising in this way may be increasingly constrained (Healy and Meagher, 2004). Only through collaborative effort, both within the profession and across other human service occupational and service user groups, can social workers promote the industrial and cultural valuation of social services work as a professional activity (see Healy and Meagher, 2004).

Yet, even in the current contexts of practice, some opportunities for professional practice remain, and so clarity about the theoretical foundations of our practice can help us to seize these opportunities.

Why Theory Matters

Social workers often find it difficult to name the theoretical frameworks they use in practice (Howe, 1987, p. 17). We may even encounter social workers who profess to have 'thrown theory out of the window' once they have finished their formal education. Yet all social workers base their practice on theoretical assumptions, whether they are aware of them or not (Munro, 1998, p. 6). Our theoretical framework guides us in deciding who or what should be the focus of assessment or intervention and, as we shall see, different frameworks offer varying ideas about the focus, objectives and processes of social work practices. Although research has repeatedly shown that few social workers use theories in a formal and explicit way (Fook et al., 2000, p. 189; Munro, 1998, p. 46), there are a number of reasons why we should develop our capacity to identify, use and develop formal social work theory in our practice.

The first reason is accountability to service users, employers and funding agencies. Drawing on research about service users' experiences of social work practice, Howe (1987, p. 164) reports that service users preferred 'social workers who appeared clear about what they were doing and why they were doing it, and social workers who say where they were going and how they were going to get there' (see also Munro, 1998, p. 12). Similarly, the new managerial reforms of the social services sector have led to increased focus on efficiency and effectiveness of service provision (for discussion, see Healy, 2002). So service users and service managers expect social workers to be able to explain the assumptions underpinning their practice, and theory can assist us in this task. Theory, particularly theory that is grounded in direct practice, can help to develop and explain the 'what', 'why', 'how' and 'where' of our practice.

Improving service quality provides a second reason for developing our capacity to identify, use and build theory in practice. Theory allows us to critically examine common-sense ways of seeing and doing things (Thompson, 1995, p. 28). Thus theory can enable us to critically review assumptions and accepted ways of doing things that work to the disadvantage of service users. In this way, theory can enhance our capacity to explore a broader range of practice options than would be evident from a common-sense viewpoint. For example, the strengths perspective (see Chapter 8) helps us to see clients' strengths and capacities that might otherwise be invisible to us, to other service providers, or to others in the service users' personal and community networks. In addition, by creating a dialogue between the formal theories of social work and our own sense of social work purpose, as we have constructed it (see Chapter 1), we can expand our capacities for creative responses to the problems and issues we face in practice (Fook *et al.*, 2000, p. 188). By understanding a broad range of theoretical frameworks, we are in a good position to develop practice strategies that build on the strengths and opportunities provided by different theoretical frameworks. For example, in the one practice encounter, we may draw on aspects of problem solving, strengths and anti-oppressive theories in order to analyse and respond to both the local and structural contexts of the issues facing the service user.

The capacity to articulate the theoretical bases of our practice is fundamental to assessing and enhancing the quality of the services we provide. The introduction of managerial reforms to the social services sector has led to increased scrutiny of social work effectiveness. Many social workers, particularly those working within the critical tradition, regard the concept of effectiveness with some suspicion because of its relationship to managerial control of service delivery processes (Trinder, 2000, p. 143). Yet the notion of effectiveness is also relevant to core social work values of social justice and professional integrity. Writing on social work in probation services, Trinder (2000, p. 149) reminds us that 'Social workers and probation officers work with some of the most vulnerable as well as the more dangerous members of society, and have an ethical duty to offer the most effective help.'

A further reason for engaging with the formal theoretical base of the profession is that we all share a responsibility for developing this base. All professions, including social work, rely on formal theoretical frameworks for practice. As Rojek *et al.* (1988, p. 174) assert, 'general, transferable knowledge is indispensable. Without it, social workers would be forced to invent social work from scratch every time they started work with a new client.' Yet, in social work, the discussion about theory development and use is often seen as the realm of academics. The non-participation of practitioners in debate about, and development of, formal theory means that the profession is denied insights from a broad range of practice perspectives. Of course, practitioners do use and create knowledge in practice but, by and large, this knowledge work occurs informally and remains in the heads of individual practitioners or, at best, is transferred orally through supervision. The informal and individualistic character of this knowledge means that it is unavailable to the social work profession more broadly and can be used in only very limited ways in educational processes. Kirk and Reid (2002, p. 203) criticize social workers' oral tradition of knowledge development and dissemination on the grounds that

> as long as observations are communicated only informally, verbally, and among a
> few colleagues, they remain apart from the profession's established knowledge.

Adding to the knowledge base involves making thoughtful, written contributions to the literature.

In addition, while informal knowledge remains inside our heads, we fail to subject it to the external scrutiny required to further our understanding of its strengths and limits both within our practice contexts and across other sites of service provision. In other words, informal knowledge-building processes allow us a great deal of freedom, but they can also foster delusion about our effectiveness in achieving our practice purposes.

Creating and Using Theory in Practice: Evidence based or Critical Reflection?

While many social work commentators agree that theory is vital to professional social work practice, social workers continue to debate how best to develop and use it in practice. Two prominent schools of thought about theory development and use can be identified. These are: the empirical practice movement, also known as evidence-based practice; and the reflective tradition. In the social work literature these two schools are often polarized, yet in practice many social work theorists and practitioners draw on both. For this reason, the distinction between the two schools is better understood as a continuum rather than as an opposition. At their most extreme, these schools foster entirely different ways of developing and using knowledge in practice. It is these distinctions that I will draw out here.

Reid (1994) uses the term 'the empirical practice movement' to describe the growing interest over the past three decades among some social work researchers and practitioners in evidence-based approaches to practice. Advocates of empirical practice, also known as evidence-based practice, argue that social work should be grounded in rational knowledge validated through scientific methods (Reid, 1994, p. 166; see also Munro, 1998). The reason for the burgeoning interest in evidence-based practice, at least among social work academics, can be attributed to growing demands by employing organizations, and the general public, that service providers articulate the knowledge base for decision making, especially when such decision making interferes with the civil liberties of service users.

During the 1960s and 1970s, a series of high-profile evaluation studies on social work practice studies in the USA raised serious questions about the effectiveness of social work intervention (Kirk and Reid, 2002, p. 38; Trinder, 2000, p. 143). This sent shock waves through the profession, which had prided itself on responsiveness to service users and led to the establishment of evidence-based social work projects aimed at providing a scientifically grounded social work practice. William Reid and Laura Epstein's task-centred practice approach is one of the best-known examples of this drive to create scientifically grounded social work practice (see Chapter 6). Today, while social workers continue to debate the merits of evidence-based practice, the movement continues to gain strength in some fields of practice, particularly in areas of high-risk decision making, such as child protection (see Munro, 1998), and in institutions that value evidence-based approaches, such as many arenas of health service delivery.

While the empirical practice movement is a relatively recent arrival in the social work field, the quest for a scientific base for practice is not. The leaders of the Charity Organisation Society (COS) founded in London in 1869 were keen to develop a scientific basis for practice. Leaders of the COS envisioned that ideally 'Charity would be, like science, an orderly systematic process in which practitioners gathered fact, made hypotheses, and revised them in the light of the additional facts from each case' (Evans, cited in Kirk and Reid, 2002, p. 27). Mary Richmond (1917), a social work pioneer, described social diagnosis as 'a product of a scientific process. Facts are gathered to serve as the basis for hypotheses, when are then tested by using the relevant evidence' (Reid, 1994, p. 166). While Richmond and her colleagues sought to develop a systematic framework for practice, their research was limited to single case studies. By contrast, members of the empirical practice movement seek to use more robust scientific methods, preferably experimental designs, for designing and testing social work approaches.

Today, social workers continue to face growing pressure from funding bodies and the general public to demonstrate their effectiveness 'as concern about the effects of social provision on recipients and the public purse has deepened' (Taylor and White, 2000, p. 181). In this context of increasing external pressure, leaders of the empirical practice movement continue to agitate for change from within the social work field. These leaders are often highly critical of social work theory development and use, charging it with failing scientific standards of knowledge development. Kirk and Reid (2002, p. 20) argue that 'The knowledge base of social work is ill defined and difficult to identify, delimit, or organize. Moreover, most of it is not the product of rigorous scientific testing.' Advocates of the empirical practice movement argue that social workers should become more research literate, that is, they should use research findings in practice and should use scientific methods to evaluate their own effectiveness. According to Munro (1998, p. 23), 'This movement encourages social workers to use empirically tested methods of helping to formulate their reasoning, and to evaluate their own work rigorously.' One of the key strengths of this movement is that it provides a framework for social workers to critically review the sources and forms of the information they use in decision making. According to Munro (1996, 1998), attention to the sources, and processes, of decision making can enable us to avoid 'avoidable' mistakes; this is especially important for decision making in high-risk situations in fields such as child protection and mental health.

Yet, while the empirical practice movement encourages social workers to engage with research findings, ultimately it promotes a 'top–down' approach to theory development and use. In this 'top–down' approach, the social work researcher develops and tests social work theory that the practitioner then applies in practice (Taylor and White, 2000, p. 184). In short, the social worker is the subject and user of knowledge, not the maker of it. In this approach, knowledge development and use are separated on the grounds that practitioners do not have the time or the scientific tools to develop robust theories of practice (see Kirk and Reid, 2002). The principles of scientific neutrality on which evidence-based social work is founded also call into question the capacity of practising social workers to objectively evaluate their own practice outcomes. The separation of knowledge development and knowledge use in the evidence-based tradition gives practitioners little scope for questioning how the knowledge was developed or how it might be challenged in practice. Another problem is that the evidence-based tradition does not provide us with strategies for sorting through the large volume of research evidence that may exist about specific practice situations. This is a key issue as research findings may contradict one another, thus leaving the practitioner none the wiser about how to act.

By contrast, social workers within the reflective tradition argue for recognition of practitioners' lived experience of practice as a basis for making and using knowledge in practice. Donald Schön (1983, 1995), a leading scholar on reflective knowledge use and development in human services professions, argues against what he describes as the 'technical rationalist' approach that underpins the evidence-based approaches to knowledge development. In the technical rationalist approach, professional knowledge is derived from a scientific knowledge base and applied to clearly defined and well-bounded scientific problems (Thompson, 1995, p. 57). For example, a civil engineer could use a technical rationalist approach to design a bridge; but a technical rationalist approach would be of more limited use to resolve public concern about where the bridge is to be built. Schön (1995, p. 34) critiques the application of a technical rationalist approach to human services work on the grounds that

> By defining rigor in terms of technical rationality alone, we exclude, as *non*rigorous, much of what competent practitioners actually do in the indeterminate zones of practice where they confront problematic situations, unique cases, and conflicts of values or objectives – we exclude the artistry they sometimes bring to technical problem solving and the judgments on which it depends.

In this excerpt, Schön does not entirely dismiss technical rationality (that is, evidence-based knowledge) but, rather, he insists that this sort of knowledge alone cannot provide the basis for knowledge development and use in human services. In part, this is because the evidence available in social work decision making, which usually involves perceptions and feelings as well as material facts, is often ambiguous. In addition, many of the problems we deal with in social work are 'messy' and 'indeterminate' and 'cannot be "solved" in any clear, measurable or calculative way' (Parton, 2000, p. 452; see also Trinder, 2000, p. 149). For example, when we are directed to assess whether a family is neglecting their baby, we may see some signs of neglect, such as the baby's bottle filled with curdled milk, and other signs of care, such as the baby's age-appropriate weight and the mother's and extended family members' physical affection for the child. In making our decision about intervention we should prioritize the safety of the baby, and we might also take into account structural factors (such as the effects of structural disadvantage on the service user), institutional factors (such as balancing the potential benefits and harm arising from child protection and family support intervention), and local factors (such as whether we can work with the family and local support services to assess, and to ensure, that the baby's care needs are met).

In contrast to the evidence-based tradition, Schön (1995) proposes a reflective approach to knowledge development and use which comprises 'knowing in action' and 'reflection in action'. The term 'knowing in action' refers to the process of developing knowledge in practice, rather than applying pre-existing theories to it (*ibid.*, p. 39). In contrast to evidence-based practitioners, advocates of reflective practice view intuitive and tacit knowledge as an essential dimension of effective practice (Fook *et al.*, 2000, p. 222). Schön (1995, p. 40) uses the term 'reflection in action' to refer to processes of refining knowledge in action so as to promote new ways of responding to the problems we encounter in practice. The capacity to reflect in action, akin to learning through 'trial and error', is important for responding to non-routine events in practice. For example, practitioners working in the field of palliative care will usually develop a repertoire of processes for helping service users deal with grief and loss. In practice, they are likely to find that in each case this repertoire of processes must be adapted to respond to the unique circumstances of the service user. The capacity to reflect in action is central to using our knowledge and skills flexibly in response to the specific characteristics of the service user and our institutional contexts.

The reflective approach places the practitioner, rather than the academic or researcher, at centre stage in knowledge development and use. A key strength of this approach is that it recognizes, and indeed values, social work practitioners as active creators and users of theory and other forms of knowledge. Taylor and White (2000, p. 196) contend that 'By introducing subjectivity, reflective writing brings us much closer to practice than objectivist accounts.' It also promotes open-ended approaches to practice that allow for the local complexities of defining issues and responding to them. In endorsing a reflective approach, Parton (2000, p. 452) argues: 'Uncertainty, confusion and doubt should form an essential part of any theoretical approaches which are serious about being useable in practice.'

Yet this emphasis on the practitioners' reflections as the basis for knowledge creation and use is problematic in a number of ways. The emphasis on intuitive and tacit knowledge means that the basis of our knowledge claims remains inaccessible to other stakeholders, such as service users, employers or funding agencies (Taylor and White, 2000, p. 193). Also, by holding the practitioners' reflections to be a true account of social work practice, this approach leaves no room to critically interrogate the knowledge claims made by the practitioner. As Taylor and White (*ibid.*, p. 200) warn,

> Whilst critical reflective practice opens up the possibility of a more uncertain, ambiguous and complex world, it tends to close much of this down again by obscuring clients' perspectives and freezing practitioners' confessional accounts as true representations of what happened.

The intuitive knowledge valued in reflective practice is also difficult to use in formal educational purposes. As, according to Schön, our knowledge is developed in and through action, our capacity to transfer this knowledge outside specific practice contexts is limited. Furthermore, in some contexts of practice involving safety-critical or legally binding decision making a primary reliance on intuitive and tacit knowledge may elevate the risk of incorrect decisions. It may also lead to the production of knowledge that is not recognized by formal decision-making institutions such as courts. For example, if we are to present our case to courts for, say, taking a child or an apparently suicidal person into the care of the state, we need to be able to articulate the basis of our professional judgements in terms of the current state of 'scientific' and professional knowledge in our field, especially if we are called upon to act as expert witnesses.

Finally, by focusing primarily on inductive knowledge building, that is, building knowledge from our practice experiences, we may fail to fully utilize formalized theories for practice as a basis for creating theory and knowledge in practice. We are in danger of expending energy on constantly 'reinventing the wheel' rather than developing and extending both existing theory and our own knowledge base using existing theories. In short, this approach does not establish a dialogue between the practitioner's intuitive knowledge and the formal theories for social work practice, but instead prioritizes the practitioner's experiential knowledge above all else. Similarly, by focusing on uncertainty and complexity, the reflective approach may lead practitioners to ignore those aspects of social work where some degree of certainty is possible and necessary. For instance, a great deal of empirical work has established effective strategies for working with involuntary clients, and some of these approaches run counter to established practices within the profession (see Trotter, 1999). Information of this type, that is, empirically developed knowledge of the field, is especially important for novice practitioners whose lack of substantive knowledge of the specific practice domain may act as a barrier to purposeful reflection on their practice situation.

Approaching Theory Reflexively: Creating Theory in Practice

Carolyn Taylor and Susan White (2000) have developed a third approach to knowledge use, the reflexive approach, as a way of overcoming the limitations of both evidence-based and reflective traditions of knowledge use in practice. Whereas the evidence-based approach separates knowledge development from practice knowledge, reflexive practice recognizes that social workers are always making knowledge in practice. Yet, although the reflective tradition, as outlined in Donald Schön's work, recognizes that social workers construct knowledge, it prioritizes the practitioner's experiential and tacit knowledge over other formal knowledge, including formal theories. In so doing, the reflective tradition can diminish the role of formal theories of practice as a basis for critical reflection on our practice and it does not adequately scrutinize practitioners' accounts of the truths of their practice.

Consistent with a reflexive approach, I recognize that knowledge and theory use is constantly being constructed in part through practitioners' experiences, and also through sources such as our practice context and formal theoretical base. In this second part of the book, we subject the formal theoretical base of practice to critical scrutiny. We do so by examining the historical, geographical and institutional base of key contemporary theories for practice, core practice principles and applications, and the strengths and weaknesses of approaches within specific practice contexts.

Five Theories of Social Work Practice

In this book we will focus on five contemporary theories of professional practice. The theories we will discuss and analyse over the next five chapters are:

- Problem solving

- Systems perspectives

- The strengths perspective

- Anti-oppressive social work

- Postmodern, poststructural and postcolonial approaches.

I have selected these theories on a number of criteria, all centred on the relevance of theories to social work practice. The first criterion is relevance to the contemporary institutional contexts of health and welfare services. Social work is usually performed by social workers in health and welfare agencies, rather than by independent service providers; this is especially the case for novice social workers. In these contexts, social workers often face significant time and other resource constraints. These constraints make resource-intensive approaches, such as psychodynamic approaches, unfeasible. Indeed, while as I have outlined the continuing influence of psychodynamic ideas on mainstream practice, the complete psychodynamic framework is rarely used as a guiding theory for practice in mainstream service agencies. For this reason, and because of the extensive criticism of psychodynamic approaches by social workers (outlined in Chapter 3), I have not included them here. These same constraints make more structured and time-limited approaches to practice, such as task-centred practice (see Chapter 5), relevant to many practice contexts.

  The privatization of social services, associated with the rising influence of neo-classical economic discourse in the public health and welfare agencies, is also leading to demand for practice approaches that are relevant to practice in non-government services. Social workers working in non-government agencies do not usually carry the same level of statutory authority as social workers working in government organizations. Thus social workers in the former may be freer to pursue support and advocacy roles with service users than social workers working in the latter, and so we might expect a growing interest among social service agencies and social workers in approaches that enhance support and advocacy work. Strengths perspectives, systems and anti-oppressive practice approaches have been included in this book because they provide relevant frameworks for delivering support and advocacy services, particularly, but not only, in the non-government sector.

  The second criterion is relevance to the purpose of social work as it is constructed through our value base and within contemporary practice contexts. All the social work theories we will discuss in the next five chapters emphasize, and promote, partnership between service providers and service users. Partnership approaches are consistent with the core social work values of promoting client self-determination and equity. In addition, in recent years, the notion of partnership has become enshrined in policy and legislation in a range of health and welfare fields from disability to child protection services (for discussion see Campbell and Oliver, 1996; K. Healy, 1998). The new emphasis on partnership can be ascribed to the convergence of influences from both the political Right (as seen in the increasing influence of neo-classical economic discourse), which has tended to emphasize service user self-responsibility, and from the political Left (as reflected in the new social movements associated with consumer rights discourse), which has supported a rights-based approach to service provision. In various ways, these divergent political forces and discourses have led to growing concern about professional expertise and welfare state paternalism. This, in turn, has contributed to increased policy support for partnership-based approaches to practice.

The third criterion is relevance of the theories to the formal knowledge base of social work. All the theories of social work practice we consider are substantially developed within social work practice and by researchers and practitioners associated with the social work field. For example, I have not included cognitive behavioural therapy for, despite its popularity in some practice contexts, it has been developed in and primarily for psychological practice (Payne, 1997, p. 114). While it is still relevant to social work, I consider it to be a borrowed theory for practice and one that remains substantially owned by the 'psy' disciplines, especially psychology.

A fourth criterion is that of extending the boundaries of the social work theory base. In recent years, 'post' theories such as postmodernism and poststructuralism have influenced social sciences and social work theory development. The strong reputation, and popularity, of narrative therapy, which is derived from postmodern theories, has also contributed to growing practitioner interest in these theories. Yet many social workers are deterred by the obtuse ways in which 'post' theories are presented. In Chapter 10 of this book I aim to provide an accessible introduction to 'post' theories and to show that social workers are often using postmodern concepts in practice as we recognize context and individual differences in constructing our understanding of client needs and our practice purposes.

Assessing Theories of Professional Practice

As we shall see over the next chapters, as social workers we have a smorgasbord of theoretical frames from which to create social work practices. But how should we choose which theories to use? According to the view, outlined in this book, that social work practice is constantly constructed, and negotiated, in context, decisions about theory use can only be made in specific institutional contexts of practice and in relation to specific practice purposes. None the less, the different approaches to knowledge use that we have discussed in this chapter raise useful questions for guiding and evaluating our use of social work theories for practice.

From an empirical point of view, Munro (1998, p. 172) asserts, 'Social workers need to evaluate explanatory theories and therapeutic approaches and decide which is the most probable or effective.' Thus, in assessing theories of practice from an empirical practice viewpoint, we could ask:

- What research evidence do we have about the effectiveness of this theory in practice?

- In what practice context was this theory developed and tested? How transferable is this knowledge to my practice context and the specific service users' situation?

- How has this theory stood up to testing compared to its rivals? (Munro, 1998)

- What is the strength of the research evidence? Was it assessed in accordance with scientific standards of evidence? Have the findings been confirmed through repeated research?

Alternatively, from a reflective perspective, we might ask:

- How well does this theory fit with my practice experiences?

- What and whom does it include or exclude?

- How might I use it to develop my understanding of my practice experiences and those of service users?

From a third viewpoint, the reflexive approach, we recognize that we not only use theory in practice, but that we are always involved in making theory and other forms of knowledge. This approach encourages us to subject all elements of our practice framework, including our contexts and our sense of purpose, to critical scrutiny. The questions that this approach raises about the theories we will consider over the next five chapters include:

- What are the historical, geographical and institutional contexts in which this theory was developed? How relevant is this to my context(s) of practice and my purposes within it?

- How does this theory of practice construct the purpose and process of social work practice? What constructions of practice does this theory make possible, what possibilities does it marginalize?

Conclusion

As we discussed in Chapter 1, our purpose in social work is constructed through negotiation between our institutional context, our professional knowledge and skills base, and our frameworks for practice. In addition, our purpose is renegotiated in each practice interaction. The ongoing construction of our practice purpose means that it is unlikely that one theory of practice will be sufficient to guide us in all situations and, so, instead, we should be able appropriately and flexibly to draw on a range of theories in practice. The three approaches to knowledge outlined in this chapter offer differ ways of evaluating theories in each context of practice. In the following chapters, we consider the historical development, practice principles and application of five contemporary theories of practice. This analysis is intended to provide a foundation for considering the uses as well as the limitations of each of these perspectives for achieving our purposes, as we have constructed them and as they are constructed for us, within our specific contexts of practice.

Summary Questions

1. According to proponents of evidence-based practice, what sorts of knowledge should social workers rely on for decision making in practice?

2. What does the term 'reflective practice' mean for knowledge development and use in social work practice?

3. What elements of the evidence-based and reflective traditions does the reflexive approach to knowledge development draw upon?

Reflection Exercise

Using and creating theory in practice

Reflecting on the purposes of social work, within your specific context(s) of social work practice, list and discuss the strengths and weaknesses of the three approaches to social work theory development and use I have outlined in this chapter. These are: evidence-based practice; reflective practice; and practising reflexivity. Compare your list with those of colleagues working in similar, different, contexts of social work practice.

Recommended Reading

The following three publications present different perspectives on debates about knowledge development and use in social work. Eileen Munro argues for an empirical approach, while Nigel Parton presents a powerful case against evidence-based practice and for a reflective approach. Carolyn Taylor and Susan White present the case for bringing both dimensions together in a reflexive approach to making and using theory in practice.

Munro, E. *Understanding Social Work: An Empirical Approach* (London: The Athlone Press, 1998).

Parton, N. 'Some Thoughts on the Relationship Between Theory and Practice in and for Social Work', *British Journal of Social Work*, **30** (2000), 449–63.

Taylor, C. and S. White. *Practising Reflexivity in Health and Welfare: Making Knowledge* (Buckingham: Open University Press, 2000).

6

Problem-Solving Approaches: Focusing on Task-Centred Practice

Problem-solving approaches are characterized by collaborative, highly structured, time-limited and problem-focused approaches to practice. Of all the
approaches we will consider in this book, problem-solving models provide
the most comprehensive frameworks for direct practice. These models
define social work purpose and practice strategies at each phase of assessment and intervention. As such, problem-solving frameworks are among
the most readily usable by inexperienced social workers, though there is
also scope to develop advanced practice within these approaches (Reid,
1977, p. 11). Most commentators, including the critics of problem-solving
approaches, acknowledge that these models enable workers to meet the
growing demand from funding agencies for cost-efficient and accountable
services (Kanter, 1983; Epstein and Brown, 2002). Yet, as I will discuss later
in the chapter, these approaches remain the subject of debate despite their
extensive use in many fields of social service delivery.

In this chapter, I discuss the origins of the problem-solving approach.
We then consider the features and application of the task-centred model and
briefly compare it with crisis intervention. I will explore the strengths
and weaknesses of problem-solving approaches. Let's turn first to the relationship of problem-solving approaches to service discourses and practice
purposes discussed in the first half of this book.

Problem-Solving Practice in Context

In Figure 6.1 I highlight problem-solving approaches and position them
below the service discourses and practice purposes. This reflects the origins
of problem-solving approaches in psychological discourses. Crisis intervention, a form of problem-solving practice, was originally developed by

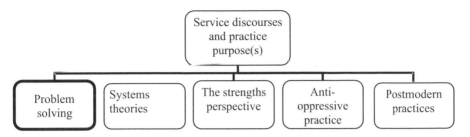

Figure 6.1 Problem-solving social work in context

psychiatrists for the treatment of trauma, while task-centred interventions draw extensively on ideas from cognitive and behavioural psychotherapies. In addition, as we shall see, the emergence and continuing popularity of problem-solving approaches can be partly attributed to growing institutional expectations that social service interventions should be focused and time-limited. I have also positioned the problem solving approach to the left-hand side of the model, next to systems theories, to represent their longer historical presence in the formal base of social work, dating back to at least the 1960s, compared to the theories that we will consider later in the book, which have become established over the past two decades. Indeed, while systems theories have a longer presence in the formal base of social work compared to problem-solving practice, they fell out of favour during the psychodynamic phase of professional social work, and only re-emerged as a major influence in the 1960s and 1970s by which time problem solving had become a significant force in the formal base.

The Origins of Problem-Solving Practice

In 1957, Helen Harris Perlman, a leading social work scholar from University of Chicago, published *Social Casework: A Problem-Solving Process*. This seminal text positioned problem solving as the central task of social work practice (Epstein and Brown, 2002, p. 46). This idea was controversial given the powerful influence of psychodynamic theory on social work practice at that time (see Chapter 3). Perlman (1957, p. xi) remained strongly committed to psychodynamic ideas and saw the problem-solving process as reforming, rather than replacing, psychodynamically oriented casework. Indeed, the crisis intervention approach to problem-solving practice incorporates psychoanalytic ideas about the psychological usefulness of trauma.

Also, the ideas of pragmatist philosopher John Dewey strongly influenced Perlman and later advocates of problem-solving practice. Dewey paved the way for collaborative and goal-focused problem solving in his view that 'human activity is an instrument for problem-solving and that truth is evolutionary and based on experience that can be tested and shared by all those who investigate' (Epstein and Brown, 2002, p. 70). This perspective offered profound challenges to psychodynamic ideas that had emphasized the hidden and unconsciousness nature of service users' problems.

Perlman proposed a highly structured and focused approach to social work intervention. She believed that a structured approach, paradoxically, unleashed the creative potential of social work. In a precursor to the modern slogan 'Think global, act local', Perlman urged social workers to adopt different levels of analysis for understanding and responding to problems. Perlman (1957, p. 29) asserted that

> It is quite possible to understand the nature of a problem in the whole, but it is rarely possible to work on the whole. In casework, as in any other problem-solving activity, the overt action must be partial, focused, and sequential even though the mental comprehension may be total.

Perlman's separation of the process of analysis from response has resonance for social workers today as many of us find our work constrained by resource and time limits. In its emphasis on partial and focused activity, Perlman's problem-solving model suggests that meaningful work is possible despite these constraints.

Perlman (1957, p. 87) stressed that problem solving should be a joint effort between social workers and service users and should aim to develop service users' capacity to solve problems independently of the worker. These principles of collaborative action and developing clients' capacities remain central to contemporary problem-solving approaches. The ideal of partnership enshrined in Perlman's approach was not intended to imply that both parties' contribution was the same. Indeed, Perlman (*ibid.*, p. 166) insisted that in the early stages of assessment the social worker should develop a 'diagnosis' that incorporated the worker's and client's view of the situation and which outlined the resources both would bring to bear on the problem-solving effort. Consistent with the principle of mutual clarity that characterizes contemporary problem-solving practices, Perlman (*ibid.*) insisted that diagnosis is 'simply an argument for making conscious and systematic that which already is operating in us half consciously and loosely'.

The Rise and Rise of Problem Solving

While Perlman's model of problem-solving practice offered profound challenges to the social work profession, it also found fertile ground within it. In part this was because of changes afoot in the organizations of social services when the model first appeared. During the 1960s in particular, social workers experienced considerable growth in employment opportunities in an expanding public sector and this was accompanied by changing tasks and expectations for social workers (Dominelli, 1996, p. 155). The psychodynamic framework that had dominated social work during the middle of the twentieth century was unsuited to practice in these new environments, which focused on a far broader range of concerns than the psychological health of the service users. The problem-solving model found receptive terrain within the profession, too, as a series of landmark studies began to call into question the long-term and relatively unstructured interventions that had become accepted practice in clinical work (Kirk and Reid, 2002; Trinder, 2000). In addition, in these new service organizational contexts, social workers faced increased demand for accountability to their employing body. Today, this focus on effectiveness and efficiency has intensified in most contemporary contexts of social service provision, and problem-solving approaches are embedded within popular practice approaches, such as case management, that pervade these contexts.

Task-Centred Practice: A Brief History

While Perlman's problem-solving formulation set a new direction for social work practice, it was soon superseded by other models of problem-solving practice. One of the most prominent and perennial of these is the task-centred approach. This model was originally espoused by North American social work scholars William Reid and Laura Epstein (1972), and was intended for therapeutic practice with individuals and families who had voluntarily committed to social work intervention (Reid, 1977, p. 2). Social workers have now adapted this approach to practice in a broad range of settings, including statutory probation and child protection and various community service fields (Epstein and Brown, 2002, p. 99; see also Doel and Marsh, 1992; Trotter, 1999).

The task-centred approach grew out of Reid and Shyne's (1969) comparison of brief and extended therapy and from Studt's work on structured intervention (Reid, 1977, p. 1). These projects suggested that clients made comparable and sometimes better progress in short term interventions (limited to about eight sessions) than clients in longer-term intervention. Moreover, researchers found no statistically significant differences in the durability of changes made in short- and long-term intervention (Reid and Shyne, 1969, p. 151). Reid and Shyne (1969, ch. 7) proposed that time-limited, structured and focused interventions led workers and service users to a greater concentration in the problem-solving effort. The positive findings about short-term structured intervention were controversial from the beginning, in part because of their challenge to the psychodynamic paradigm, but also because social workers questioned claims about the generalizability of the model (see Kanter, 1983). We shall discuss these concerns later on.

In 1970, in response to the findings on the relative effectiveness of short-term therapy, William Reid and Laura Epstein established the Task-centred Project at the University of Chicago. The objective of this project was to develop scientifically valid social work approaches 'that could be learned efficiently, increase the effectiveness of direct services, and increase the ability to conduct research on treatment practices' (Epstein and Brown, 2002, p. 92). The model was aimed at 'problems in living', which Reid and Epstein (1972, p. 20; see also Reid, 1977, pp. 2–3) referred to as the following:

- interpersonal conflict;

- dissatisfaction with social relations, such as social isolation;

- problems with formal organizations;

- difficulty in role performance;

- problems in social transition, such as entering or leaving an institution;

- reactive emotional distress, such as anxiety provoked by a traumatic experience;

- inadequate resources, such as a lack of money or housing.

Some problems, such as practice with people suffering from chronic psychiatric illness, were excluded from this list. More recently, however, task-centred practitioners have added another category of 'Other: Any problem not classifiable' to the list of issues that this model can be used to address (see Epstein and Brown, 2002, p. 135). Some proponents of task-centred practice now suggest that this model offers a unifying approach for social work (see Doel, 1998), though others, as we shall see, have significant reservations about the theory.

One way of thinking about the task-centred framework is that it provides a 'shell' in which other theoretical perspectives can be incorporated so long as they do not disrupt the requirements that intervention is structured, focused and time-limited. Indeed, Reid and Epstein encouraged social workers to draw thoughtfully on a broad range of theoretical perspectives in developing practice interventions (Epstein and Brown, 2002, p. 103; see also Reid, 1992). British social work theorist Mark Doel (1998, p. 197) contends that the task-centred approach has moved 'into more radical territory, embracing notions of partnership, empowerment and anti-oppressive practice, and signalling practical ways of realising these ideas'. In short, this model appears to offer practitioner and service user a great deal of discretion about the approaches they use to achieve target goals.

Key Principles of Task-Centred Practice

Practice Principle 1: Seek Mutual Clarity with Service Users

Task-centred practitioners seek to maximize clarity between social workers and service users about the purpose and the process of intervention (Ford and Postle, 2000, p. 53). Clarity is important for promoting a constructive working relationship based on realistic expectations of the intervention process. Clarity is achieved by the worker and service user jointly determining the focus and processes of intervention, the establishment of written or oral contracts, and the regular collaborative review of progress towards target goals.

Practice Principle 2: Aim for Small Achievements rather than Large Changes

Task-centred practice focuses on enabling clients to make small and meaningful changes in their lives. Doel and Marsh (1992, p. 106) assert that this is 'a departure from the grand reformism of social work in bygone days. The desire for radical change, at either a personal or societal level, is understandable, but leads to disappointment.' This focus on small, local and achievable change activity is based on the assumptions that: it is beyond the scope of social work practice to produce large-scale change; and, in any case, it is not necessary to address all the problems we identify because successful problem-solving experiences will have knock-on effects for other problems in the clients' life that may enable them to live with these problems or to deal with them without the intervention of social service agencies (Epstein and Brown, 2002, p. 144).

Practice Principle 3: Focus on the 'Here and Now'

The task-centred approach is structured around a limited number of problems, no more than three, which are the targets of intervention. Drawing boundaries around the problem to be worked on increases the effectiveness and the efficiency of the practice process and limits the potential for 'loose, diffuse, and rambling work' (Epstein and Brown, 2002, p. 143). In contrast to practitioners of the psychodynamic models which preceded them, task-centred practitioners have little interest in the client's personal history, other than in understanding historical factors that may directly impact on the current problem-solving effort. Indeed, Epstein and Brown (2002, pp. 102–3) assert that 'accumulating substantial past history is inefficient and may mislead the client about the intentions of the practitioner'.

Practice Principle 4: Promote Collaboration Between Worker and Service Users

Like Perlman's problem-solving model, task-centred practice is based on the active participation of worker and service user as partners in the problem-solving effort. Each is expected to take an active, though different, role in the problem-solving process. According to Epstein and Brown (2002, p. 73), task-centred practitioners 'tend to be active, and direct, to teach, advise, and instruct'. Through their mutual contract, the client also is held accountable for developing, implementing and monitoring change strategies.

Practice Principle 5: Build Client Capacities for Action

Task-centred practitioners focus on responding to client problems in localized and practical terms. According to Epstein and Brown (2002, p. 99), most troubles have two components: the client lacks the resources or the skills required to alleviate a problem. While acknowledging that the problems may have their origins in other 'causes', such as 'deeper' psychological problems or unjust structural conditions, task-centred practitioners aim to build client capacities to deal with the identified target problems. While not necessarily ignoring the personal or structural origins of client problems, task-centred practitioners see dealing with these original causes as beyond the scope of the problem-solving effort and unnecessary for addressing the target problems of the service user (Reid, 1977, p. 12).

Practice Principle 6: Planned Brevity

Reid and Epstein used the term 'planned brevity' to refer to intervention processes that are limited to no more than 15 sessions over a short period of up to three months (Reid, 1977, p. 7). In many practice contexts today, this would not be considered brief intervention, but at the time that task-centred casework was introduced, long-term therapeutic interventions were common. Proponents of task-centred practice argue that planned brevity of intervention carries benefits for both service users and service provider organizations. Service users benefit because, as practice research shows, deadlines motivate change and also because in short-term intervention the problem-solving efforts of workers and clients are concentrated (Reid and Epstein, 1972). Service provider organizations benefit as brief interventions allow for the cost-effective deployment of staff resources in increasingly stretched welfare agencies.

Practice Principle 6: Promote Systematic and Structured Approaches to Intervention

The task-centred model offers a standardized approach to social work inter vention that is also sufficiently flexible to apply in a broad range of practice contexts. The standardization of the model helps to ensure mutual clarity between service provider and service user, and external accountability as the practice proceeds sequentially through a predetermined, and scientifically tested, intervention framework. Epstein and Brown (2002, p. 96) assert: 'Being systematic can protect clients and practitioners from extremes of bewilderment, frustration, and irrelevancy. Systematic practice minimizes waste of time, effort, and money and encourages effective practice.' Yet, within this overall model, practitioners and service users have considerable discretion in determine the actual content of intervention (Reid, 1977, p. 11).

Practice Principle 7: Adopt a Scientific Approach to Practice Evaluation

The task-centred model emerged during a period of growing scepticism within the profession about the validity of established practice methods, and external demands for accountability. These pressures have continued to intensify in the intervening years. In response to these concerns, Reid and Epstein (1972) were committed to developing a model of practice that was based on scientific findings, developed through scientific methods and amenable to scientific research. Most proponents of task-centred practice argue that social workers should systematically review and monitor the casework process using scientific methods and scientific research, rather than rely on intuition or anecdotal evidence of progress (Epstein and Brown, 2002, pp. 217–18; Trotter, 1999, p. 86).

Task-Centred Practice: Putting the Model into Practice

In the task-centred model, workers and service users work intensively on a mutually agreed set of target problems. 'Tasks' are the vehicle through which target problems are addressed and clients' skills are developed. Reid (1992, p. 38) asserts that 'An ultimate goal in the use of tasks is empowerment of the client – to enable the client to design and carry out their own problem-solving actions.' The following description of the model draws primarily on the original model devised by Reid and Epstein (1972) as well as Epstein and Brown's (2002) further development of the approach and Trotter's (1999) application of these ideas to work with involuntary clients. The task-centred approach has five phases, which should flow sequentially in order to maximize client outcomes (Epstein and Brown, 2002, p. 93). Occasionally, it may be necessary for us to revisit earlier stages of the process with service users, and, in such cases, we should aim to return to the stage we were at before the interruption of the sequence. Assuming that our problem-solving intervention will occur over eight sessions, I have indicated the approximate point in the intervention process where each step should occur. We will use a case study to assist us to demonstrate the phases of the approach and to practise some of the skills associated with it.

Practice Exercise

Task-centred practice

You are a social worker in a large teaching hospital, and one of your responsibilities is discharge planning for older people where there are complex personal or family situations.

You receive a referral for George, who is in his late seventies. He was admitted two days ago for urgent investigation of chest pains. He cares for his wife Flo, who is in her early seventies and has Alzheimer's disease. In the notes, you read that George needs to do everything for her, including dressing, bathing and helping her go to the toilet. You also read that when George was admitted, the Carer Respite Centre arranged for a live-in careworker to look after Flo, as it became apparent that George would only need to be in hospital for about four days.

After the first day, the careworker tells her supervisor that while she was helping Flo shower and dress she noticed that Flo looks very underweight and may be malnourished. The careworker also found that the cupboards and

> ## Practice Exercise (*cont'd*)
>
> fridge had little food in them. The Carer Respite Centre then contacts you. When you first meet George, he is very anxious to get home to look after Flo, and he insists he doesn't need any help, and no one but he can understand her and care for her.

Pre-Intervention Phase: Understanding the Context of the Intervention (Prior to, and During, Session 1)

The purpose of this phase is to understand and establish the context of intervention. This involves understanding the reasons for referral (if referral has occurred) and clarifying with the service user any limits or boundaries to the practice relationship.

The task-centred model was originally designed for clinical practice with voluntary clients. In this context it was understood that the target problems would be identified by clients as something they 'recognize, understand, acknowledge, and want to attend to' (Epstein and Brown, 2002, p. 93). Yet, as social workers moved increasingly into public welfare agencies, advocates of the task-centred model have recognized that tasks other than those identified by the clients themselves may have a bearing on the problem-solving effort (see Trotter, 1999). If a referral is involved, we should clarify the referral source's goals and:

(a) whether any compulsion, legal or otherwise, underpins these goals. For instance: is their contact with you compelled by a third party such as the courts or another service agency?

(b) what reporting requirements do you or the service user have to the original referral source? If so, who is responsible for feedback to the referral source?

In the process of understanding the source of the referral you may also need to negotiate expectations with the referral source, bearing in mind the respective agency policies about confidentiality and the like. The practice principle of mutual clarity means that you should communicate any obligations you have to the referral source, or anyone else, to the service user. Moreover, understanding the referral agency's view does not mean that one necessarily accepts it as the focus of work. As we work with the client on defining the target problem it may be necessary to defer or even reject the referral source's view of the most pressing problem.

The principle of mutual clarity requires us to clarify the role of the agency and service providers with service users, whether voluntary or involuntary, in this pre-intervention phase. Trotter (1999, p. 48) suggests that the themes that should addressed before to beginning assessment and intervention include:

- the role of the worker – such as case planner, case manager or case-worker;

- the nature of the social worker's role in their specific practice context, particularly any legal or other obligations we bear that may impact on the social work process. For example, you should inform the client of your reporting requirements, if any;

- confidentiality and its limits. The client should be aware of in what conditions information disclosed in the casework process might be shared with others and how, if at all, the client would be informed about this;

- the client's expectations of the casework process;

- what is negotiable and what is not. The former might include places and times of meetings, while the latter might include processes for dealing with allegations of abuse or violence.

Practice Exercise

Beginning work with George and Flo

Focusing on the case study of George and Flo, discuss with a partner whom you see as the referral source for this case study and what issues you would like to clarify with them.

- What issues would you raise with George in this pre-intervention stage?

- Role-play with a partner how you would approach the referral source and George in this pre-intervention phase.

Step 1: Defining Target Problems (Session 1)

The purpose of this step is for the worker and service user to arrive at a shared understanding of the issues of concern and to begin to narrow down the focus of intervention. Task-centred practitioners seek to explore and, as far as possible, prioritize the service user's view of the problem, though, in many instances, the worker's perspectives and those associated with external mandates, such as the courts, must be taken into account. The achievement of a mutually agreed definition of the target problem is no easy task given differences between service providers and service users. These differences may include: different world-views; obligations; values; and identifications such as – age, gender, class. These differences are likely to be especially pronounced in practice with involuntary clients who may hold ambivalent, and even hostile, feelings about the intervention process (see Trotter, 1999, ch. 5). The strategies of understanding a problem survey and problem ranking are intended to ensure that the client's view, and that of relevant stakeholders, is understood before reaching a shared definition of the target problem(s).

The focus on understanding the client's view of the problem is consistent with the social work credo of 'starting where the client is at' and it is also vital for building a working relationship with the service user. Beyond this, task-centred practitioners also recognize that the client's involvement in defining the problem is critical to concentrating their efforts on the change process (Epstein and Brown, 2002, p. 136). For example, George is more likely to be motivated to work on target problems that are consistent with his definition of the problem and his goals rather than those that he regards as imposed from an external source, such as the carer or the hospital.

The problem survey

In this first step, task-centred practitioners use a problem survey, or problem search, to develop a comprehensive understanding, for both themselves and service users, of the issues at hand. In this process, the service user and provider list the issues as they see them in as concrete and a practical way as possible and in the client's own words (Trotter, 1999, pp. 86–7); this is to ensure that workers and service users are both clear about the problem and what needs to be done. For example, in undertaking a problem survey with George, he may suggest the following issues:

- I want help to return home as soon as possible;
- I am finding it difficult to cope with basic jobs around the house like preparing meals.

As our purpose is to develop understanding of the target problem, the worker should encourage discussion of a brief history and context of each problem. For example: how long has this been a problem? How severe is the problem? What is its impact on your life? What strategies have you used to manage it so far?

While the views of the client are central to the problem clarification process, so too, it is usual for the worker to take an active role in raising issues to be resolved. In this role, workers may challenge definitions of the problem that are unrealistic or undesirable. For example, in working with George we may acknowledge his strengths in caring for his wife, Flo, while also challenging his view that he doesn't require further support. In this framework, 'undesirable' definitions of the problem are those that conflict with our legal mandates or professional value base. For example, if the hospital team were to define the problem as 'George cannot manage Flo's care and thus Flo should be referred to a nursing home', we might also challenge this definition as inconsistent with our professional ethic of self-determination.

How we manage competing definitions of the problem is largely dependent on our practice context. Where the service user is a voluntary client and where there is no overriding threat to others, the service user's definitions of the problems should prevail (Epstein and Brown, 2002, p. 162). However, there are at least two contexts in which the worker is duty bound to insist on specific problems being considered in this phase. The first occurs when the worker is legally mandated to address specific problems, such as child protection or self-harm concerns (see Trotter, 1999, ch. 5). The second is where the worker has formed a judgement of a potential risk the service user might pose to themselves or others. In terms of our professional accountability to the service user and to our employing agency, and to our professional value base, it is vital that we raise these issues in this initial phase. Returning to the case study then, we should raise our concerns about Flo's possible state of malnourishment as a problem for further investigation, if George has not already raised this concern.

Problem ranking

Once a list of problems is established, the worker and service user analyse priority areas of intervention. Task-centred practitioners insist that only a limited number of problems can be addressed within any task-centred intervention cycle. Epstein and Brown (2002, p. 155) suggest a 'rule of three', that is, to limit intervention to no more than three issues. In the problem-ranking process, problems that the client is most anxious to resolve are usually given highest priority (Reid and Epstein, 1972, p. 21), though, again, legally mandated problems should be prioritized as well. Some of the questions we might ask at this stage include:

- What is the most urgent problem and why?
- What problem is the service user most motivated to work on?

● What, if any, problems are the worker and service user required by external mandate to work on? For example, the health team you work with may insist that concerns about Flo's care are addressed with George.

Practice Exercise

Defining our problem focus

With a colleague, role play the two strategies of problem survey and problem ranking. Each of you should take a turn playing the social worker and the service user roles. Discuss what each of you found useful about this way of approaching problem assessment and what concerns, if any, this process raised for you.

Discuss the application of these strategies to your practice context. Where, if at all, would these strategies apply; where might they be problematic?

Step 2: Contracting (Session 2)

The aim of this step is for the worker and service user to reach an explicit agreement about the target of their intervention and how the target problem(s) is to be addressed. This agreement will form the basis of a contract between service worker and service user (Epstein and Brown, 2002, p. 189). The main purpose of the contract is to ensure mutual clarity and accountability between the worker and service user. In contexts where clients are involuntary or reluctant participants in the intervention process, the contracts are more likely to be written (*ibid.*, p. 167). A contract should include practical information about the working relationship between service provider and service user, such as the duration, frequency and location of meetings, as well as detailed information about the following elements.

Goals of intervention

Drawing on the work completed in step 1, the worker and service user should identify up to three target problems that will be the focus of their work together. The client should be primarily responsible for determining the order of problems to be addressed. The goals should be stated in the client's own words and on their own terms. If the service provider has other goals on behalf on the agency, such as goals related to legal compliance, then these need to be indicated as the service provider's goal in the contract. So, in working with George, possible goals for intervention include:

- Flo's health status to be investigated by a medical team and a plan of action to address her apparent health problems;

- for George and Flo to get more home help so that George remains in the primary care role for as long as possible;

- for George's health problems to be thoroughly assessed and monitored.

A statement of the tasks

In task-centred practice, tasks have a dual purpose: to directly address the target problem(s); and to develop the service user's problem-solving skills. With this purpose, and our target goals in mind, we work with the client in determining practice tasks. Once tasks are decided, they should be spelled out in detailed and concrete ways. For example:

- George will contact the home help service to arrange an assessment for home care support by 3 February;

- Karen (social worker) will arrange for the community health team to investigate Flo's health status by 3 February.

The responsibilities of worker and service user

In the process of completing our detailed task list, we must also clarify who is responsible for task achievement. In assigning responsibilities we should bear in mind that a key intention of task-centred practice is to develop the client's problem-solving abilities; hence we must resist any temptation to do 'for', rather than do 'with', the service user. In developing our contract, we should also be mindful of the time limits and ensure that tasks are achievable within our time frame (Epstein and Brown, 2002, p. 183).

Discussion Point

With a colleague discuss what you see as the strengths and weaknesses of contracting in practice. Provide practical illustrations for each point you make.

Task-centred practitioners argue that contracts help to maximize clarity between workers and service users and can provide a vehicle for collaboration in defining practice goals and processes. The establishment of a contract can also provide concrete evidence of a commitment to the intervention process (Epstein and Brown, 2002, p. 169). On the other hand, social work commentators have raised numerous concerns about contracting. Dominelli (1996) questions the mutuality of the contracting process, arguing that clients may have little option but to enter into contractual arrangements. For example, a client seeking only material assistance may feel forced to enter into a contract for other assistance as a condition of receiving the aid they seek. Questions are raised about client and worker accountability to practice contracts. In each practice context we need to be clear about the legal and other practical ramifications of the contract; who may have access to the contract; and what are the consequences of failing to meet the contractual obligations.

Step 3: Problem-Solving Implementation (3–7 sessions)

Most of the change work occurs in this step of the model. In this phase we will refine the problem and the tasks, and support and review task performance. Let's consider each aspect of this step.

Refining the problem and tasks

In earlier stages, we defined the target problem. As we begin to act on the problem it may be necessary to review our definitions of it. For example, the medical team may discover that Flo's low weight is due to a disease, not malnutrition, and thus we may need to review our plan of action with George altogether. In order to ensure both mutual clarity and that our tasks fit the target problem, it is important that we continually review our definition of the problem and tasks throughout this phase.

Supporting task performance

Consistent with the aim of by client's problem-solving capacities, the worker facilitates the service user's performance of agreed tasks. The worker may foster skill development through, for example, encouraging the service user to rehearse task activities. For instance, if George has never previously contacted a service agency, we may role-play with him the task of contacting the home help agency. The worker may encourage the service user to anticipate obstacles to successful task completion and discuss strategies for overcoming these problems. For example, as we assign tasks, we might probe what George will find easy and difficult about each task and consider how we will help him to address the identified problems. In order to support task performance, we might also discuss incentive and reward strategies for task achievement. For instance, if George enjoys a game of bowls and lunch at the bowling club, we might encourage him to schedule in an extra visit to the club as a reward for completing tasks associated with his target problem.

Reviewing task performance

Recall the importance that task-centred practitioners place on systematic intervention and evaluation as opposed to anecdotal evidence or intuitions about performance. At the very least, this requires us systematically to gather information with the client about task performance and the status of the target problem. By regularly reviewing task performance we can acknowledge the gains made by the client and also address task non-performance. Task-centred practitioners view the non-performance of tasks as indicating that something is going wrong in the intervention process. Review of non-performance of tasks provides an ideal opportunity to address issues with the service user and revise our contract. For instance, we may find that George has not contacted the local home help service. As we probe the reasons for this, George reveals to us that he is worried about losing his independence. We might use this revelation to explore ways in which George can access support for Flo so that he maintains his sense of dignity and self-control.

Practice Exercise
_____

Assessing and promoting task performance

Imagine you are meeting with George in session 4, the first meeting after the contract. Role-play with a partner how you would discuss and support task performance with George. Each of you should take a turn playing the social worker role and the role of George. Discuss what you found useful and what was unhelpful in supporting task performance.

Step 4: Termination (Last Session)

The well-planned termination of intervention is integral to the overall structure of the task-centred approach. Recall that task-centred practitioners believe that a clear and looming deadline is vital for concentrating worker and service user efforts on change (Reid and Epstein, 1972). For this reason, task-centred practitioners are cautious about the extension of intervention beyond the agreed contract between worker and user; any such extensions should be strictly time-limited and focused. As Epstein and Brown

(2002, p. 230) warn, 'The practitioner should be vigilant about the tendency to drift into open-ended treatment (driven perhaps by desires to attain elusive goals) without a clear contract.'

From the outset, the worker should have communicated the time limits to the intervention and this should be reinforced throughout the process. For example, if we have contracted with the client to meet for eight sessions, we might remind them of the place of the current session in relation to other overall sequence: for example, 'This is our fourth meeting. We have four more meetings to go; how are we doing so far?'

The key purpose of the termination meeting is to review our overall progress towards addressing the target problem and to point to the future (Epstein and Brown, 2002, p. 230). In line with the principle of systematic intervention and review, the review of what was, and wasn't, accomplished should incorporate a range of information sources: client's and worker's perceptions of the process; any 'evidence' parties have gathered about accomplishments, such as data collected over the course of the intervention; and reflections on key learnings and expectations for the future. Epstein and Brown (2002, p. 233–4) suggest also that we should initiate discussion of how the service user might maintain any progress made during intervention. For example, we might probe how George will get the support he needs to continue in his role as carer for Flo.

Comparing Task-Centred and Crisis Intervention

We should not leave this discussion of problem solving without reference to 'crisis intervention', another popular model of practice. A comparison of the two methods is useful for highlighting the different ways the principles of problem-solving practice can be applied. This comparison will also further illuminate the practical applications of these two models.

While social workers sometimes use the term 'crisis intervention' to refer to practice in high-stress or high-risk situations, the term also refers to a distinctive approach to problem solving. Crisis intervention first emerged in the 1940s through the work of American psychiatrists Gerard Caplan and Eric Lindemann (Kanel, 2003, p. 14). Crisis intervention was introduced to social work in the 1960s through social workers in the field of mental health, particularly through the work of Howard Parad (1965; see also Parad and Parad, 1968) and later by Naomi Golan (1978).

Caplan defines a crisis as 'occurring when a person faces an obstacle to important life goals that is, for a time, insurmountable by the customary means of problem-solving' (Golan, 1986, p. 302). Within crisis intervention models, crises are both an inevitable part of the life course, often associated with life changes such as the transition from childhood to adolescence, and also arise through hazardous events, for example, the loss of a job or serious illness. The model centres on the idea that crises present both threats and opportunities and that, if handled well, can contribute to personal growth. Caplan argued that not only are crises inevitable; they are actually essential for personal growth (Kanel, 2003, p. 3). Like the task-centred model, crisis intervention is characterized by distinct phases of intervention, each with a clear purpose and specific tasks.

Like task-centred practice, crisis intervention offers a time-limited, structured approach. Both models are oriented towards long-term empowerment of clients by developing their capacities for independent problem resolution. Both models, in their contemporary forms, draw heavily on cognitive and behavioural ideas (see Kanel, 2003, p. 39). However, these models differ markedly in some key theoretical assumptions and the rationale behind their shared practice principles.

While both task-centred and crisis intervention models are eclectic, the crisis intervention model is more strongly aligned with psychodynamic ideas focusing on the internal world of the client. For example, crisis intervention is intended to promote psychological growth, whereas task-centred practitioners aim to resolve 'problems in living'.

In addition, both models promote brief intervention but for different reasons. Whereas task-centred practitioners limit the duration of intervention, in part because they believe that people are motivated by limited time lines and achievable goals, crisis intervention practitioners insist on time limits because they believe that the period of crisis and, thus, the window of opportunity for change, is brief (see Golan, 1986, p. 298; Kanel, 2003, p. 3).

A further difference is that the crisis intervention model puts far greater emphasis on the exploration and ventilation of client feelings. This is because crisis intervention theorists view the ventilation of feelings as a precursor to meaningful change. Finally, differences also exists in the role of the worker in the two models. Both models assume that the worker should adopt an active role in problem-solving activity, though in the crisis intervention model the worker becomes less directive over time as the client becomes 'ready to 'take charge of himself' once more' (Golan, 1986, p. 324).

Discussion Point

Returning to the case study of George and Flo introduced earlier in the chapter, discuss what you see as the advantages and disadvantages of a crisis intervention approach, compared to a task-centred approach, for working with this situation.

Strengths, Weaknesses and Issues in Problem-Solving Approaches

In the following discussion we will focus mainly on the task-centred approach, though many of these points also have relevance for crisis intervention.

Strengths

Problem-solving processes are consistent with case management – or care management – models, which is now a dominant framework for social service provision (Dominelli, 1996). Task-centred practice, in particular, allows the social worker to provide time-limited, highly structured and problem-focused services that are relatively easy to administer and evaluate by social service agencies. In other words, social service agencies can see the value, or otherwise, of these services (Doel, 1998, p. 198). In this way, task-centred practice can contribute to the revaluing of social work practice by service agencies and can lessen the conflict social workers sometimes feel between their institutional contexts and their professional practice frameworks. Aside from this point of consistency between practice contexts and intervention methods, proponents of task-centred practice identify a number of key strengths of this approach.

A major strength of task-centred practice is that it promotes clarity of thinking and action between service providers and service users. This limits the potential for confusion and frustration between service providers and service users. Also, the principle of mutual clarity encourages service providers and service users to think through carefully what can be achieved in their time together, thus enhancing service provider and service user accountability to the problem-solving process and reducing the scope for unrealistic expectations and disappointments.

In addition, by involving service users in determining practice goals, processes and outcomes, the approach is consistent with core social work values of respect and self-determination. Doel and Marsh (1992, p. 97) go even further to argue that task-centred practice promotes an openness to the client's world-view and, as such, is consistent with anti-oppressive practices. Consistent with the value of respect, it challenges us all to recognize and support service users' capacities to address the problems they face (*ibid.*).

Also, the model aims to empower service users to address the problems they face in daily living without ongoing support from social service agencies. Given the well-known problems of long-term involvement with social services, such as scope for surveillance by the state, the quest to promote independence from social services, wherever possible, should be appreciated by service users and providers.

A further strength is its commitment to accountability. Research suggests that social workers' evaluation of their own practice tends to be highly subjective, irregular and difficult to assess by others (see Healy and Meagher, 2001; Munro, 1998). By placing the issue of continuous practice evaluation at the centre of direct practice, task-centred practitioners challenge us to look squarely at our effectiveness and how we develop strategies for communicating this to other stakeholders, particularly those using and funding services.

Weaknesses and Issues

Yet, despite their popularity in some practice and academic contexts, problem-solving models are also the subject of extensive critique. Some commentators question the generalizability of the model, arguing that it is only suitable for relatively superficial problems with people who are atypical of social service users. Kanter (1983, p. 229) criticizes Reid and Shyne's study of brief intervention, on which the task-centred model is founded, on the grounds that 'the study's participants tended to be young, middle income, motivated, and free of gross pathology'. Thus, according to Kanter (1983), the task-centred model is simply irrelevant to the vast bulk of service users who have to face entrenched and complex issues. Furthermore, proponents' claims about the scientific soundness of the model can give practitioners an unwarranted level of confidence in it and leave little room for individual doubt or complaint from service users. Thus there is considerable risk that problems encountered in the application of the model will be attributed to the service user, who may be placed in the 'too hard' basket; rather than lead to further questioning of the model.

A related concern is that the structured, time-limited, goal achievement framework is inappropriate for practice with some kinds of issues, especially those with significant emotional content. Or, to put it differently, there are some areas of social work practice in which goal achievement is less important than simply 'being with' the client. Consider, for example, a young mother dying of breast cancer. A task-centred approach may help us to assist her in practical preparations for her death, but could lead us to be grossly insensitive to the likely significant emotional issues arising in this situation. To some extent, crisis intervention models may provide an alternative approach for emotionally charged situations, but its underpinning assumption – that crises are resolved in four to six weeks – is problematic in enabling the worker to provide longer-term support as may be required in the case example mentioned here.

Using insights from sociological discourse (Chapter 3), we can critique the model's failure to adequately acknowledge the social and structural contexts of service users' problems. Proponents of this model tend to see problems of social disadvantage as outside the ambit of problem-solving intervention, preferring instead to concentrate on local, small-scale achievements (Doel and Marsh, 1992, p. 93). According to Payne (1997, p. 113), the effectiveness of the model in offering short-term piecemeal responses to service users' immediate concerns 'may result in society's avoiding longer-term and more deeply seated responses to social oppressions'.

From a consumer rights discourse perspective, we might also question the scope for partnership and participation within the model. Dominelli (1996) criticizes this model on the grounds that its claims to partnership are illusory in the context of inequalities within the practice context and in society more generally. Of course, we know that power inequities are an ever-present reality in social work practice – between service user, services providers and service agencies – however, for Dominelli (1996, p. 157) the problem is that the task-centred model does not adequately acknowledge these differences, nor does it 'encourage challenges to a system that causes a client's distress'.

Partnership is also problematic in contexts where service providers and service users have vastly different, and possibly irreconcilable, views of a problem. The value given to partnership in this model reflects its therapeutic origins and its intended use for practice with voluntary clients. But what of situations in which the client is not entirely voluntary or where your concerns, as the worker, are in conflict with the client's views? For example, returning to our case study, we can see that working with George would become more problematic if there were a concern about domestic violence between the couple. In that situation it may be difficult to reach an agreement with George about the focus of our intervention for we would be duty bound by our professional ethics, and in some contexts by law, to prioritize our concerns about possible abuse of Flo above all else. Indeed, we need to thoroughly investigate our concerns before we can be sure that helping George with his target goal – to return home – will not worsen matters for Flo. Similarly, in statutory social work contexts, the social worker is mandated by the courts to work on specific problems. If the client is unable to agree to contract to work on these problems – even as part of a more extensive contract – then task-centred practice is not appropriate.

The emphasis on a structured, time-limited intervention can be problematic with clients from some cultural groups. While Anglo-Saxon cultures tend to value ideals such as time effectiveness and structured and linear intervention efforts which are consistent with problem-solving approaches, other groups, such as Indigenous cultural groups, often hold a different view. Members of the cultural groups with a more cyclical view of time and which place a great deal of emphasis on, say, relationship building and sharing of stories, are likely to be alienated by this approach.

The emphasis on strict time limits to each practice step also poses a problem even for the mainstream health and welfare institutions for which it was originally intended. In many of these contexts practitioners and clients have little choice about the duration of their work together. The eight-session time frame, on which task-centred practice is based, may be too lengthy in some contemporary contexts of social work practice, such as acute hospital wards where the practice relationship may be limited to one or two sessions. Alternatively, in other contexts where protracted involvement is inevitable, such as some community support programmes, the time-limited model is also not feasible. In these contexts, Doel and Marsh (1992, p. 85) suggest that longer-term involvements can be broken down into 'manageable chunks of work'. However, this appears to be a contravention of the principle of planned brevity which is central to problem-solving models.

Conclusion

For the novice practitioner, problem-solving models offer comprehensive and structured frameworks that are readily applicable to practice; for the advanced practitioner they provide an overall direction for practice within which increasingly sophisticated and creative approaches can be developed. Yet we have also seen that many social work commentators express strong reservations about these models. Nothwithstanding these debates, problem-solving approaches have enjoyed enduring popularity in many fields of practice and this seems unlikely to subside in the near future. It is important, then, that we have a thorough critical understanding of these models and recognize their uses as well as their limits within our specific contexts of practice.

Summary Questions

1. Briefly describe the four steps of task-centred practice outlined in this chapter.

2. Briefly describe how the seven principles of task-centred intervention would apply to social work practice with a specific client group, such as young people or survivors of mental health conditions.

3. How does task-centred practice differ from crisis intervention?

Reflection Exercise

Outline the uses and limits of problem-solving approaches for realizing the social work values of promoting client self-determination and social justice in your actual (or intended) context of social work practice.

Recommended Reading

Doel, M. and P. Marsh, *Task-centred Social Work* (Aldershot: Ashgate, 1992).
This book provides a thorough introduction to task-centred practice focusing on social work in Britain. In chapter 7, the authors respond to various criticisms of the task-centred approach; this is useful for critically thinking through this model.

Epstein, L. and L. Brown. *Brief Treatment and a New Look at the Task-Centered Approach* 4th edn (Boston, MA: Allyn and Bacon, 2002).
This book provides a comprehensive framework for task-centred practice and addresses some of the issues in using this framework within contemporary practice contexts.

Reid, W.J. and L. Epstein, *Task-centered Casework*. (New York: Columbia University Press, 1972).
In this seminal text on task-centered practice, William Reid and Laura Epstein outline the rationale for, and the processes of, this practice approach.

Trotter, C. *Working with Involuntary Clients: A Guide to Practice* (St. Leonards, New South Wales: Allen and Unwin, 1999).
Chris Trotter provides a comprehensive guide to task-centred practice with involuntary clients.

7

Three Waves of
Systems Theories

Systems perspectives have had considerable influence on the formal base of social work. Indeed, some social work theorists argue that a systemic perspective distinguishes social work from other human service professions (see Meyer, 1976). Systemic analyses focus on interactions within and across multiple 'social' systems, which can include the interpersonal system of family and friendship ties, neighbourhood system, organizational systems, social policy systems and social structural systems. Systems theory emphasizes the role of these systems in contributing to individual and community well-being.

The enduring popularity of systems theories in social work texts and in practice can be attributed to their consistency with social work's long-standing mission to understand and respond to people in their environment (Bartlett, 1970, p. 89; Gordon, 1969, p. 6). Systems theories provide ways of understanding problems and issues; however, it is widely agreed that systems frameworks do not provide intervention methods (see Mattaini and Meyer, 2002; Leighninger, 1978; Wakefield, 1996a and b). Recently, debate about complexity and chaos theories has renewed social workers' interest in the application of systems ideas to social work (see Hudson, 2000; Warren *et al.*, 1998).

In this chapter, we will consider the origins of systems perspectives in social work. We will discuss the assumptions and practice applications of three waves of systems perspectives. These are: general systems theory; eco-systems perspectives; and complex and chaos theories.

Systems Theories in Context

Systems theories, like all the theories for practice we consider in this book, draw on the discourses originating, and operating, outside the field of social work. So while systems theories have helped to guide and explain our work,

132

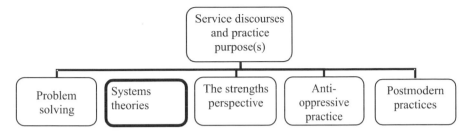

Figure 7.1   Systems theories in context

the core concepts within these theories were not developed in, or intended for, social work practice. Figure 7.1 highlights systems theories in relation to the service discourses and social work theories discussed in this book.

I have positioned systems theories below the service discourses to reflect the origins of systems approaches in sociological discourse. In addition, I have placed them next to problem-solving approaches to reflect the similar historical epoch in which these theories (re-)emerged as powerful influences in contemporary social work. While systems theories arguably have a lengthier history in social work than problem-solving approaches, having been introduced in the 1930s, it was not until the 1960s that systems approaches re-emerged as a powerful theoretical foundation for the profession. Let's turn now to consider these origins in more detail.

The Origins of Systems Theory in Social Work

According to Woods and Hollis (1990), Hankins, a sociologist in the Smith School of Social Work, first introduced the term 'systems theory' to social work in 1930. Yet even before the term 'systems theory' was proposed, social workers in the emerging profession adopted a 'person-in-environment' perspective (Kemp *et al.*, 1997, p. 23; see Richmond, 1917). Richmond (1917, p. 365) argued that social workers must balance personal and social change orientations as she asserted that 'social reform and social case work must of necessity progress together'.

As outlined in Chapter 3, during the middle part of the century, a psychological focus dominated the formal base of social work (Kemp *et al.*, 1997, p. 21). It was not until the 1960s that a dual focus on person and environment returned to prominence in the formal base of social work. In 1964, leading social work theorist Florence Hollis urged social workers to adopt a 'psychosocial' perspective, that is, to recognize both the 'social and psychological' aspects of assessment intervention (Woods and Hollis, 1990, p. 14). Systems theories provided an intellectual foundation for reintegrating the psychological and sociological discourses by recognizing that a range of systems, including the intrapersonal and interpersonal, as well as neighbourhood and society, impacted on service users in a myriad of ways. Recognizing the potential of systems theories to integrate the base of social work during this period of extreme tension in the human science foundations of the formal base of social work, some commentators argued that systems theories could provided a unifying framework for the profession (Bartlett, 1970).

The First Wave: General Systems Theory

While systems theory has been used in social work since at least 1930, it was not until the 1960s that social workers articulated a distinctive systemic approach to practice. During the period, Gordon Hearn and his colleagues in the National Association of Social Workers in the USA pioneered the application of this theory to social work (Hudson, 2000, p. 216; see also Hearn, 1969). The initial proponents of systems theory emphasized its potential to provide scientific credibility to the profession and to develop an integrated theoretical foundation that would 'capture the central elements of social work practice in all its varied forms' (Gordon, 1969, p. 5). General systems theory challenged the profoundly individualistic focus evident, particularly in American social work, during the middle part of the twentieth century and encouraged social workers to give 'substantially more attention to environmental change' (Hearn, 1969, p. 65).

General systems theory was derived from the work of Ludwig von Bertalanffy, a biologist, and from sociological attempts to apply biological systems theories to the social world (Leighninger, 1978, p. 448). From his earliest writings, in the 1920s onwards, von Bertalanffy (1968, pp. 11–12) argued that systems approaches were more appropriate than 'causal' models for dealing with complex interactions in all types of systems: biological, mechanical and social. Bertalanffy (1968) argued that systems ideas were relevant to human service professions, particularly psychology and psychiatry. He challenged behaviourist views that presented humans as 'reactive automatons' and instead argued for recognition of 'active personality systems' (*ibid.*, p. 207). By drawing attention to the *transactions* between the individual and their social environment, Bertanlaffy (*ibid.*, p. 219) proposed that an individual's mental health can only be understood in relation to whether the individual has 'an integrated framework consistent within the given cultural framework'; in other words, from a general systems perspective psychological pathology is considered to be socially and culturally produced rather than primarily arising from the individual psyche. Bertanlaffy (*ibid.*) challenged psychotherapists to redirect their attention from 'digging up the past' to a focus on insight into current conflicts, attempts at social and psychological reintegration, and orientation towards future goals. This proposal was a radical departure from the psychoanalytic frameworks that dominated the 'psy' disciplines and social work during the middle part of the twentieth century. Today, systems perspectives can be used to challenge the individualistic focus of the dominant discourses shaping health and welfare services (see Chapter 2) as well as 'psy'-based approaches to social work.

General Systems Concepts

The original proponents of general systems theory used biological terminology to explain client needs, situations and the purpose of social work practice. Some of the core concepts included transaction, homeostasis, entropy, equifinality and feedback. For example, the concept of homeostasis refers to 'the tendency of a biological organism to seek and keep some kind of operating balance in its internal processes, or, at least to seek and keep processes within certain limits' (Leighninger, 1978, p. 448). Social workers took this concept to mean that the maintenance of a steady state is 'essential for growth of the human organism' (Bartlett, 1970, p. 103; see also Gordon, 1969). Hence, using a general systems approach, social workers focused on identifying states of 'entropy' (or disorder) and working towards achieving a steady state, or balance, between the individual and their social system, especially their family system. Although this terminology was intended to enhance the scientific credibility of social work, many social workers were alienated by it. Indeed, while many of the core concepts on which social workers rely are often drawn from received ideas, the fact that general systems theories arose from the biological sciences rather than human science disciplines, like psychology or sociology, contributed to significant language and conceptual differences that, in the longer run, were difficult to overcome.

None the less, general systems theory contributed to the proliferation of systems-oriented practice models, most prominent among these were the unitary models presented by Pincus and Minahan (1973) and by Goldstein (1973). These models had significant international influence in the development of social work theory for practice (see Boas and Crawley, 1975). Ultimately, however, many social workers have judged general systems theory (GST) to be fundamentally flawed (Mune, 1979). Critics argue that GST's reliance on abstract concepts and the 'mechanistic, nonhuman nature of much of its language' alienated most practising social workers (see Kemp *et al.*, 1997, p. 4; see also Mune, 1979). In addition, GST maintained a relatively narrow focus on the interaction between the individual and their immediate environment and failed to address the impact of macro structures on service users' lives. A further criticism is that the concept of 'system equilibrium' led to an overemphasis on system maintenance functions and negative feedback loops in sustaining problems (Hudson, 2000, p. 217). For example, the violent behaviour of a family member could be seen as a symptom of the system and thus something for which all family members were responsible. Proponents of the second wave of systems theories attempted to overcome these problems.

The Second Wave: Ecosystems Perspectives

During the 1970s, the ecosystems approach to practice superseded general systems theory. Germain and Gitterman's (1996) life model of social work practice and the ecosystems work of Carol Meyer are widely identified as the leading formulations of ecosystems perspectives in social work (Payne, 1997, p. 143; Wakefield, 1996a; see also Kemp *et al.*, 1997, p. 41). In this discussion we will focus on the work of these social work leaders.

The ecosystems perspective brings together GST and an ecological view to expand the focus and relevance of systems perspectives to direct social work practice. The ecosystems perspective retains the GST notion of environmental wholeness, that is, recognition that the parts of the system can never be entirely separated from each other (Mattaini and Meyer, 2002, p. 6). Some of the biological terminology used in GST is also retained in ecosystems models (*ibid.*, pp. 11–13).

Ecosystems thinkers see ecology as a useful metaphor for encouraging social workers to focus on transactions within and across systems and to seek sustainable, not only short-term, change (Kemp *et al.*, 1997, p. 44; Mattaini and Meyer, 2002, p. 8). On the basis of this metaphor, systems theorists argue that social work assessment and intervention should focus on 'person : environment' transactions (Mattaini and Meyer, 2002, p. 6; see also Meyer, 1976, p. 129). Proponents of the ecosystems approach use the distinctive term 'person : environment' to 'repair the conceptually fractured relationship' between person and environment (Germain and Gitterman, 1996, p. 1). Drawing on the ecological metaphor, person:environment transactions are understood to be complex and non-linear. In recognizing complexity, Germain and Gitterman (*ibid.*, p. 7) discourage social workers from searching for 'original causes', whether they be psychological or sociological in nature, and instead encourage them to focus on person:environment exchanges.

The ecosystems perspective encourages social workers to recognize that problems arise because of 'a poor fit between a person's environment and his or her needs, capacities, rights, and aspirations' (Germain and Gitterman, 1996, p. 8). Lack of fit between the person and their environment can occur for many reasons, including anticipated life transitions such as retirement, as well as chronic environment stressors, such as poverty. Addressing earlier criticisms that the ecosystems perspective failed to address structural injustices, later formulations of this perspective incorporated recognition of power, 'habitat' or social location, and diversity of lifestyles (see Germain and Gitterman, 1996).

A core purpose of ecosystems intervention is to improve these transactions by promoting adaption between the person and their environment. According to Germain and Gitterman (1996, p. 5), 'the ecological metaphor helps the profession enact its social purpose of helping people and promoting responsive environments that support human growth, health, and satisfaction in human functioning'. The process of adaption is not passive but is an 'active, change-oriented process' (*ibid.*, p. 475). Proponents of the ecosystems approach frequently contend that it is the focus on enhancing systemic transactions, rather than on improving the functioning of isolated systems, that distinguishes social work from other human service professions such as psychiatry and psychology.

Like the general systems approach, the ecosystems perspective guides assessment and offers general directions for intervention, but it does not propose specific intervention methods (Germain and Gitterman, 1996, p. 45; Mattaini and Meyers, 2002, p. 18). The ecosystems perspective is intended to enable social workers to recognize complexity, and to avoid reductionism, in assessment and intervention.

The Life Model of Social Work Practice

In this section we will discuss the application of ecosystems perspectives using 'the life model of social work practice' formulated by Carel Germain and Alex Gitterman (1996). The life model is characterized by three stages: the initial phase; the ongoing phase; and the ending phase. We will discuss each of these phases by reference to the following case study.

Case Study

Imagine you are a social worker practising in a family support service. The social worker from the juvenile detention centre has referred Tracy to you to provide supportive casework focused on the impending birth of her first child. Tracy is 17 years old and is seven months pregnant. She has recently been released from a youth detention centre. Since she was 14, Tracy has spent extended periods in youth detention for a series of offences, primarily stealing and break-and-enter offences.

Case Study (*cont'd*)

Tracy is from the dominant Anglo-Saxon culture and her former partner, and father of the unborn child, is from an Indian community. Tracy is no longer in a relationship with the child's father and she does not plan for him to have any role in the parenting of the child. His family does not know about Tracy's pregnancy. Tracy has a difficult relationship with her parents: she was placed in foster care as a young child due to her parents' severe alcoholism. Tracy has no relationship with her foster family: she states that she was sexually abused by her foster father and wants nothing to do with that family. Apart from periods in detention, Tracy has been homeless since she was 14.

Tracy's sister Leanne has now offered Tracy a place to stay for as long as she needs. Leanne is 24 years old and has two children (six years and three years). Tracy is happy to accept Leanne's offer and she tells you that she has always had a good relationship with Leanne. In the referral file from the government authority, you learn that Tracy would like to return to school. While in detention, she made good progress with her formal education and would like to complete secondary school. You also learn that the government authority plans to monitor Tracy's parenting as there are concerns about her capacity to care for the child when it is born, given Tracy's family background and her own harmful use of drugs and alcohol.

Initial Phase: Getting Started

The primary purpose of the initial phase is for the social worker and service user to establish an active partnership based on 'mutuality and reciprocity' (Germain and Gitterman, 1996, p. 39). This partnership recognizes the social worker's and service users different knowledge and skills: 'Social worker's bring professional knowledge and skill to the therapeutic encounter. Those served bring their experiential knowledge of their life issues and their life stories' (*ibid.*). This purpose is achieved, first, by the use of empathy. Thus we would aim to clarify how Tracy sees her situation and, particularly, what she would like to achieve through her work with you. We should also clarify our role, including any obligations and constraints imposed by the agency or any other authority, such as the statutory authority.

Second, in this first phase, the worker and service user work together to identify and, where necessary, prioritize 'life stressors'. Germain and Gitterman (1996, p. 14) describe a life stressor as an event or transition that contributes to maladaption in the 'person : environment' fit. Together with Tracy we would identify her strengths and capacities as well as the stressors in Tracy's life.

Ongoing Phase: Working Toward Goals

Our primary purpose in this phase is to promote adaption in the 'person:environment' relationship so as to maximize Tracy's well-being and that of her child (Germain and Gitterman, 1996, p. 8). An ecological assessment forms the foundation of practice in this phase. The central skills involved in this phase are: goal clarification, facilitation, coordination, and individual and systemic advocacy (Germain and Gitterman, 1996).

In an ecological assessment, the service provider and service user work together to gather data about, and analyse the impact of, multiple systems on the service user's situation. Many ecosystems theorists use an ecomap to assist the assessment process (see Meyer, 1993; Mattaini and Meyer, 2002). The ecomap is a 'graphic system for viewing the relevant connected case-elements together, within a boundary that clarifies for the practitioner the case system as the focus of work' (Mattaini and Meyer, 2002, p. 4). This pictorial representation enhances our capacity to see the complexities in the service user's situation much more powerfully than words alone (Meyer, 1994, ch. 6). In addition, the use of an ecomap can also enhance client opportunities to participate in the assessment.

There are many ways of representing an eco-map (see Meyer, 1993). Many social work commentators use Bronfenbrenner's (1979) approach in which a series of concentric rings is used to represent different system levels. In this model, the term micro-systems refers to informal systems such as home, the family and the local community, meso-systems refers to formal systems that have a direct impact on service users' lives, such as schools and social services, and finally, macro-systems refers to the society as a whole and to the large social institutions of government and business. The model is illustrated in Figure 7.2.

Using an ecomap, we would assess the impact of different systems on Tracy's situation and, on this basis, develop a plan for action directed at each of these systems as illustrated in Table 7.1.

The practice process

Within the overaching goal of enhancing the person:environment fit, one of our primary purposes in this phase is to enhance and strengthen service users' 'adaptive capacities and problem-solving abilities' and, concurrently, we aim to promote environmental adaptedness (Germain and Gitterman, 1996, p. 50). The social worker's role, then, is to promote change at the micro-, meso- and macro-levels. Germain and Gitterman (*ibid.*) suggest that the social worker enhances service user capacities through 'the methods of enabling, exploring, mobilizing, guiding, and facilitating'. One way we could enhance Tracy's capacity is by recognizing the strengths she already

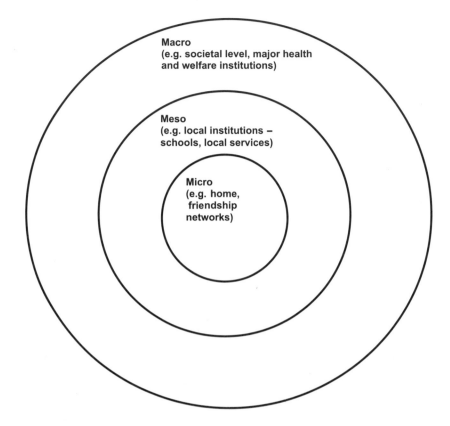

Figure 7.2 Mapping ecosystems

possesses. For instance, we acknowledge the capacities Tracy has demonstrated by surviving her abuse experiences and life on the streets. In the role
of 'guide', we could help Tracy identify strategies for meeting identified
needs such as ante-natal care.

From an ecosystems perspective we would promote a supportive
community for Tracy. Community support would ensure that she has
some independence both from her personal supports, such as her sister, and
also from the health and welfare systems that have had such a dominant
influence on her life. At a micro-level, we may seek to link Tracy to peers,
such as young mothers, or young people returning to secondary education.
If these community networks are absent, we may take an active role in
creating them with Tracy.

At an institutional level, we could support Tracy in her wish to return to
school by identifying and facilitating her access to educational institutions.
If we are unable to locate supportive institutions, we may need to advocate

Table 7.1 Ecosystem intervention plan for working with Tracy

System level	Action	Methods
Micro-systems (home and family)	Strengthen tie with sister	Casework, family support skills, knowledge of support agencies
	Address estrangement with family of origin	Family mediation and family therapy skills
	Address peer isolation	Link to peer network, work on social skills
Micro-systems (community and neighbourhood)	Address local community isolation	Link to community development initiatives, e.g. local family day care, neighbourhood house
Meso-systems (institutions)	Promote educational pathways for Tracy	Access information on educational opportunities; challenge barriers that might prevent return to school (e.g. absence of child-care facilities)
Macro-systems (policy change)	Address lack of support services, educational options, child-care options for young parenting and homeless women, address injustices faced by young people abused in foster care	Research and policy development on support services, educational, child-care, and alternative care systems. Use this research to promote policy change. Link Tracy to peer support and advocacy networks where she may work collectively with others to address the injustices confronting her

both at local institutional and broader policy levels for increased access to education for Tracy and for other young people in similar situations.

Within life-modelled practice it is important that social workers are aware of, and responsive to, the need for policy change. According to Germain and Gitterman (1996, p. 53), 'social workers and clients seek to influence organizational practices and legislation and regulations at local, state, and national levels in the cause of social justice. The influencing method includes such skills as coalition-building; positioning; lobbying; and testifying.' Tracy's situation points to a number of public policy issues. Aside from the issue of support for young people to access to educational opportunities, Tracy's situation also raises issues about the plight of young people abused in alternative care systems and the importance of early intervention and support systems for young parents.

Phase Three: The Ending Phase

As in the task-centred approach, a well-planned termination of intervention is integral to the overall structure of the systems approach (Germain and Gitterman, 1996, p. 56). Some practical ways we could prepare Tracy for the termination phase of our work together include discussing duration of intervention at the outset and regularly referring to this throughout the intervention process. Unlike task-centred practice, Germain and Gitterman (1996, p. 59) stress that the social worker should encourage the service user to discuss their responses, such as anger, sadness or relief, about the conclusion of the intervention. Consistent with the emphasis in the eco-systems approach's stress on comprehensive service delivery, in this final phase we should engage Tracy in an evaluation of our work together and ensure that adequate plans are in place for her to access support once our intervention is complete.

The Third Wave: Complex Systems Theories

In recent years, a third wave of systems theories has entered the social work field. These systems approaches, known as complex systems and chaos theories, emerged originally in the disciplines of maths, physics and engineering (Bolland and Atherton, 1999; see also Capra, 1996). Over the past two decades, these theories have had a growing impact on a range of fields including information technology, business, management, social sciences and the humanities. The Australian social work theorist, Colin Peile was among the earliest proponents of complex systems ideas in social work as exemplified in his work on the creative paradigm (see Peile, 1988, 1994). By the late 1990s, a number of social work theorists were applying complex systems ideas to social work practices (see Bolland and Atherton, 1999; Hudson, 2000; Warren *et al.*, 1998). Some theorists argue that complexity theories provide a way of articulating the intuitive knowledge possessed by most social work practitioners about the non-linearity and unpredictability of change processes (see Bolland and Atherton, 1999; see also Warren *et al.*, 1998). These theorists argue that complex systems ideas enrich, rather than replace, existing ideas about systems theories in social work (see Hudson, 2000, p. 227; Mattaini and Meyer, 2002, p. 9).

A complex system is one in which the behaviour of the whole system is greater than the sum of its parts. Darley (1994, p. 1) states that 'The defining characteristic of a complex system is that some of its global behaviours, which are the result of interactions between a large number of relatively simple parts, cannot be predicted simply from the rules of those underlying interactions.' Complex systems researchers use inductive approaches to consider how local phenomena, including apparently simple interactions, contribute to evolution to larger complex systems.

Complex systems are characterized by non-linearity. Linearity implies a constant relationship between two variables; for example, if the rate of unemployment in an area increases, there is a proportionate increase in the rate of crime. By contrast, in non-linear relationships, a change in one variable, or set of variables, will be associated with disproportionate changes in another variable, or set of variables. For example, as the rate of unemployment in an area rises, there is a sudden and disproportionate increase in the rate of crime. The popular saying 'the straw that broke the camel's back' captures the idea of the disproportionate relationship between an event and an outcome (Hudson, 2000, p. 220).

Whereas general systems theorists suggest that, typically, social systems are stable, complexity theorists argue that change is a usual feature of complex social systems (Warren *et al.*, 1998, pp. 364–5). Feedback mechanisms contribute to the growing complexity of these systems over time (Capra, 1996, p. 123). In particular, the complexity of relationships within systems is amplified by 'repeatedly self-reinforcing feedback' (*ibid.*); this is similar to the concept of positive feedback in general systems theory. Within non-linear systems certain events, or experiences, can have a snowballing effect: there is a repetition (or iteration) of the effect of the event or experience so that it has a disproportionate effect on the life of the individual, group, family or community. For example, some settings of institutional care can exacerbate, rather than alleviate, a person's distress and illness by repeatedly reinforcing the 'sick role' to the point where the person becomes the role (see Goffman, 1991). Again, common expressions such as 'downhill slide', or conversely the idea of 'going from strength to strength', capture something of the concept of 'self-reinforcing feedback'.

Another feature of complex systems is extreme sensitivity to initial conditions, that is, small changes at initial phases in the system's development can lead to substantial and complex changes in the behaviour of the system (Capra, 1996, p. 132). Complexity theorists refer to this extreme sensitivity as the 'butterfly effect'; this metaphor is used because of the 'half-joking assertion that a butterfly stirring in Bejing today can cause a storm in New York next month' (*ibid.*). The concept of a 'butterfly effect' is relevant to a globalized world, where changes in one part of the world have immediate and substantial impact on other parts. Similarly, in social work practice we sometimes see that a short-term, and well-timed, intervention can have a disproportionately positive impact on the capacity of service users to achieve their goals. Indeed, the recognition of the potential for high impact in short-term intervention underpins practice models such as problem-solving and solutions-focused therapy.

Complex systems are characterized by complex, rather than random, behaviour. Warren *et al.* (1998, p. 363) describe this as 'deterministic chaos'. Importantly, complexity or chaos theories do not imply that the 'real world' comprises of random unpredictable events, but rather that the behaviour of complex systems shows 'a deeper level of patterned order' (Capra, 1996, p. 122) than is suggested by the 'linear cause and effect models familiar to social scientists' (Warren *et al.*, 1998, p. 358). For example, recent discussions on social capital suggest that the choices parents make (and are constrained to make) about where they live can have a long-term and substantial impact on the life chances of their children. Complex systems theory recognizes that any 'outcome', such as children's well-being, is determined by the interaction of multiple factors across interpersonal, community and structural contexts (Mainzer, 1996, pp. 279–80). Overall, complexity theorists do not see people as victims of their social context; nor do they see them as entirely free agents.

Finally, the notion of 'phase change' used by complex systems theorists is particularly relevant to social workers in community development contexts. The term 'phase change' refers to the moment at which the system switches from one pattern of complexity to another (see Mainzer, 1996, p. 10). For example, human systems can shift rapidly from one form of organization to another (Warren *et al.*, 1998, p. 364), so that critical periods of phase change are often observed in communities undergoing processes of urban deteroriation or gentrification. During these periods, there are times when the community becomes a qualitatively different place to be, whether for better or worse. Understanding of the processes of phase change could help us to advocate for policies that can promote or sustain positive changes in communities. For instance, if we can show that a certain level of social mix, such as numbers of home owners compared to renters, affects other outcomes such as child protection risk, we may use this information to argue for strategies to improve home ownership options in some communities (see Manzer, 1996, p. 277).

Social work researchers have a developing interest in the application of complex systems ideas to the discipline. Social work researchers Warren *et al.* (1998, p. 366) assert that 'nonlinear dynamics offers the possibility of a far deeper and more nuanced understanding of the ways in which human systems arise and change than is now available'. In addition, Bolland and

Atherton (1999) contend that these theories affirm the understandings already held by most practising social workers of the non-linearity of human systems. For example, the recognition of the complex interactions between individual systems and social structures is consistent with social workers' long-standing focus on 'person in environment' approaches.

Yet despite the intuitive appeal of complex systems theories, we can also identify a number of limitations to the application of these theories to social work. The importance of specialist mathematical knowledge for describing and analysing complex systems is a major barrier to social workers' use of complex systems ideas. As Bolland and Atherton (1999, p. 369) point out, 'Strictly speaking, then, chaos theory is a mathematical way of understanding complex nonlinear behaviour in systems.' The reliance of complexity theory research on specialist mathematical knowledge, such as fractal geometry, limits the application of complex systems theories in social work, and indeed in many human science fields at the 'conceptual or hypothetical-deductive level' (Hudson, 2000, p. 227). We must question how realistic it is to expect social workers to develop expertise in complex mathematics given the breadth of terrain already covered by our discipline. Moreover, we must be wary of the potential of complex systems theory research, given its foundations in disciplines that are markedly dissimilar to social work, to further deepen the divisions between social work research and social work practices.

A related concern is whether research techniques used by complexity researchers to simulate complex weather systems or even economic systems should be applied to the study of social processes. Puddifoot (2000, p. 84) points out that 'there remains a considerable gap between idealized theoretical models and anything resembling real social behaviour' (see also Hudson, 2000, p. 228; Mainzer, 1996, p. 280). At best, the application of complex systems theories to social work research is in its early exploratory phases and certainly does not warrant a paradigm shift.

Complex systems ideas have potential to affirm the complexities of social work practice and policy processes. Yet, as criticisms of these ideas show, we must be wary of the simplistic application of these models to social work. Two questions seem pertinent here: first, what aspects of social work can complex systems theories illuminate that escape current practice models? (Puddifoot, 2000, p. 92). For example, complex systems theories renew our appreciation of the important role of local social interactions in creating, not only reflecting, broader social processes (see Mainzer, 1996, pp. 276–9). A second question is: how might we use these models in ways that bridge, rather than widen, the gap between social work research and practice? Some researchers suggest that qualitative research methods, which incorporate inductive and non-linear knowledge development processes, can help to illuminate complex social processes (see Vallacher and Nowak, 1997).

Discussion Point

Reviewing systems theories

What are the strengths and limitations of systems theories for social work practice within your practice context, or a context of practice that interests you?

Strengths and Limitations of Systems Theories in Social Work

Throughout this chapter we have considered arguments for and against each wave of systems theory. In this final section, we will summarize the overall strengths and weaknesses of systems theories for achieving our purposes in social work practice.

Strengths

A key strength of systems perspectives is that they provide a framework for understanding and responding to people in their environments. Systems approaches discourage the pathologization of either the individual or their environment, instead encouraging the social worker to analyse the interactions within and across systems. According to Mattaini and Meyer (2002, p. 4), 'The ecosystem perspective is a way of seeing complex phenomena (the person and the environment) in their interconnected and multilayered reality, to order and comprehend complexity and avoid oversimplification and reductionism.'

In addition, systems theories can provide a unifying conceptual foundation for social work as a profession focused on understanding and responding to people in their environment. As neo-classical economic discourses increasingly dominate social work practice contexts, we will face intensified pressure to identify our contributions to social service delivery. The systems perspective offers the profession an option for defining this contribution. For example, as systems 'specialists', professional social workers can provide forms of assessment at individual, group, community and organizational levels that promote systemic understanding and sustainable systemic change.

Systems approaches encourage social work professionals to respect the contributions different methods make to practice and to develop basic competencies across the range of intervention approaches. Gitterman (1996, p. 474) points out that

> An ecological view helps us appreciate that no theory, concept, model or approach can take everything into account. The complexity of the human condition requires that we develop both a broad perspective as well as specific accommodations and competencies.

This framework can provide an antidote to competition between practice methods; the message of systems theories is that we need a range of perspectives and intervention methods

Weaknesses

Despite the considerable influence of systems perspectives on the knowledge base of social work, we should also recognize their substantial limitations. Some social work commentators criticize the lack of clarity about core systems concepts, such as what constitutes a system, what are the boundaries of a system, and what are the attributes of a system (see Mune, 1979, p. 65). This lack of clarity contributes to an absence of both theoretical and empirical justification of systems viewpoints in practice (Wakefield, 1996b, p. 206). Instead, practitioners are invited to accept central claims derived from systems theories, such as the claim that all parts of a system are complexly intertwined and that changes in one part of the system will inevitably lead to changes in other parts without any external justification of these claims. In short, systems theories present an intuitively appealing, yet largely untested, viewpoint for social work practice.

Some commentators point to inconsistencies between social work values and systems theories (see Wakefield, 1996a and b). A focus on function and exchange within systems can leave out questions of structural injustice and abuse of power (Wakefield, 1996b, p. 201). For example, feminist theorists have shown that family system functioning often depends on the exploitation of women's labour. Moreover, as Wakefield (*ibid.*) also points out, the systemic focus on interactions and networks can cause social workers to lose focus on the uniqueness of the person. In practice we may also encounter concerns that a focus on individual and environment interactions downplays the individual's capacity and responsibility for change.

Critics are concerned that systems perspectives draw on discourses that have little relevance to social work. For example, the first wave of systems theory draws heavily on biological discourses, while the third wave draws extensively from maths and physics discourses. Some commentators question whether concepts from these discourses can be applied directly to social processes, such as social service delivery (Mune, 1979; Puddifoot, 2000; Wakefield, 1996b). In addition, as we discussed earlier, the specific language used to describe key concepts, whether this is the language of the biological sciences, physical sciences or complex mathematics, is likely to alienate practitioners who already cover considerable conceptual terrain in their work. If so, the importation of systems ideas from other disciplines will further entrench the division between formal knowledge and practice knowledge in social work.

A further issue is that systemic perspectives provide little guidance on how to move from a holistic analysis to systemic intervention. All three waves of systems perspectives help us to perceive the person-in-environment as a unity, but to act we may need to break down this gestalt into smaller pieces. One problem here is that a systems perspective recognizes all information available to us but does not help us to prioritize it.

Finally, a systemic analysis does not necessarily enable us to use the enormous bank of information gathered in the development of a systemic analysis to form systemic action strategies; indeed, the sheer amount of information may be prevent such action. As Leighninger (1978, p. 454) provocatively asks: will social workers, 'while recognizing the social nature of many problems, find them so complex that they despair of solving them and go back to individual therapy as the only profitable use of their talents?' Proponents of systemic approaches, particularly ecosystems perspectives, have argued that social workers should have a generic skill set in order to practise holistically. This seems an incredible demand given the growing diversity of social work practices. As Wakefield (1996a, p. 196) points out, in most complex endeavours 'specialisation rather than a comprehensive approach by each individual increases efficiency and effectiveness'.

Conclusion

Systems perspectives have had substantial influence on the knowledge base of professional social work. In this chapter we have explored three waves of systems theories and their influence on social workers' knowledge bases. We can see that systems perspectives remain a contested view in social work. At the very least, they provide a way of articulating the complexity of interactions between individuals and their environments. For many social workers this is an intuitively appealing framework. Even so, we can see substantial concerns about the extensive adoption of these viewpoints in practice. Notwithstanding these limitations, however, systems theories remain key conceptual frameworks for contemporary social work practice.

Summary Questions

1. What common criticism can be made of the applicability of each of the three waves of systems theory to social work practices?

2. What are the key stages of ecosystems practice?

3. What are the characteristics of a complex system?

Reflection Exercise

Thinking about your role as a social worker, or your likely role in an area of practice that interests you, discuss the comparative strengths and limits of ecosystems and complex systems theories for extending your analysis of service user needs.

Recommended Reading

Germain, C. and A. Gitterman *The Life Model of Social Work Practice: Advances in Theory and Practice*, 2nd edn (Columbia University Press, New York 1996).
This book offers one of the leading formulations of the ecosystems perspective as a practice model. It provides a thorough overview of the theory and practice of ecosystems perspectives in practice.

Hudson, C.G. 'The Edge of Chaos: A New Paradigm for Social Work?', *Journal of Social Work Education*, **36**(2) (2000), 215–30.
This article offers an excellent overview of the application of complex systems theories and chaos theories to social work.

Meyer, C.H. *Assessment in Social Work Practice* (New York: Columbia University Press, 1993).
The late Carol Meyer is a key leader in ecosystems perspectives in social work. This widely cited text provides an accessible introduction to the use of ecosystems perspectives in social work assessment. Chapter 6 provides an excellent explanation of the use of ecomaps in social work assessment.

Wakefield, J. 'Does Social Work Need the Eco-Systems Perspective? Part 1: Is the Perspective Clinically Useful?', *The Social Service Review*, **70**(1) (1996a), 1–32.
Wakefield, J. 'Does Social Work Need the Eco-Systems Perspective? Part 2: Does the Perspective Save Social Work from Incoherence?', *The Social Service Review*, **70**(2) (1996b), 183–213.
In these companion articles, Wakefield makes a powerful case against ecosystems perspectives in social work and his argument has relevance for the application of

other waves of systems theories. Wakefield argues that social work is unified by a common purpose of promoting minimal distributive justice, and that an ecosystems perspective is unnecessary and may be unhelpful for achieving this aim. These articles provide an excellent critical analysis of the development and deployment of systems perspectives in social work.

8

The Strengths Perspective

The strengths perspective is a relatively recent development in social work theory. While social work theorists have long emphasized the strengths and capacities of service users, it was not until the late 1980s that the strengths perspective was fully articulated as a practice approach. The strengths perspective hails from North America, primarily from the work of Dennis Saleebey, Charles Rapp and Anne Weick from the University of Kansas. In recent years, the strengths perspective has gained popularity in many countries and practice contexts (see Parton and O'Byrne, 2001). Originally developed in mental health practice contexts, this perspective is now adapted for a broad range of practice contexts including: child protection (see Turnell and Edwards, 1999); addictions (van Wormer and Davis, 2003); developmental disabilities (Quinn, 1998); and corrections (van Wormer, 2001).

The growing popularity of the strengths perspective can be partly attributed to its embodiment of social work values, particularly its emphasis on respect and service user self-determination. The strengths perspective emphasizes optimism and creativity, and, in so doing, offers an alternative to increasingly defensive and risk-averse practices that have become commonplace as a result of the growing influence of the dominant discourses we discussed in Chapter 2. In this chapter, we will define the strengths perspective, its origins and its theoretical foundations. We will overview the practice principles arising from this perspective and consider its application to practice with individuals and communities. We turn first to consider how the strengths perspective draws on the service discourses discussed earlier and its relation to the other theories for social work practice outlined in the book.

The Strengths Perspective in Context

Figure 8.1 highlights the strengths perspective in relation to services discourses and other theories for practice.

151

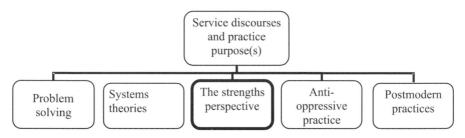

Figure 8.1   The strengths perspective in context

Like all theories for practice considered in this book, the strengths perspective draws its intellectual foundations from service discourses as well as, of course, from practice within specific service fields. This perspective was originally founded in mental health services and 'psy' perspectives, especially ideas of psychological resilience, inform this theory. In addition, as we shall see, sociological discourse, especially the work of Erving Goffman, also contributes to this approach. In contrast to problem-solving and systems approaches, the strengths perspective also draws on the alternative discourses discussed in Chapter 4. In particular, many aspects of the strengths perspective are consistent with consumer rights discourses, which challenge professional expertise by highlighting clients' expertise about their concerns and also the importance of promoting supportive communities for recognizing and fostering service users' capacities. In addition, consistent with discourses associated with religion and spirituality, the strengths perspective also recognizes that responses to the spiritual needs of the service user are a dimension of holistic service provision. I have positioned the strengths perspective after problem-solving and systems perspectives to reflect their more recent influence on the formal base of social work practice. I have located them alongside anti-oppressive and postmodern approaches which, like the strengths perspective, have become established in the formal base of social work over the last two decades.

The Strengths Perspective: What Is It?

The strengths perspective focuses on the capacities and potentialities of service users. It concentrates on enabling individuals and communities to articulate, and work towards, their hopes for the future, rather than seeking to remedy the problems of the past or even the present. According to Saleebey (1997, p. 4), the strengths perspective formula is simple: 'Mobilize clients' strengths (talent, knowledge, capacities) in the service of achieving their goals and visions and the clients will have a better quality of life on their terms.' The strengths perspective requires practitioners to adopt an optimistic attitude towards the individuals and communities with whom they work.

Many proponents of the strengths perspective debate whether this approach is a theory, a distinct way of seeing the world, or a value position. Weick *et al.* (1989, p. 354) suggest that

> If anything, a strengths perspective is a strategy for seeing; a way to learn to recognize and use what is already available to them [the service users]. The professional person thus becomes a translator who helps people see that they already possess much of what they need to proceed on their chosen path.

In this book, we will refer to the strengths perspective as a theory of social work practice. This is because, like other theories of practice, it offers guidelines for analysing and developing practice responses. In this sense, it fits the definition of social work theory outlined in Chapter 4.

Origins of the Strengths Perspective

The approach first emerged among social workers in North America practising in mental health contexts, mainly with people diagnosed with severe and chronic psychiatric conditions (Saleebey, 1996, p. 296; see also Rapp, 1998). Saleebey (1996, p. 296) states that the strengths perspective was developed in opposition to 'U.S. culture and helping professions [that] are saturated with psychosocial approaches based on individual, family, and community pathology, deficits, problems, abnormality, victimization and disorder'.

As the strengths perspective gains increasing international attention, it is important for us to understand how the geographical and institutional settings in which this approach originated have shaped its development and application. The origins of the strengths perspective in the USA is significant because North American social work is more strongly aligned with the professions of psychiatry and psychology than is the case in other countries, such as Australia, New Zealand, the UK and Scandinavia. The origins of the strengths perspective in mental health contexts is important also as this provides the primary frame of reference for the development of this approach. The original advocates of the strengths perspective sought to challenge key concepts in biomedical – and more specifically, psychiatric – discourses, particularly the emphasis on individual pathology, that, in their view, dominate conventional mental health agencies. While biomedical and psychiatric discourses shape social work practices in many practice domains, as we have seen, in many agency contexts other discourses, such as law and neo-classical economics, are also influential in shaping social work practice and our understandings of client 'needs', 'strengths' and 'deficits'.

Despite these contextual differences, the strengths perspective's core critical insight that social work is based on a deficit model resonates with social workers across many countries. Weick *et al.* (1989) attribute this common focus on deficit to the historical foundation of social work in religious charities and the assumption that service users' problems could be attributed to moral failings. Also, the psychodynamic tradition of social work, influential in shaping the modern profession, focused on uncovering and treating psychopathology (*ibid.*, p. 350). Today, proponents of the strengths perspective argue that despite the profession's stated commitment to values of client self-determination and respect, dominant practice approaches remain mired in the language of pathology and deficit (Saleebey, 1996; Weick *et al.*, 1989).

Let's consider an example. Problem-solving approaches (see Chapter 6) aim to help service users identify their problems and goals for change, based on the assumption that they lack the skills or resources to resolve these problems. You will recall that the social worker's role was, in part, to help the service user develop realistic and desirable goals for change, thus suggesting that some of the client's own hopes and dreams might be beyond them and may even harm them by creating unrealistic expectations. By contrast, in the strengths perspective, we turn our attention to the capabilities and assets of service users and their communities, and use service users' hopes and dreams, however unrealistic they may seem to us, as our guide for our practice.

Knowledge Foundations of the Strengths Perspective

Before turning to the practice principles of the strengths perspective, let's consider the sources of intellectual and practice inspiration for this approach. The strengths perspective draws on a broad scope of theoretical knowledge and empirical research in the social sciences and social work, and is strongly aligned with solution-focused and empowerment approaches.

Proponents of the strengths perspective acknowledge Bertha Capen Reynolds as an influential figure in the development of this approach (Saleebey, 1997, pp. 15–16; see also Kaplan, 2002). Reynolds was a social work practitioner and educator whose work with the Maritime Union during the 1940s shaped her outlook on professional work practice. Drawing on this practice experience, Reynolds (1951, p. 130) criticized the profession's growing attachment to professional status and its uncritical adoption of psychoanalytic discourse. Reynolds challenged the fledgling profession of social work to reject notions of professionalism that emphasized detachment, diagnosis and individualized treatment as ultimately destructive to the well-being of service users. In turning away from a psychological treatment orientation, Reynolds (*ibid.*, p. 175) advocated that the profession recognize its political responsibilities for enhancing the social and political inclusion of service users. Reynolds also urged social workers to focus on clients' strengths and capacities rather than concentrating on personal pathology. In a statement consistent with the strengths perspective, Reynolds (*ibid.*, p. 34) asserted:

> Recognition of what a client has to work with, in himself, is a better starting point than an attempt to make him accept his failure, and ... building him up as a person makes him more ready, rather than less so, to go on to further growth and accomplishment.

The work of Erving Goffman, the eminent sociologist, has also had a profound influence on the strengths perspective. Goffman's (1991) research on social labelling, stigma and marginalization showed that many of the practices adopted by human service institutions and human service professions contributed to the problems they were intended to overcome. For example, by using the label 'schizophrenic' one is imposing a stigma on a person that has a range of negative ramifications for their self-understanding and the way others respond to them. In recognition of the power of language to 'elevate and inspire or demoralize and destroy' (Saleebey, 1997, p. 8), advocates of the strengths perspective urge workers to be sensitive to their language use, particularly in their description of clients' perceived capacities and deficits.

The strengths perspective draws also on empirical research about psychological resilience. Dennis Saleebey (1997) points to research demonstrating that adverse life events are not strong predictors of future capacities. Reviewing research on childhood trauma and adversity, Saleebey contends that the majority of people do not reproduce the problems to which they were exposed as children (see Saleebey, 1997). The resilience research also suggests that people can actually benefit from difficult life events (see McMillen, 1999). This is particularly true for adults' acute experiences of adversity, such as surviving a life-threatening illness or natural disaster (*ibid.*, p. 456). In our discussion of the weaknesses of the strengths perspective, later in the chapter, we will discuss problems in the strengths perspectives theorists' interpretation of the resilience research.

The strengths perspective also has some similarities with ego-psychology concepts. Psychodynamic and psychosocial casework theorists argue that social workers should seek to identify and reinforce 'ego strengths'. Both the strengths perspective and ego psychology emphasize the links between psychological strengths, such as ego strengths, and personal resilience in the face of adversity (see Garrett, 1958, p. 44). Interestingly, the proponents of the strengths perspective themselves do not usually link their approach to ego psychology. This may be because ego psychology was part of, and reinforces, a pathological view of service users. For example, Hamilton (1951, p. 296), a proponent of ego psychology in casework, warned that 'caseworkers must not only ally themselves with the healthy parts of the personality ... but also make a new appraisal, as it were, of how the ego is weakened and dependency needs exacerbated by illness'. None the less, given that the strengths perspective first arose among social workers in the mental health field, where 'psy' discourses are ubiquitous, it is likely that these ideas have contributed to the development of this approach.

A strong interchange of ideas and practice techniques exists between strengths perspectives and solution-focused brief therapy practice (see Turner and Edwards, 1999; see also O'Connell, 1998). Proponents of the strengths perspective and solution-focused brief therapy share an intellectual debt to Geoffrey Bateson and researchers from the Brief Therapy Centre, particularly Watzlawick, Weakland and Fisch (Weick *et al.*, 1989, p. 351; De Shazer, 1985, p. 6). These researchers challenged the conventional psychotherapeutic wisdom that effective therapy should be long-term and insight-oriented. Instead, they focused on the use of paradox and recognition of small changes as ways to unlock problem systems (see Weakland *et al.*, 1974). Drawing on features of solution-focused brief therapy as outlined by Barret-Kruse (cited in O'Connell, 1998, p. 3), we can identify similarities between this approach and the strengths perspective; for example both approaches:

- recognize and focus on the strengths and capacities of service users to respond the problems facing them;

- view service provision as a mutual learning process for service provider and service user;

- seek to depersonalize the problems facing the service user. In other words, both approaches emphasize that the person is not the problem, rather the problem is the problem;

- are oriented towards the exploration of future possibilities rather than an excavation of the past.

Proponents of solution-focused brief therapy and the strengths perspective see these features as radical departures from established models of interpersonal work (see O'Connell, 1998, pp. 3–4; Saleebey, 1997; Weick *et al.*, 1989).

Some proponents of the strengths perspective link it with empowerment approaches (see Saleeby, 1997; van Wormer, 2001). Many features of the empowerment approach (see Parsons *et al.*, 1998; Payne, 1997) are consistent with the strengths perspective. Both approaches aim to recognize and build service users' capacity to help themselves and their communities and to promote a mutual learning partnership between workers and service users. However, advocates of empowerment perspectives focus more strongly on the social and structural origins of service users' difficulties than do proponents of the strengths perspective. In concert with anti-oppressive practice perspectives, empowerment theorists (Parsons *et al.*, 1998, p. 5) contend that social workers should 'help individuals see the roots of their problems in society' and foster collective action among service users directed at both 'internal and external' social structures. The empowerment perspective articulated by Parsons *et al.* (1998) can be seen as a bridge between the strengths perspective and anti-oppressive approaches in that it combines core elements of both practice perspectives.

Practice Assumptions and Principles

The strengths perspective involves much more than a mantra emphasizing client capacities. The perspective refers to a distinct set of assumptions from which flow core practice principles. In this section, we will turn to these assumptions and principles.

Drawing on the work of Saleeby (1997) and Weick *et al.* (1989), we can identify the following key assumptions of the strengths perspective:

- All people have strengths, capacities and resources.

- People usually demonstrate resilience, rather than pathology, in the face of adverse life events. This is because, according to strengths perspective theorists, 'all human organisms have an inclination for healing' (Saleebey, 1996, p. 10).

- Service users have the capacity to determine what is best for them and they do not need human service workers to define their best interests for them.

- Human service professionals, including social workers, tend to focus on perceptions of clients' problems and deficits while ignoring their strengths and resources. Saleebey (1996, p. 297) warns that 'Pursuing a practice based on ideas of resilience, rebound, possibility, and transformation is difficult because, oddly enough, it is not natural to the world of helping and service' (Saleebey, 1996, p. 297).

- Collaborative partnerships between workers and service users reflect and build service users' capacities. Yet human service professionals, including social workers, are reluctant to collaborate with service users in a spirit of mutual learning and genuine partnership, preferring instead to protect their professional power.

Now we'll turn to the practice principles arising from these assumptions. In this discussion, we will also consider practical strategies for applying these principles.

Practice Principle 1: Adopt an Optimistic Attitude

Social workers have a professional duty to assume a positive and optimistic attitude towards service users. Optimism is essential because our outlook determines whether we can see, let alone build on, service users' strengths and resourcefulness (Turnell and Edwards, 1999, p. 62). This positive attitude requires us to be sceptical about labels that construct service users as incompetent or incapable of achieving an improved quality of life; instead we should seek to fully recognize clients' capacities and resources, as well as their hopes and dreams for the future.

How: In practice, we must challenge ourselves, and others, including those in formal and informal helping networks, to question pathological and deficit-oriented views of service users and to seek out instead evidence of clients' strengths, capacities and resourcefulness. For example, in working with families identified by authorities as being at risk of abusing their children, we could explore the relationships that they feel positive about and that could help them build a support network for themselves and their children, such as extended family relationships, friendships, professional helpers and community networks (Turner and Edwards, 1999).

In addition, we must convey to service users our belief in their capacities to resolve the immediate problems facing them and to achieve quality of life on their own terms. Sensitivity to our use of language is also vital here, as Kaplan and Girard (cited in Saleebey, 1996, p. 304) assert:

> People are more motivated to change when their strengths are supported. Instead of asking family members what their problems are, a worker can ask what strengths they bring to the family and what they think are the strengths of other family members ... The worker creates a language of strength, hope, and movement.

At a minimum, this approach requires that we separate the person from the problem that brings them to the social service agency. So instead of describing a person as schizophrenic we might refer to them as the person with schizophrenia. Better still, if we must refer to the issues facing service users, then we should describe them in terms that convey our respect for their resilience; thus the service user is described as a survivor of schizophrenia.

Practice Principle 2: Focus Primarily on Assets

While advocates of the strengths perspective do not deny the reality of problems such as mental illness and addiction, they assert that we should resist making them the focus of our assessment and intervention. Rather, we must primarily recognize the assets of the service user because we can build only on strengths, not on deficits. For example, in a corrective services setting, we would balance our focus on the service user's criminal behaviour with recognition of those aspects of the service user's life 'upon which a non-offending future might be built (O'Connell, 1998, p. 145).

We should focus on eliciting the full range of assets of the individual, including their personal capacities as well as resources embedded in their social networks. For example, Quinn (1998, p. 105) argues that

> It is easy to assume, for example, that any adult with Down syndrome will be a happy, placid person who is satisfied performing routine, repetitive tasks … Instead, the entire range of possible cognitive abilities, physical capacity, and personal interests must be evaluated. The assumption should be made that the young adult can accomplish any task, until this is proven wrong.

How: Strengths-oriented practitioners argue that we, as practitioners, must change the way we listen to the client's account of their situation. A strengths approach to listening requires us to be on the lookout for signs of capacity and resourcefulness, rather than problems and deficits in service users' lives. Van Wormer (2001, p. 32) describes a strengths approach to listening thus:

> Listening is the method; listening to the client's story, not passively, uncreatively, but with full attention to the rhythms and patterns, and then, when the time is right, observing, and sharing until through a mutual discovery, events that can be seen in terms of some kind of whole. The challenge is to find themes of hope and courage and in so naming to reinforce them.

A strengths-oriented approach suggests that the process of identifying and reinforcing service users' capacities, of itself, contributes to positive change as it reveals existing strengths that might otherwise be overlooked. For example, let's say we are working in a school context and a young person is referred to us because of their absenteeism. The referral from the school principal tells us that, on average, the young person misses two days of school per week. From a strengths perspective we would not focus on the two days missed per week, but rather, we turn our attention to what keeps the young person at school three days per week. Moreover, using a strengths perspective approach to listening we would seek out strengths, not only within the individual, but also within their formal and informal networks. So we could say to the young person: 'Tell me about someone who wouldn't be surprised to know that you had managed to get yourself to school three days per week despite everything that is going on for you.' The focus on strengths within the young person's network helps us, as workers, and the service user to gain a comprehensive list of the resources available to address the problem at hand.

Practice Exercise

Strengths-focused listening

For this exercise you will need to work in pairs. Each person is to take a turn at being the social worker and the service user. You should each take the assigned role for five to ten minutes. The conversation is focused on the service user telling of a challenge they have faced and the social worker listening for, and reflecting back to the service user, signs of strength in the service user's story.

In preparing for the role of service user, think about a challenge you have faced in your life. It should be something that had a serious impact on your life, such as your decision to undertake a career in social work, a decision to leave a relationship, a situation of loss or grief you have experienced, or a decision to make a significant lifestyle change.

In the role of social worker, ask the other person to talk with you about a challenge they have faced in their life. Using the strengths perspective, listen and probe for signs of strength in the story; highlight these strengths to the 'service user'.

Reflecting on the exercise, discuss:

(a) From the perspective of being in the social worker role:
  – what, if anything, did you find useful about this approach?
  – what, if anything, did you find limiting about this approach?

(b) From the perspective of being in the service user role:
  – what, if anything, did you find useful about this approach?
  – what, if anything, did you find limiting about this approach?

A few words of clarification would probably assist here, lest a strengths approach to listening be dismissed out of hand as naïve or even dangerous. First, proponents argue that a strengths approach to listening does not require us to ignore evidence of risk, only that such evidence is put within a comprehensive understanding of the service user's situation (Turnell and Edwards, 1999, p.65). For example, if we are child protection workers working with a young mother (Sally) suspected of neglecting her child (Ben, two years old), we might assess not only the risks to the child but also times when the young mother has found the resources within herself and her community to give the child the care he needs. In some situations, this information can be used to promote change in the service user's life.

In addition, while strengths-oriented listening requires us to question the labels applied to the service user, this does mean that we should ignore these categories altogether. Indeed, in some situations, labels, such as diagnoses, can bring clarity and relief. For instance, some people may find relief in diagnosis of medical or psychiatric conditions to explain symptoms that are puzzling and distressing to them. According to van Wormer (2001, p.75), 'the secret' lies in how these labels are used. In the strengths perspective, the labels applied to the service user become a point of discussion and investigation with the service user rather something to be used by professionals over them.

A final concern is that too great a focus on strengths may lead us to either naively or insensitively gloss over service users' negative feelings and perceived deficits and, in so doing, cause us to lose credibility with service users and other service providers. Therefore it is important that we find ways of acknowledging service users' and other service providers' interpretations, while also promoting the strengths-oriented view. For example, returning to the example of Sally, the young mother suspected of neglecting her child, we might say: 'From what you've told me, I can see that you've found being a young mother, alone, very difficult and that you feel that Ben has suffered a great deal. What good might come out the struggles you've had for your relationship with him?'

Practice Principle 3: Collaborate with the Service User

Like all the practice approaches we consider in this book, the strengths perspective emphasizes the importance of partnership between worker and service user. Again, as in the other approaches, proponents of the strengths perspective recognize that a partnership approach is consistent with social work values and, also, at a practical level, the solutions developed collaboratively are likely to be more useful to the service user than those imposed by others, such as experts. In addition to these arguments, proponents of the strengths perspective argue that the formation of a practice partnership increases the resources available to solve the problem at hand. Through alliance, service providers and service user are best able to harness the resources and capacities of the service user, including their capacities for self-help. Second, partnership work, of itself, is a necessary, though not sufficient, condition for service user empowerment. Advocates of the strengths perspective contend that people can grow only when others, particularly 'helpers', 'actively affirm and support their capacity to do so' (Weick *et al.*, 1989, p. 354; see also Saleebey, 1997). Finally, in contrast to problem-solving approaches, proponents of the strengths perspective argue that finding solutions is a creative process that must engage all the understandings, including emotional and spiritual perspectives, and capacities of the service worker and service user (see Weick *et al.*, 1989). In the solution-focused approaches, on which strengths practitioners often draw, there is recognition that solutions to problems often lie in emotional and irrational knowledge; that is, that this non-rational knowledge provides the 'keys' to unlock problems. Steve de Shazer (1985, p. 7) asserts that 'All that is necessary is that the person involved in a troublesome situation does something different, even if that behavior is seemingly irrational, certainly irrelevant, obviously bizarre, or humorous.'

How: There are many ways we can encourage collaboration between service workers and service users. These include:

- *Promoting a collaborative physical environment.* For example, we seek to ensure that the space in which we work with the service user is free of interruptions and that our work furniture is arranged in ways that promote collaboration, such as ensuring that worker and service user are sitting at the same level, face to face, with nothing obstructing our view of each other, such as a desk.

- *Promoting a collaborative interpersonal relationship.* Strategies for achieving collaborative interpersonal relations are highly context-specific and so it is important that, in seeking to enhance mutuality, we do so in ways that are appropriate to the environment. Some general ways of achieving mutuality may include: encouraging mutual use of first names; the use of appropriate self-disclosure, particularly to indicate resources and assets you may use in responding to the service user's concerns; paying attention to the service user's perceptions of the situation, especially their interpretations of the key issues and how these might be resolved; encouraging the service user to participate in setting the agenda for your work together and evaluating the effectiveness of your shared work; being alert to opportunities for demystifying professional intervention processes, for example by clarifying biomedical terminology that has been applied to the service user or their situation;

- *Encouraging collaborative and creative solution seeking.* We can encourage collaborative solution seeking by, for example, working with service users to 'brainstorm' possible solutions to their identified concerns. Consistent with the principle of optimism, we should encourage service users to put forward all possible responses to identified concerns, no matter how outlandish and unrealistic they may seem to us.

Practice Exercise

Comparison of expert-centric and collaborative styles

Again working in pairs, let's imagine that one of you is the social worker and one is the young mother, Sally, whose situation was described earlier in the chapter. In one scenario adopt the expert model of practice in which you, as the social worker, are the child protection expert, and the client, Sally, is dependent on the social worker's decision as to whether or not she is allowed to maintain care of her child. Try working from this perspective for at least five minutes.

Now, staying in the same roles, start the role play again but, this time, adopt a strengths-oriented collaborative approach. Again, try working from this perspective for at least five minutes.

Once you have attempted the role play using both the expert model and the strengths-oriented collaborative approach, then, with your role-play partner, discuss your experiences of being a social worker or service user using both approaches. The following questions may help you begin your reflections.

- From within each of your roles, what did you find easy and what was difficult about each approach?
- What effects did each approach have on you as the social worker or as the service user? For example, did either approach make you feel more or less confident in the role of social worker or as service user? What else did you experience when working from each perspective?
- What do you see as the likely outcomes of each approach in practice?

Practice Principle 4: Work Towards the Long-term Empowerment of Service Users

According to Rappaport (cited in Saleeby, 1997, p. 8), a commitment to service user empowerment 'requires us to create opportunities for the alienated and distressed to seize some control over their lives and the deci- sions that are critical to their lives'. In part, this involves recognizing and affirming service users' resilience and capacities in the face of adversity. Thus we recognize that people are not only unharmed by negative life events but may actually develop capacities from them. In addition, the strengths perspective is aimed at achieving practical outcomes that enhance service users' capacity to improve their quality of life. The social worker's role is to facilitate service users' capacity to use existing strengths and resources, as well as developing new ones, to achieve their hopes and dreams.

How: From a strengths perspective, empowerment is achieved, in part, by a focus on the future possibilities rather than past problems. Thus, rather than seeking to excavate the causes of problems, our work is oriented towards uncovering the service users' hopes and dreams for the future. From the strengths perspective, it is vital that we affirm service users' resilience and capacities, including those developed via adversity, rather than view them as victims of their situation or social structures. In addition, strengths-oriented practitioners seek to enhance empowerment by achieving practical out- comes with service users that are consistent with their hopes and dreams for the future.

Practice Principle 5: Create Community

Advocates of the strengths perspective stress the importance of social support for achieving resilience and enhancing quality of life. According to Saleeby (1996, p. 299), belonging to a community is first step towards empowerment, because

> Membership means that people need to be citizens – responsible and valued
> members in a viable group or community. To be without membership is to be
> alienated, and to be at risk of marginalization and oppression, the enemies of civic
> and moral strength.

Just as social workers' recognition of service users' strengths can enhance their capacity to activate these strengths, so too, community recognition of, and support for, service user strengths can help them to mobilize their capacities in the achievement of their hopes and dreams. In addition, from a strengths perspective, community support can build and draw on the capacities of service users to help themselves and to help others.

How: In working with service users' strengths, we should recognize the strengths and assets embedded in service users' social networks. These strengths could include people whom the service user experiences as affirming and supportive and roles that service users perform in their 'community' that develop or reflect their capacity for self-help and/or the help of others. Social workers can be alert to opportunities to link service users to community networks that could affirm and build their capacity for self-help and community service. If such networks are absent, social workers can contribute to the development of support networks. For example, young mothers can benefit from peer support networks that both offer them support and build their capacity to offer support and advocacy to others (see Healy and Walsh, 1997).

The Strengths Perspective in Community Development: An Asset Approach

While the strengths perspective emerged in a casework practice, its key themes are applicable to other practice methods, such as community development. Community development is a method used by social workers and others, such as town planners, that focuses on developing the resources of communities (Green and Haines, 2002, p. vii). The asset-based community development approach (often referred to as ABCD practice) shifts away from the needs-focused approach that, according to Kretzmann and McKnight (1993, p. 25), has characterized community development and instead focuses on the gifts, skills and assets within a community (Green and Haines, 2002, p. 9). According to Kretzmann and McKnight (1993, p. 13), 'strong communities are basically places where the capacities of local residents are identified, valued and used'.

The key features of the asset-based approach, as outlined by Kretzmann and McKnight (1993), are:

- *Change must begin from inside the community.* The community must drive the change process. This is important because the community will own and support changes and initiatives that it has developed. When the community 'owns' initiatives, the process of creating and sustaining change will build pride and independence within the community. But there is a further pragmatic reason why proponents of ABCD practice promote change from the 'inside out'. According to Kretzmann and McKnight (1993, p. 5), in the current climate of neo-classical economic reform, it is futile to depend on outside help and so 'the hard truth is that development must start from within the community'.

- *Change must build on the capacities and assets that already exist within communities.* There are at least four sites where assets can be uncovered.

These are: individuals; informal networks, such as neighbourhood ties; civic institutions, such as sporting organizations, and self-help groups; formal institutions, such as schools, charitable institutions, businesses or government agencies.

- *Change is relationship driven.* The asset approach fosters collaboration across different sectors, such as informal, community service, business and government agencies.

- *Change should be oriented towards sustainable community growth.* Advocates of the asset-based approach are critical of community development approaches that focus primarily on community maintenance, and also on approaches that look outside the community for change initiatives (Green and Haines, 2002, pp. 9–11; Kretzmann and McKnight, 1993). Instead, they seek to achieve the long-term social and economic empowerment of disadvantaged communities by building assets within the community and using these as a basis for partnership with other communities and other sectors (see Green and Haines, 2002, p. 11). According to Kretzmann and McKnight (1993, p. 354), 'Clearly a community which has mobilized its internal assets is no longer content to be recipient of charity. Rather, this mobilized community offers opportunities for real partnerships, for investors who are interested in effective action and in a return for their investment.'

If you are interested in an asset-based approach to community development, please see the references at the end of this chapter.

Discussion Point

Thinking about your context of practice, or contexts of practice that interest you, and the social work role(s) within that context, identify the strengths and weaknesses of the strengths perspective.

The Strengths of the Strengths Perspective

So, finally, we turn to a consideration of the strengths and weaknesses of the strengths perspective. Many practitioners, service provider organizations and social work commentators regard the strengths perspective as a valuable addition to the professional base of social work. A key strength of this approach is that it recognizes the power of optimism, on the part of both service worker and service user, for achieving significant improvements in the quality of service users' lives. It challenges us, as service providers, constantly to reflect on the subtle ways in which our attitudes and language as 'helping professionals' can be used to enable or, conversely, to disempower service users. The strengths perspective provides a necessary corrective to the assumptions underpinning many other practice approaches that service users' destinies are constrained by the problems and issues they face. Indeed, this negative and limiting view of service users' capacities underpins many apparently humanistic and critical approaches to social work practice. For example, many contemporary practice perspectives portray service users as victims of circumstance or social structures and as lacking the skills needed to achieve their goals.

In addition, the strengths perspective can provide challenges to the dominant discourses shaping social work practice contexts. Whereas the biomedical and legal discourses promote professional detachment and privilege professional expertise, the strengths perspective promotes collaboration between workers and service users and encourages a sceptical stance towards expert knowledge. Of course social workers, particularly inexperienced workers, employed in practice contexts where these other discourses prevail will need to take great care to communicate the theoretical foundations and principles of this approach as well as to understand its limitations within their practice context. Otherwise, there is a risk that practice based on the strengths perspective will be misinterpreted as merely naïve, inexpert or even dangerous, within the practice context.

The strengths perspective also encourages us to focus on the social, as well as the individual, context of service user concerns. In contrast to the individualistic orientation of the dominant discourses shaping social work practice, the strengths perspective draws our attention to how the resources within the service users' informal and formal networks can be used, or developed, to assist them achieve their hopes and dreams (see Quinn, 1988). This focus on building sustainable community support networks for and with service users provides a useful framework for practice in situations where service users' concerns are not amenable to the types of short-term, structured interventions considered in Chapter 6. Indeed, this perspective is now widely utilized in community support work in a broad range of fields including mental health, disability support, and child and family support agencies, though, as we have seen in this chapter, this approach is not limited to these contexts.

Weaknesses and Concerns

Despite its considerable value as a contemporary practice perspective, we can also identify some criticisms of the strengths perspective. The strengths perspective appears naïve in relation to the barriers, particularly the structural obstacles, that many service users experience in realizing small goals, let alone their hopes and dreams. Cowger (1998, p. 33) argues that

> The models and perspectives of strengths-based practice must become conceptually more holistic to include the political, structural, and organizational ramifications of the approach and to move beyond the narrow focus on promoting client strengths in direct practice perspectives to critical analysis and action at the institutional, organizational and policy levels.

At best, the strengths perspective adopts a liberal perspective which focuses change aspirations at the individual and the community levels. For many social workers working in anti-oppressive and empowerment traditions, this change focus is too narrow. Moreover, from an anti-oppressive perspective we would ask whether the concept of collaborative partnership, which is advocated by proponents of the strengths perspective, is meaningful in the context of this perspective's failure to acknowledge the continuing inequalities between service providers and service users (see Dominelli, 1996).

A related concern is that the strengths perspective places too much responsibility on individuals and communities for achieving change. Seemingly resigned to the dominance of neo-classical economics in public policy, Kretzman and McKnight (1993, p. 5) argue that disadvantaged communities have 'no other choice' than to create change themselves (see also Weick *et al.*, 1989, p. 354). Many social change advocates, such as anti-oppressive workers and members of consumer rights movements, would argue that there is another choice: to transfer economic and social resources to disadvantaged communities as a way of minimizing the impact of global economic and technological change upon them (see Dominelli and Hoogvelt, 1996; see also Chapter 3, this volume).

The strengths perspective is inconsistent with core components of the social work role in some contexts of practice. For example, in contexts such as statutory child protection work, mental health risk assessment and corrective services, social workers have a statutory, and an ethical, obligation to assess the risk the clients present to themselves or to others. In these contexts, a primary focus on clients' strengths is unviable and may exacerbate some clients' vulnerability to harm themselves or to harm others. Further criticism is that proponents of the strengths perspective have, to this point, failed to account for how certain attitudes and behaviours are counted as strengths. There are two problems here. One problem is that, although strengths-oriented social workers claim a non-judgemental stance, the concept of 'strength' is a culturally loaded term, for what counts as strength is one context may be seen as weakness in another. For example, in presenting evidence of resilience, Saleebey (1996, p. 3000) reports on a study that found that two out of three children identified as at 'significant risk' for adolescent problems 'had turned into caring and efficacious adults by age 32'. There is an implicit assumption here that certain dispositions, such as being 'caring' and 'efficacious', are strengths, yet the bases of these assumptions are not articulated. This failure to reflect on why certain attitudes and behaviours count as strengths leads to a second concern: what are the boundaries of dispositions and behaviours we will endorse as strengths? A strength in one context, such as assertiveness of rights, might become dominance in another context. The lack of direction as to how a worker determines a strength is a weakness of this perspective.

The strengths perspective appears to be based on a questionable interpretation of the research on resilience. In his review of the resilience literature, McMillen (1999, p. 458) reports that people are more likely to become resilient in the face of adversity when they face acute events rather than chronic adversity. McMillen (*ibid.*, p. 462) also reports that 'children and people from lower socio-economic classes might have the most difficulty benefiting from post adversity changes in life structure.' These two findings are significant given that the adversity faced by many social service users is chronic rather than acute and, furthermore, social service clients are disproportionately drawn from socioeconomically disadvantaged backgrounds. Similarly, if we return to Saleebey's (1996) report on longitudinal research findings that the majority (66 per cent) of people who had been identified as being at risk of significant adolescent problems had turned out to be caring and efficacious adults by age 32. Yet Saleebey does not address the fact that a further interpretation of this research is that one-third (33 per cent) of those identified at risk had experienced serious psychological problems into adulthood; this is a much higher rate than one would expect for the general population. In short, while the strengths perspective's emphasis on hope and human resilience is an important corrective to a pathologizing view of human service clients, we must careful also of underestimating the elevated risks facing vulnerable populations. Understanding this risk is important for promoting preventive and protective measures for 'at-risk' populations.

Conclusion

The strengths perspective is a valuable addition to the social work practice literature. It embodies many of the humanitarian values on which the social work profession is founded. One of its key strengths is that it provides social workers with a framework for promoting respect for client capacities and potential. Yet, as we have seen, critical questions are raised about this approach. Some of these concerns rest upon the perspective's lack of recognition of the structural barriers to service user empowerment. In the next chapter, we will consider the anti-oppressive approach – an approach that, by contrast, focuses on understanding and responding to structural injustices.

Reflection Exercises

1. The strengths perspective has been introduced to practice with a wide variety of client populations. To what extent is the strengths perspective relevant to practice with culturally and linguistically diverse communities?

2. Many social workers claim to already operate from a strengths perspective in practice, even without direct knowledge of theory for practice outlined in this chapter. In your observation or experience of social work practice, what elements of the strengths perspective have you observed in practice and what elements appear to be missing in the practice you have observed?

Summary Questions

1. What ideas from the service discourses discussed in earlier chapters underpin the strengths perspective?

2. What is involved in the practice skill of strengths-focused listening?

3. Outline the five principles of practice using the strengths perspective.

4. What are the features of an assets-based approach to community development?

Website

http://www.northwestern.edu/ipr/abcd.html
This is the website for the Asset-Based Community Development Institute where John Kretzmann and John McKnight, widely regarded as the founders of the ABCD approach, are located. The website includes references to research papers, seminars and practice projects on ABCD practice.

Recommended Reading

Green, G. and Haines, A. *Asset Building and Community Development* (London: Sage, 2002).

This book provides a good introduction to the theory and practice of a strengths approach to community development.

Kretzmann, J. and J. McKnight. *Building Communities from the Inside Out* (Chicago: Center for Urban Affairs and Policy Research, 1993).
This workbook offers a practical guide to the application of assets-based community development. It can be ordered from the website cited above.

Saleebey, D. (ed.) *The Strengths Perspective in Social Work Practice* 3rd edn (Boston, MA: Allyn and Bacon, 2002).
This collection is edited by one the leading figures in the strengths perspective and offers a comprehensive introduction to the theory of the strengths approach and its application to a broad range of practice fields, including mental health and addictions. If you only read one collection on the strengths perspective, this one should be it!

Turnell, A. and S. Edwards. *Signs of Safety: A Solution and Safety Oriented Approach to Child Protection Casework* (New York: Norton, 1999).
This book demonstrates how strengths perspective and solution-focused approaches can be practically applied to child protection work.

9

Modern Critical Social Work: From Radical to Anti-Oppressive Practice

In this chapter we will focus on anti-oppressive practice, which is part of the critical social work tradition. In its broadest sense, critical social work is concerned with the analysis and transformation of power relations at every level of social work practice. In this chapter and in Chapter 10, we will discuss critical approaches to social work. Here we will focus on modernist forms of critical social work and in the next chapter we will consider postmodern forms. In this book, we use the term modern critical social work to refer to a broad range of practice perspectives, from radical to anti-oppressive. These perspectives draw on critical social science theories and focus on understanding and addressing the impact of broad social structures on the problems facing service users and the social work process itself. In this chapter, we will discuss the historical foundations of modern critical social work and the radical approaches that preceded anti-oppressive practice. We will outline and apply anti-oppressive practice principles to a case study and consider the strengths and weaknesses of this practice. We turn first to a consideration of the location of anti-oppressive practice approaches in relation to service discourses and other theories for practice.

Anti-Oppressive Practice in Context

Like all other theories for social work practice, anti-oppressive practice draws on received ideas from service discourses and insights from specific practice contexts. Anti-oppressive practice draws on sociological discourses, especially critical social science ideas, and concepts from the consumer rights movements, to construct understandings of client 'needs' and appropriate social work responses to them. The anti-oppressive approach highlights the

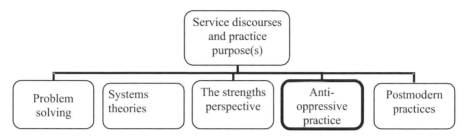

Figure 9.1   Anti-oppressive practice in context

structural contexts of service users' problems and urges social workers to facilitate service users' critical consciousness of, and collective responses to, the
causes of the problems they face. Unlike other theories we've considered in
this book, this theory for practice is built on rejection of some aspects of
psychological discourses that have made such significant contribution to
modern social work (see Chapter 3). Yet, as we shall see, some core concepts from 'psy' discourse, especially the importance of self-reflection and
the 'relationship' between worker and service user, have been incorporated
into anti-oppressive theory for practice. In Figure 9.1, I have located this
theory between the strengths perspective and postmodern practices to
reflect the common historical lineage of these theories for practice, all
of which have only emerged as significant influences in the formal base of
social work since the 1990s. None the less, while the term 'anti-oppressive
practice' was not widely used in social work until the 1990s, many of the key
ideas and practices associated with this theory are well established within
the professional base. We turn first to the historical foundations of anti-
oppressive theory.

The Foundations of Modern Critical Social Work

The term 'modern critical social work' is used here to refer to a broad range
of practice approaches including: Marxist social work; radical social work;
structural social work; feminist social work; anti-racist social work; and anti-
oppressive and anti-discriminatory social work. Despite their considerable
diversity, the approaches share an intellectual debt to the critical social
science paradigm (Healy, 2000, p. 18).

The key features of the critical social science paradigm that are especially
relevant for modernist forms of critical social work include the claim that
macro-social structures shape social relations at every level of social life
(Healy, 2000, pp. 19–21). For example, some critical social science theories
assert that capitalism shapes relations between middle- and working-class

people, or that patriarchy shapes relations between men and women, or that imperialism constrains relations between European and non-European peoples. Drawing on these understandings, critical social workers seek to understand the original causes of oppression, within overarching social structures, and are committed to transforming these structures (see de Maria cited, in Reisch and Andrews, 2001, p. 5).

Critical social scientists also hold that the world is divided between 'haves' and 'have nots' and that the interests of these groups are opposed and irreconcilable (Healy, 2000, p. 19; see also Mullaly, 1993, pp. 142–3). The 'haves' are those who are members of the privileged groups, such as the middle class, males, Europeans, heterosexuals, and the able-bodied, while the 'have nots' are located on the other side of the social divide, that is, the working class, women, non-Europeans, gays and lesbians, and people with disabilities. In terms of these divisions, social workers are presented as powerful, because of their professional status and access to institutional power, while service users are represented as relatively powerless. As we shall see, modernist forms of critical practice require social workers to reflect on their access to power and to develop strategies for sharing power with service users who are assumed to be less powerful (see Dalrymple and Burke, 1995; Dominelli, 1988, pp. 10–11).

Another feature of the critical social science paradigm is the view that the oppressed are complicit in their oppression. This complicity is secured by dominant ideologies that present the current social order as just (Fay, 1987, p. 70). For example, the dominant discourse of neo-classical economics focuses on individual choices and responsibilities but obscures the way in which these choices are constrained by social patterns. Critical social workers argue that social workers should raise the consciousness of the service user; that is, to help them see that the causes of the problems they face lie not in themselves but in unjust social structures.

A final feature of the critical social science paradigm relevant to modern critical social work is the emphasis on empowering oppressed people to act, collectively, to achieve social change. In all forms of critical social science, the ideal goal of collective action is for a society free of all forms of oppression and domination (Fay, 1987). In this paradigm, it is in service users' collective self-interest to agitate for social change. Drawing on these ideas, critical social workers aim to create opportunities for service users to participate in collective, rather than individual, responses to their concerns. So, for example, in responding to young mothers' experiences of violence, we would see individual support and counselling as precursors to these young women's participation in the development of collective, and consumer-run, initiatives for challenging violence against young mothers (see Healy, 2000; Healy and Walsh, 1997).

The Early History of Critical Social Work

Although critical social work theories gained prominence during the 1960s and 1970s, critical social workers have always existed within the professional of social work. In the late nineteenth century, critical elements within the profession highlighted the impact of socioeconomic disadvantage on service users and encouraged social workers to forge links with social movements and the trade union movement (Reisch and Andrews, 2001, p. 35). Perhaps the best internationally known 'first-wave' critical social worker is Jane Addams, who worked in the Settlement House Movement in Chicago from the 1890s onwards and who later won the Nobel Prize for peace in 1931 for her pacifist activities.

During the middle part of the twentieth century, a small number of leading social work commentators challenged the profession to move beyond its increasingly individualistic orientation. For example, in 1949, Norma Parker (see Parker, 1969), a leading Australian social work academic, advocated a human rights framework for analysing social issues and for promoting service users' well-being. The historical evidence suggests that, often, these social workers paid a high personal and professional price for their views as, often, they were professionally isolated and vulnerable to persecution (see Reisch and Andrews, 2001). For example, in the USA, during the McCarthy era of the 1940s and 1950s, Bertha Reynolds, a prominent early critical social worker, was forced to resign from her academic post and was effectively blacklisted from service organizations because of her association with the Communist Party (*ibid.*, p. 115).

The Birth of Radical Social Work

During the 1960s and 1970s radical social work emerged as a distinctive practice approach and had a significant influence on social work education. The dramatic expansion of radical social work literature during this period can be attributed to a number of factors, including: the growing influence of sociology, particularly critical sociology, on social work and social policy; critical social change movements; and the discovery of poverty as a public policy concern (Reisch and Andrews, 2001; see also Thompson, 1997). Across what we now know as the post-industrial world, a cadre of radical social work academics drew on Marxist philosophy to reorient social work towards its 'true' purpose–radical social change (Martin, 2003, pp. 23–4; see Bailey and Brake, 1975; Corrigan and Leonard, 1978; Galper, 1980; Throssell, 1975).

Drawing on critical social science theories, particularly Marxism, radical social workers argued that social workers should recognize that the origins of service users' problems lay primarily in unjust social structures, rather than in their personal histories. Radical social workers highlighted the inherent contradictions of social workers' role. They questioned the potential for truly progressive practices in capitalist societies and urged social workers to constantly reflect on the social control dimensions of their ostensibly caring role (see Corrigan and Leonard, 1978, pp. 90–93). Radical social workers encouraged social workers to eschew individualistic practices that characterized 'psy' approaches in favour of working collectively with service users for social change. For example, Throssell (1975, p. 21) argued that

> Any substantial change in the current oppression of whole groups of people requires not diagnosis and treatment of those groups but change in the others – the non-deviant, the 'normal' or 'healthy'. Thus, to overcome poverty (and its consequences), there needs to be a relinquishing of wealth by the rich ...

Consistent with critical social science principles, radical social work theorists argued that service users would only act rationally in their own best interests once they understood that the true origins of their problems lay not in themselves but in oppressive social structures. Thus critical consciousness raising was a key practice strategy employed by radical social workers.

The Diversification of Critical Practice Models

Radical social workers had probably anticipated that their perspectives would contribute to tensions within the profession. What may have been less expected was the growing discontent among them about the limited scope of radical analysis and practice. Many critical commentators saw radical social workers' primary, if not exclusive, focus on class as too constraining. In the 1980s and early 1990s, critical social workers critiqued, extended and diversified radical practice theories beyond their concentration on class-based oppression. The most prominent of these new critical practice models were: feminist social work; anti-racist social work; and structural social work.

Feminist social workers critiqued the gender blindness of radical social work. Feminist social workers sought to broaden radical definitions of social oppression by placing women's experiences of gender oppression on the agenda of critical social work, alongside other forms of oppression, such as classism, racism and heterosexism (Dominelli and McLeod, 1989, p. 2). These social workers argued that a gender analysis must be central to radical practice because the vast majority of social service workers and service users are female (Hanmer and Statham, 1999). In practice, feminist social workers drew attention to women's specific experiences of oppression, such as their vulnerability to domestic and sexual violence, which had been largely unrecognized in the radical paradigm (Hanmer and Statham, 1999; Weeks, 1994). Like radical social workers, modern feminist social workers asserted that the true origins of women's oppression lay in the macro-structures, particularly those associated with patriarchy (Dominelli and McLeod, 1989, p. 33).

From feminist social movements, feminist practitioners incorporated practice principles that have influenced other forms of modern critical practice. One of these principles is that 'the personal is the political'. By this, feminist practitioners meant that personal experiences have their origins in political structures, and, also, that personal behaviour reflects and reinforces broader political processes (Dominelli and McLeod, 1989, p. 33). Thus we should reflect in our personal and professional relationships the kinds of political change we would like to effect. Another powerful idea in feminist social work is the notion of radical egalitarianism. By this feminist social workers emphasize that service providers should seek to minimize power differentials between service workers and service users (Dominelli, 2002b, p. 39).

Among critical social workers, there was also a concern that issues of racial injustice were inadequately addressed by class-focused analyses. On the bases of these concerns, distinctive anti-racist approaches emerged during the 1980s, not as a threat to radical social work, but rather as a necessary extension of the apparently myopic focus on class-based oppression. Anti-racist social workers sought to show that racial oppression was a significant and distinct form of oppression, rather than merely an effect of class-based injustices (Dominelli, 1988; Hutchinson-Reis, 1989; Shah, 1989). Like radical social workers, anti-racist social workers adopted a critical stance towards modern professional social work, but extended the radical analysis to recognize racial oppression. For example, Dominelli (1988, p. 33) asserts that

> As their [social workers'] attention is deflected onto resolving 'clients' personal problems', social workers expend considerable energy teaching clients to change their behaviour, making it conform to more closely 'acceptable' standards. For black clients, this has led white social workers to ignore the specific circumstances and avenues through which racism holds black people back and deprives them of resources, power, justice and dignity.

Anti-racist social workers sought to reform social work practice towards recognition and collective responses to racial injustice (see Dominelli, 1988).

Structural social work represented a further extension of radical social work. One of the earliest references to 'structural social work' occurred in 1974 when American social work scholars Middleman and Goldberg published a book on this topic. Since the late 1970s, Canadian scholars have been strongly associated with the development of this practice theory, initially in the work of Maurice Moreau (1990) and, more recently, in publications by Bob Mullaly (1993), and Ben Carniol (1992). In common with the other theories we have discussed in this chapter, structural social work is based in the critical social science paradigm (Mullaly, 1993, p. 141). As their name suggests, structural social workers are primarily concerned with analysing and confronting structural injustices, particularly 'how the rich and powerful within society constrain and define the less powerful' (Martin, 2003, p. 24; see also Mullaly, 1993, p. 143). However, in contrast with radical social workers, who focused on class-based oppression, structural social workers insist that 'all forms of oppression are, in reality, mutually reinforcing and overlapping' (Moreau, 1990, p. 64; see also Mullaly, 1993, p. 146).

Structural social workers' practice strategies draw not only on critical social science, but also on ideas from critical social movements, particularly the women's movement, gay and lesbian rights movements, and the trade union movement (see Mullaly, 1993). In addition, structural social workers draw on the insights of a range of critical social work theories including radical, anti-racist and feminist social work (*ibid.*, pp. 148–9). Again, like the critical practice models we have discussed so far, structural social workers promote consciousness raising on the grounds that 'the social order may seriously impair a client's capacities to accurately construe reality' (Moreau, 1990, p. 54). Also, structural social workers aim to facilitate collective rather than individualistic responses to structural injustices (*ibid.*, p. 53). Structural social workers urge social workers to engage with progressive social change activities in order to address the structural injustices that lie at the heart of the issues facing most service users.

Anti-Oppressive Practice

Over the past decade anti-oppressive social work has emerged, and developed, as a dominant theory of critical social work practice. Anti-oppressive practice first arose in the UK in the late 1980s (Martin, 2003, p. 29). During the 1990s, a series of landmark publications on anti-discriminatory and anti-oppressive practice, primarily by British authors (see Dalrymple and Burke, 1995; Dominelli, 1997; Thompson, 1997), led to the international recognition of this approach. Dominelli (cited in Dominelli 2002a, p. 6) defines anti-oppressive practice as

A form of social work practice which addresses social divisions and structural in-equalities in the work that is done with 'clients' (users) or workers. Anti-oppressive practice aims to provide more appropriate and sensitive services by responding to people's needs regardless of their social status. Anti-oppressive practice embodies a person-centred philosophy, an egalitarian value system concerned with reducing the deleterious effects of structural inequalities upon people's lives; a methodology focusing on process and outcome; and a way of structuring social relationships between individuals that aims to empower service users by reducing the negative effects of hierarchy in their immediate interaction and the work they do.

In this definition we can see the intellectual debt anti-oppressive theorists owe to debates among critical social workers we discussed in the last section. For example, like other modern forms of critical social work, anti-oppressive theorists emphasize: the structural origins of service users' problems; an orientation towards radical social change; and a critical analysis of practice relations and an attempt to transform these relations in practice. Yet anti-oppressive theory extends existing critical practice theory in a number of ways, most particularly in its insistence that the personal and cultural bases of oppression must be integrated with the structural analysis of oppression and its recognition of interpersonal and statutory work as legitimate sites of anti-oppressive practice.

In this discussion we refer to anti-discriminatory theory alongside anti-oppressive theory on the grounds that both theories share many core assumptions. However, we also alert the reader to debate among theorists about the commonalities and differences between the two schools. Dalrymple and Burke (1995, p. 3) claim that anti-oppressive practice places greater emphasis on changing social structural arrangements, while, they contend, anti-discriminatory theorists rely more heavily on anti-discriminatory legislation as a vehicle for achieving change. However, anti-discriminatory theorists may contest this claim on the grounds that they, too, offer a comprehensive theory of practice aimed at challenging existing structural arrangements (Thompson, 1997, pp. 157–9).

Core Assumptions of Anti-Oppressive Practice

A key assumption of anti-oppressive practice is that social workers must recognize multiple forms of oppression and further that all forms of oppression should be acknowledged as harmful (Thompson, 1997, p. 22). In anti-oppressive theory, oppression arises from unequal power across social divisions (Burke and Harrison, 2002, p. 229; Dalrymple and Burke, 1995, p. 16). For example, Mitchell (cited in Dalrymple and Burke, 1995, p. 16) argues that women are oppressed by men, children and old people by adults, disabled people by able people and so on. Anti-oppressive theorists urge social workers to be constantly alert to the social divisions affecting service users' lives.

Anti-oppressive social workers argue that social divisions shape practice relationships and, further, that we can reduce the disempowering effects of these differences by critical reflection on our position within the social structures. According to Thompson (1992, cited in Thompson, 1997, p. 11), social workers must make a stand in relation to the contradictions associated with their structural location and service role, as he writes:

> There is no middle ground; intervention either adds to oppression (or at least condones it) or goes some small way towards easing or breaking such oppression. In this respect, the political slogan 'If you are not part of the solution, you must be part of the problem' is particularly accurate. An awareness of the sociopolitical context is necessary in order to prevent becoming (or remaining) part of the problem.

Anti-oppressive theorists emphasize that the social work role is an intensely political role in which social workers occupy a privileged status, at least in contrast with service users. Hence social workers must adopt an ongoing critical and reflective stance so as avert as far as possible replicating oppressive social relations in practice (see Burke and Harrison, 2002).

Anti-oppressive theorists highlight the multiple levels of oppression, including, but also going beyond, structural oppression. Thompson (1997, p. 20) proposes a three-dimensional model of discrimination, the 'PCS' analysis, that describes the interaction across the personal or psychological, the cultural, and the structural sources of oppression (see also Dalrymple and Burke, 1995, p. 12; Mullaly, 2002). For Thompson (1997, p. 20) the personal level of practice refers to the personal feelings and attitudes of the service user as well as the interpersonal relationships established between service providers and service users. The cultural level 'represents the interests and influence of society as reflected in the social values and cultural norms we internalize via the processes of socialization' (Thompson, 1997, p. 20). Anti-oppressive theorists require social workers to constantly reflect on the ways in which social structures associated with capitalism, patriarchy and imperialism contribute to, and interact with, the personal and cultural levels of oppression (*ibid.*, p. 22).

Anti-oppressive theorists emphasize that various forms of oppression interact with each other. For analytic purposes, anti-oppressive theorists identify specific kinds of oppression, such as ageism and sexism, while also recognizing that, in practice, different forms of oppression 'occur simultaneously and affect people in combination' (Thompson, 1997, p. 12; see also Mullaly, 2002, ch. 7). Recognition of this complexity has significant implications for collective action in so far as anti-oppressive practitioners do not assume that a specific kind of oppression will necessarily provide the basis for commonality. For example, the experience of oppression encountered by a black single mother will, of necessity, differ from that of a black, disabled man, and shared racial oppression cannot be assumed as a basis for commonality in all contexts. According to Mullaly (2002, p. 153), 'making links between oppressions, therefore, will require the recognition of both commonalities and specificities across different forms and experiences of oppression'. In addition, Mullaly (*ibid.*) argues that we must recognize that complex interactions across oppressions can intensify the experience of oppression. So, for example, a person subject to two forms of oppression, such as class- and race-based oppression, may suffer more than twice the level of oppression experienced by a person subject to only one of these forms of oppression (see *ibid.*, pp. 153–6).

Anti-oppressive social workers recognize and seek to support a broad range of intervention strategies. A key strength of anti-oppressive theories is that they recognize interpersonal and statutory practice as legitimate sites of social work practice and, in so doing, seek to develop the potential for critical practice at these sites. For example, in contrast to radical social workers' wholesale rejection of statutory power (see Simpkin, 1979, ch. 7), anti-oppressive social workers assert that, particularly in high-risk situations, 'At the end of the day no action at all can be as oppressive as intrusion into people's lives' (Dalrymple and Burke, 1995, p. 83).

We turn now to a case study of the Hayden family. In the following section, we will discuss the key principles of anti-oppressive practice and you will be invited to apply these principles to this case study.

Case Study

The Hayden Family

Imagine you are working as a social worker in a community-based child and family welfare service. The service you work for is staffed by social workers, psychologists and a family worker. The service provides child and family welfare services to those with ongoing involvement from the statutory authority and service providers can work for up to three years with a family requiring long-term support and therapeutic intervention. Your service works closely with the statutory authority and other agencies, as many families referred have a broad network of services involved in their lives. You have received the following referral from the statutory child protection authority.

Case Study (cont'd)

Family history of Hayden family re: Child Protection Concerns
Julia – 35 years
Kathleen (subject child) – 12 months
Max (subject child) – 4 years
Cynthia – 14 years
Delia – 16 years
Jonathan – 18 years

Julia is a woman of Anglo-Saxon background whose own childhood was characterized by instability, loss and abuse. Julia's mum and dad split up when she was nine years old. Initially Julia lived with her mum, but when her mother's new partner moved in Julia was sent to live with her dad. Her father proceeded to sexually and physically abuse her – until Julia turned 14 and ran away to a refuge.

Julia experienced bouts of homelessness and, though a good student, found it hard to maintain her schooling. She became pregnant at 16 to her boyfriend at the time, and gave birth to her first child at 17. Later she married the father of her two daughters but the relationship was characterized by violence and drug abuse, and she has been struggling with a drug habit ever since. Her oldest three children were placed in care because the violence and drug abuse affected her parenting; she had irregular contact with them for several years. Three years ago the children re-established contact with Julia and the two girls returned to her care six months later.

Julia has had a number of male partners, but most of these relationships have been characterized by domestic violence and criminal activity. The family has been residing in public housing ever since the birth of her four-year-old.

Despite her history of severe abuse, Julia has a clear picture of the sort of parent she would like to be and is able to articulate the steps she needs to take to get there. Concerns focus on her capacity to reach her goals.

Julia has a supportive drug and alcohol worker who is a very effective advocate – however, there have been concerns that this worker, and the drug and alcohol service generally, minimize the impact of the drug abuse on Julia's ability to parent. In this case there has been a history of conflict and poor communication between the services involved with the family.

Reasons for referral to the child and family welfare service
Julia is experiencing difficulties in her ability to adequately parent her two youngest children in particular. The statutory child protection officer tells you that there have been a number of reports on the two younger children related to neglect – in particular, emotional neglect of the children and whether or not Julia has the capacity to be a good enough parent. At one stage, she left her two young children with her mother and disappeared for two weeks on a

---

Case Study (*cont'd*)

'drug binge'. After this incident, the youngest child was placed in the grandmother's care and has recently returned to Julia.

The concerns of the statutory child protection agency include: Julia's long history of drug use; her criminal activity in relation to this; her history of being involved in violent relationships; her ability to understand the impact of drug use on her parenting capacity; and the impact of disrupted attachment on her youngest child.

She struggles to respond to her children's needs and also has a tendency to rely on her older children to provide the parenting of the younger children. For example, her 16 year old daughter, Delia, failed to attend college because she had to stay home to look after the youngest child.

Practice Principle 1: Critical Reflection on Self in Practice

Anti-oppressive social workers seek to maintain an open and critical stance towards their practice (Thompson, 1997, p. 159). This approach demands that we reflect on the ways in which our own biographies, especially how our membership of particular social divisions, shapes our practice relationships (Burke and Harrison, 2002, p. 231). We are also challenged to reflect on how the biographies of other professionals involved in intervention and assessment might affect their capacity to truly empathize with and understand the clients' experiences. The assumption is that, first, by reflecting on our membership of social categories, and where possible, replacing ourselves with workers of similar social backgrounds, we can begin to address power differentials in practice.

Practice Exercise

Critical reflection on self

Referring to the case study introduced here, discuss your answers to the following questions. From the perspective of you as a worker in the case study, identify:

- who you see as the service user(s);

- who would you see as the service user if you were working in a different service, such as the drug and alcohol service, or the local statutory authority;

Practice Exercise (*cont'd*)

- using the anti-oppressive framework, what social divisions are you a member of (for example, gender, class, race identities)?;

- how might your membership of these identity groups enhanced and limit your capacity to work with the client(s)?

Practice Principle 2: Critical Assessment of Service Users' Experiences of Oppression

Anti-oppressive practitioners assess how personal, cultural and structural processes shape the problems service users present to social service agencies. An anti-oppressive assessment requires us to consider how the service users' membership of specific social divisions and their historical and geographical context shape their experiences and the options for action available to them (Burke and Harrison, 2002, p. 232). In our analysis of service users' oppression it is important that we consider the impact of major social divisions such as race, class and gender, as well as other divisions arising from inequality and discrimination, such as 'geographical location, mental distress and employment status' (*ibid.*). In addition, the anti-oppressive assessment process turns social workers' attention to the critical analysis of prevailing ideologies shaping agency policies and resource allocation. For example, we might consider how the discourses of biomedicine, neo-classical economics and law might shape various professionals' assessment of the Hayden family and the services available to them.

The processes of critical reflection extend also to reflection on how the language one uses in assessment is shaped by dominant ideologies that convey and sustain oppressive power relations. Dalrymple and Burke (1995, p. 82) argue that in our practice 'we have to be aware of the way in which language can reflect power differentials and have an impact on the people with whom we are working ... It [the power differential] enables workers to label others and define what is acceptable and unacceptable behaviour. Terms such as *disturbed, at risk* and *in need* describe behaviour from a particular value perspective' (italics in original). Anti-oppressive theorists contend that while they do not negate social workers' responsibilities towards the assessment of phenomena such as 'risk' and 'need', they insist that any assessment must also be 'theoretically informed, holistic, empowering and challenging' (Burke and Harrison, 2002, p. 234).

Practice Exercise

Undertaking critical assessment

Using an anti-oppressive framework, discuss:

- what forms of oppression these service users' are subject to (Remember to consider both major social divisions, e.g. class and sex, and also other forms of discrimination, such as unemployment, isolation);

- in your role as a child and family welfare worker, what dominant ideas or discourses will shape service provision to this family;

- how these ideas will shape service provision to this family.

Practice Principle 3: Empowering Service Users

Anti-oppressive approaches to empowerment seek to overcome the cultural, institutional and structural, as well as personal, obstacles to clients taking greater control of their lives (Dalrymple and Burke, 1995, pp. 52–3; Thompson, 1997, p. 156).

At the interpersonal level, anti-oppressive social workers promote service user empowerment by encouraging service users to share their feelings of powerlessness (Dalrymple and Burke, 1995, pp. 53–4). Again, as in other forms of critical social work, anti-oppressive theorists support consciousness-raising processes that enable service users to understand how structural and cultural injustices shape their experiences of oppression and which highlight that service users are not alone in their experiences of power-lessness (Mullaly, 2002, pp. 180; Thompson, 2003, p. 223).

Anti-oppressive theorists identify that a further barrier to empowerment may lie in service users' lack of capacities, or confidence in their capacities, to act. Thus social workers working in the anti-oppressive paradigm work with service users to identify areas for skills development and to facilitate opportunities for service users to exercise, and gain confidence in, their capacities. Another way service providers can empower service users is by ensuring that their views are incorporated into the assessment process, especially where the service provider and service user disagree.

At an institutional level, anti-oppressive social workers promote changes to the organization and delivery of services in ways that enhance anti-oppressive practice and service user control (see Thompson, 2002, ch. 6). Anti-oppressive theorists insist that, because the processes of service delivery can serve to oppress or empower, it is crucial that service providers have opportunities to learn about, and maximize their potential for, anti-oppressive practice. According to Thompson (1997, p. 158), 'awareness training' for service providers can help to promote anti-discriminatory practice at every level of the service organization. Additionally, anti-oppressive theorists promote service user involvement in decision making about the management of social service resources.

Empowerment at the structural level requires social workers to work towards fundamental reformation of social, economic and political structures in ways that lead to the more just distribution of material resources and social power. Mullaly (2002, p. 194) suggests that the obstacles to structural empowerment can be addressed by the development of alternative services and organizations, engagement with progressive social movements, critical social policy practice, and revitalization of the political sector. Returning to the case study, we might use the knowledge we have gained from our work with the Hayden family to expose the inadequacies of current government policy and service provision to families affected by parental drug use.

Practice Exercise

A critical and multidimensional approach to empowerment

- Referring to the case study, identify at least one barrier to empowerment facing members of this family at each of the following levels: personal; institutional; cultural; and structural.

- Identify and discuss two practical strategies you would use for addressing each of these barriers.

Practice Principle 4: Working in Partnership

For anti-oppressive social workers the term 'working in partnership' means that 'service users should be included as far as possible as fellow citizens in the decision-making processes which affect their lives' (Dalrymple and Burke, 1995, p. 64). While all the practice theories we have discussed so far in this book incorporate partnership as a practice principle, anti-oppressive theorists take the notion of partnership in a different direction. In contrast to theories such as task-centred or the strengths approach, which see partnership as something that can be achieved relatively easily given the will of both parties, anti-oppressive theorists see partnership as a vexed issue. Anti-oppressive workers contend that the potential for partnership is constrained by unequal power relations arising from: the stigma of service use; vested power interests held by professionals and service provider agencies; social control roles of service agencies; and agency accountabilities to third parties such as funding bodies rather than primarily to service users themselves (Dalrymple and Burke, 1995, p. 64).

For anti-oppressive practitioners, any gesture toward partnership must begin with the genuine sharing of power at interpersonal and institutional levels (Dalrymple and Burke, 1995, p. 65). Some ways of enhancing partnership at the personal level include open clear communication in which one fully discloses the nature and scope of one's service role. For example, it is vital that service users are made aware of your statutory responsibilities in relation to them and the organizational constraints, such as time limits, on your involvement with them. Clarity of communication may also be enhanced by written agreements in which the service worker and the service user establish a contract about their responsibilities in the intervention process (Dalrymple and Burke, 1995, p. 67). Partnership also demands that we value the individual by, for example, showing respect for their perspectives and their lived knowledge (Burke and Harrison, 2002; Mullaly, 2002).

At both personal and institutional levels it is important to maximize service users' opportunities for participation in the decisions affecting them. Some ways of achieving this include establishing an agency charter in which service users' right to participate is endorsed and mechanisms are established for redressing lack of opportunity to participate. At an agency level this will also involve the allocation of resources, such as support staff, to ensuring that service users can truly participate in decision making.

Practice Principle 5: Minimal Intervention

Anti-oppressive social workers recognize that social services work is a contradictory activity in which social care dimensions are always intertwined with social control. However, anti-oppressive theorists concede that social workers may need to enact social control to prevent harm to the service user, as is the case in high-risk environments (see Dalrymple and Burke, 1995, p. 78). Anti-oppressive theorists adopt the principle of minimal intervention in order to reduce the oppressive and disempowering dimensions of social work intervention. The principle of minimal intervention means that social workers should aim to intervene in the least intrusive and least oppressive ways possible (Payne, 1997, p. 261; see also Dalrymple and Burke, 1995, p. 81). In practice this usually means that social workers should focus on early intervention with the primary aim of preventing the escalation of risk of harm to the service user.

Dalrymple and Burke (1995, p. 83) suggest that some ways anti-oppressive social workers can achieve minimal intervention include adapting existing services to increase their accessibility. For example, service workers might adopt an outreach model of practice that increases service users' knowledge and options to access a particular service. Another way we might increase the services accessibility and comprehensiveness is by linking existing services. For example, when working with a group of young parents we might move beyond a focus on their parenting needs to increase their access to services such as literacy and educational services to address long-term barriers to social and economic participation.

Practice Exercise

Practising minimal intervention

● How might you minimize the intrusiveness of your intervention with the Hayden family?

● Imagine now that the manager at the child and family service has asked you for your ideas about how the organization might minimize the intrusiveness of its interventions with families like the Hayden's. What practical strategies would you recommend for your organization?

Anti-Oppressive Practice: Some Critical Reflections

In this section, we will consider the strengths, limits and concerns associated with this approach. The substantial body of recent publications on anti-oppressive practice attests to the contemporary popularity of this approach, at least among social work educators and authors! The key strengths of this practice model include its reconciliation of social work values and practice methods. Anti-oppressive approaches place the value of social justice centre stage in all dimensions of social work practice. It does not blame individuals for their difficulties, but encourages us to adopt a multidimensional analysis which recognizes the personal, cultural and structural dimensions of the oppression experienced by service users such as the Hayden family. It ensures that as practitioners we recognize the effects of cultural practices and social structures on services users' lives and it makes these processes and structures a legitimate site of social service intervention.

Unlike earlier critical practice models, such as radical social work, anti-oppressive practice also values the contribution local change processes can make to achieving social change. An anti-oppressive approach, then, would encourage us to consider how we can promote effective support for the Hayden family. This approach would also encourage us to constantly reflect on the subjectivities that shape our capacity to practise in an anti-oppressive way with all members of the Hayden family. For example, we would reflect on how our subjectivity as middle-class helping professionals would limit our understanding of the dilemmas faced by Julia as the parent of five children living in public housing.

Anti-oppressive practice challenges social workers to recognize the cultural and structural context of their practice. In the case of the Hayden family this allows us to move beyond a focus on family dynamics to recognize, also, the cultural and structural dimensions of their situation. Thus, for example, using an anti-oppressive approach we might become involved in establishing support and advocacy services for families with parents affected by drug and alcohol use. In this way we might prevent families such as the Hayden family from reaching the crisis points that have led to statutory intervention.

Despite the growing popularity of anti-oppressive practice in the social work literature, we can also identify many limitations of this approach. I have serious concerns about the application of this model to 'high-risk' decision making, that is, in situations where there is a significant risk of death or serious injury to a client. The strong critique of 'psy' discourse underpinning this approach, accompanied by the prioritization of structural analysis of clients' experiences, can lead social workers to neglect individual psychological and personal factors that may contribute substantially to elevated risk in some contexts, such as child protection, mental health and work in corrections. Social workers' capacity to act in high-risk situations can be further limited by the principle of minimal intervention which is based on insight into the oppressive effects of social work intervention, but with the exception of Dalrymple and Burke's (1995) work on the topic, there is little acknowledgement of the importance and helpfulness of the use of power in social service interventions. Indeed, in situations involving spousal or child assault, what is experienced as oppressive social service intervention by one party, the assailant, may be experienced as the way out of an untenable situation by another, the victim of violence. Even in less extreme situations, clients do not necessarily experience service intervention as oppressive; the anti-oppressive model fails to take account of the diversity of clients' experiences of service provision and, especially, the fact that some service users willingly seek out this form of intervention to address a wide variety of needs (Wise, 1990).

Furthermore, the anti-oppressive principle of minimal intervention is especially problematic in instances where service users present different and conflicting needs as it provides no way of prioritizing one set of service users' needs over another. For example, the framework gives us no way of prioritizing the needs of Julia Hayden (the mother in our case study) and those of her children, particularly Kathleen and Max (the two youngest children).

Another limitation of the anti-oppressive approach is its reliance on an oppositional stance in which the battle lines are clearly drawn even before we enter specific sites of practice. This conflictual stance is evident in Thompson's (1997, p. 159) assertion that 'The prefix "anti" in anti-discriminatory practice is very significant; it denotes fighting against a powerful and established ideology.' The pre-emptive polarization of positions between an 'us' and 'them' is very problematic in many areas of social work practice in which compromise and negotiation of 'grey areas' can be critical to finding a workable solution to the problem at hand. If we arrive at these situations with preconceived notions of 'enemy and ally', our capacity to respectfully listen to, and work with, a range of stakeholders will be constrained. In relation to the Hayden family, we must also be careful about what is labelled as 'powerful and established' ideology and what is recognized as genuine concerns. This case study raises some potentially painful issues, particularly for Julia, such as confronting the effects of her drug use on her parenting, and we must be careful about dismissing these concerns as evidence of a 'powerful and established' ideology, such as the ideology of parenting.

A contradiction exists between anti-oppressive theorists' claim to promote dialogue in practice and their assumptions that they hold a true and correct analysis of the world. This is evident in the practice of consciousness raising, in which the social service worker, in a spirit of dialogue, introduces a critical structural analysis of the service user's experience. For example, Mullaly (2002, p. 184) describes a three-stage model of consciousness raising in which the service user develops an awareness of their shared oppression with other members of their oppressed category and gains a sense of identification, self-respect and pride with this category. The danger of consciousness-raising efforts is that those who do not conform to the truths presented by the anti-oppressive service provider may be dismissed as lacking critical consciousness or as conservative reactionaries. For example, Dominelli (2002a, p. 10) charges those who oppose anti-oppressive practice as fearful of losing 'the taken-for-granted privileges accorded to them through an inegalitarian social order'. The issue here is that by characterizing all those who oppose anti-oppressive practice 'insights' as self-interested or conservative, anti-oppressive theorists insulate their approach from the critical practical reflection required to understand the uses and the limits of the model for promoting critical practice in the diverse institutional contexts of social work activity.

The primary reliance on a structural analysis of power relations that underpins this theory leaves little room for recognizing different power relations at local levels. For example, in reflecting on a case scenario involving a young black woman, Burke and Harrison (2002, p. 232) contend that 'A white male social worker brings to the situation a dynamic that will reproduce the patterns of oppression to which black women are subjected in the wider society.' The assumption here is that one's membership of certain identity categories associated with class, gender and race has direct and causative effects on local power relations. Yet other factors, such as organizational philosophy, current social policy and legislative dictates, and the valuing of different kinds of local knowledge, can also have profound effects on power relations (Featherstone and Fawcett, 1994; Healy, 2000). For example, while we should recognize the oppressions to which Julia has been subject by her father and her partner, we must also acknowledge and emphasize the kinds of power that Julia exercises also, in relation to her children.

I am concerned also that anti-oppressive theorists do not adequately address the impact of institutional context on the development and application of anti-oppressive principles. While proponents of anti-oppressive practice urge workers to choose this model as the best, even the only, way to achieve social justice in social work practice, they fail to reflect on how this choice may be easier for service providers in some contexts than in others. Yet our understanding of client needs as well as our role and our options for intervention are profoundly shaped by context, including institutional context, client needs, and even our own capacities as social workers. For example, referring to the Hayden case study, statutory child protection workers have obligations to the application of statutory law, while other workers, such as the drug and alcohol workers discussed in the case study, have different obligations, in this case to advocate for the mother, Julia. These context-specific obligations will shape who we see as the primary service user and what will take priority in our practice and, thus, the extent to which we can apply key anti-oppressive principles. It may even be that, in some contexts of practice, anti-oppressive practice may lead to harm by, for example, minimizing recognition of risk (K. Healy, 1998). At the very least, greater recognition of the institutional limits to the application of anti-oppressive practice is needed for the critical and grounded development of this theory.

Conclusion

Anti-oppressive social work is a practice theory that stands on the cusp of modern and postmodern practice. I have categorized it as a modern critical approach because of its continuing reliance on notions of critical consciousness raising – which imply that there is a singular underlying truth to which service users should be exposed – and also because of its continuing emphasis on a structural analysis of oppression and its orientation to large-scale structural reform, even though this is mediated by recognition of the personal and cultural dimensions of oppression. The postmodern elements of anti-oppressive practice, particularly the growing use of discourse analysis by anti-oppressive theorists (see Mullaly, 2002), also place it at the intersection of modern and postmodern practice. Yet, as we shall see in the next chapter, postmodern approaches to critical social work urge social workers to adopt a sceptical attitude towards many of the claims on which modern forms of social work, including anti-oppressive practice, are founded.

Summary Questions

1. What are the key differences between anti-oppressive theory and other forms of critical social work, such as radical social work and feminist social work?

2. From the perspective of anti-oppressive theory, why is it important that social workers reflect on their personal biography?

3. What practical strategies do anti-oppressive social workers use to promote the empowerment of service users?

Reflection Exercise

Thinking of two different contexts of social work practice that interest you, consider the uses and limits of the anti-oppressive model in these contexts. From this reflection summarize the characteristics of the institutional contexts and the client groups to whom this approach is most likely to be useful and those for whom it is more problematic or inappropriate.

Recommended Reading

Dalrymple, J. and B. Burke. *Anti-oppressive Practice: Social Care and the Law* (Buckingham: Open University Press, 1995).
This is one of the first texts on anti-oppressive practice and provides a comprehensive introduction to the theory and practice of this approach.

Mullaly, B. *Challenging Oppression: A Critical Social Work Approach* (Ontario: Oxford University Press, 2002).
This book provides a thorough introduction to the theoretical foundations of anti-oppressive practice. It explains the interactions across personal, cultural and structural dimensions of oppression.

10

Postmodern Approaches
in Practice

Since the 1990s, postmodern theories have had a growing influence on the formal base of social work and have contributed to new theories for social work practice. In this chapter, I will explain differences among 'post' theories, including postmodernism, poststructuralism and postcolonialism. These theories have been hotly contested in the social sciences and humanities since the 1960s, but their impact on the formal base of social work is relatively recent. While social work commentators debate the pros and cons of post theory for practice, a growing number of social workers apply post theories to a broad terrain of social work practices from casework to community work and policy practice. Still, the position of post theory in the formal base of social work is far from assured. None the less, despite some deserved bad press about the arcane language adopted by some postmodernists, we will see that, often, social workers are already using many similar ideas to explain the complexities of power, identity and change processes in direct practice.

In this chapter, I outline the key features of postmodernism in the human sciences and consider the historical development of postmodern ideas in social work practices. I discuss core concepts underpinning post theories and their implications for constructing service users' needs and practice responses. We will consider a theory for practice, narrative therapy, that draws on postmodern ideas and turn to a case illustration to consider the pros and cons of postmodernism in social work practice. We turn first to consider where postmodern theories fit in relation to the service discourses and the theories for practice we have discussed so far.

Postmodern Practices in Context

Postmodern practices draw on, but also disrupt, ideas from the service discourses discussed in Chapters 3 and 4. In concert with the sociological discourse which has strongly influenced the formal knowledge base, postmodernists view all aspects of social work practice, particularly concepts of client needs and social work responses, as socially constructed. In contrast to critical sociological discourse, which has focused our attention on how macro-processes associated with capitalism, patriarchy and imperialism produce client needs and social work practice processes, postmodernists are attentive to the ways discourses construct these concepts. For example, postmodern perspectives urge us to recognize the different ways discourses, like biomedicine and consumer rights, construct 'client needs' rather than view one of these perspectives as more accurate than the other. Like the anti-oppressive practice perspective, postmodern practices challenge some aspects of the 'psy' discourse, especially psychoanalytic ideas that seek the causes for the client's malaise in their past. Instead, as we shall see later in the chapter, some forms of postmodern practice seek to understand and where necessary disrupt the narratives that construct service users' self-understandings as well as the understandings of others. While postmodernism does not offer support to alternative discourses, such as consumer rights and discourses associated with religion and spirituality, it does support the possibilities these alternative discourses open up for recognizing different perspectives than have been traditionally acknowledged within formal health and welfare institutions.

As I stated in Chapter 1, this book is written from a postmodern perspective in that I seek to outline how key institutional and service discourses construct social work practices. You may be wondering why I have not positioned postmodernism as a separate, overarching discourse like the human science or alternative service discourses considered earlier in the book. The primary reason is that, at this point in the history of social work, postmodernism is a hotly contested discourse that, while offering profound contributions to theories for practice, is not yet widely accepted by either service providers or service users as a key frame of reference. Indeed, as I will explain further in this chapter, a key contribution of postmodern perspectives is to diversify that which we or others, such as colleagues and service users, hold as the 'truth' about core concepts such as client needs or practice responses.

In the first half of this chapter, I explain key themes in postmodern perspectives and how these can contribute to the formal base of social work. In the second half of the chapter, I will consider one practice approach, narrative therapy, emerging from postmodern perspectives. In Figure 10.1, I have situated the postmodern practice perspectives next to, but after, the strengths perspective and anti-oppressive practice, to acknowledge its more recent influence on the formal base of social work practice. Indeed, while these three sets of practice perspectives have grown in influence since the 1990s, the strengths perspective and anti-oppressive theory are founded in

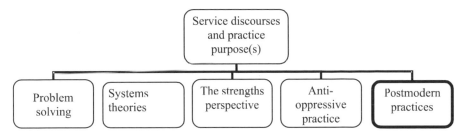

Figure 10.1 Postmodern practices in context

earlier theories for practice. By contrast, while postmodern perspectives draw on aspects of established practice approaches, they also represent a break with the discourses and theories underpinning the formal base of social work practice.

So What is Postmodernism?

Before turning to the application, and development, of postmodernism ideas for social work practice, I need first to outline the key features of postmodern theories. The terms postmodernism, poststructuralism and postcolonialism refer to a broad band of theoretical projects developed in the social sciences and humanities over the twentieth century (Weedon, 1997, p. 19). In this chapter we will discuss concepts associated with Continental European forms of postmodernism. I will refer, in particular, to the work of French postmodern philosophers, especially Foucault, Derrida, Lyotard, Kristeva and Cixous. We will focus on how social workers use these ideas to analyse and respond in direct social work practice.

Despite the considerable diversity within, and across, the 'post' schools, key thinkers in this tradition share some common ideas. Post theory represent a break with core notions of the Enlightenment. Post theorists question the narrow definitions of 'reason' on which a range of influential discourses and practice approaches depend. As we have discussed in Chapters 1 and 2, Enlightenment thinkers believed that reason could help people break free from the strictures of the Church and the State and, in so doing, achieve personal liberation, societal order and social progress (see O'Brien and Penna, 1998, pp. 9–12). Post theorists have argued against this view of reason as a liberatory tool arguing that it is also a political instrument, used to privilege the views of some groups, such as professionals, over those viewed in these discourses as less rational, such as service users (see Foucault, 1991, 1997). In social work, an exclusive focus on reason can prevent us from using other forms of knowledge such as bodily knowledge that can also provide important practice insights. For instance, when I interviewed a social worker following the death of a child on her caseload, she described to me the bodily sensation of fear (she stated that 'I felt the hair rise up on the back of my head') when she first met the stepfather, who was eventually found responsible for the death of the child. This bodily response gave her important information that she was not able to use in preparing her formal and rational assessment of the child's safety.

Post theories also require us to critically examine the ideas of progress on which many forms of health and welfare institutions rely in forming and evaluating their interventions. Post theorists question the humanistic ethos of helping/rehabilitating/empowering others. Foucault's research, in particular, demonstrates that the various institutions of the modern era, such as the modern prison, school and hospital, have become sites for the ever more detailed operation of power over subject populations (O'Brien and Penna, 1998, p. 119; see Foucault, 1973, 1991, 1997). Foucault's work urges us to be cautious in our claims to 'help', 'empower' and 'emancipate' as he shows that these practices can also be associated with the 'will to power' over others. For example, in the process of raising others' consciousness about the original causes of their oppression, we are also imposing our truth about the nature of their experience. A postmodern perspective challenges all social workers – regardless of their practice approach – to critically reflect on the ways in which our practices contribute to the control and surveillance of people we are seeking to assist.

Postmodernism challenges the idea, common to most modern discourses and theories for practice, that our identities are fixed as, for example, a 'working-class' person, or a 'woman'. Instead, post theorists assert that our identities are socially constructed through language, that is, our identities and the meanings attached to them are fluid and change according to context (Lyotard, 1984, p. 15). For this reason, post theorists often oppose practices based on fixed identities, such as the idea that people can or should form collective actions around a common identity, such as being a woman or person with a disability (see Sawicki, 1991, p. 19). According to post theorists, these fixed identities necessarily devalue differences within the oppressed group.

Postmodernists focus on understanding local details and complexities, such as the diverse experiences of people within a community, rather than trying to construct a single story or narrative about an event or a population. In short, post theorists are united in their 'incredulity towards metanarratives' (Lyotard, 1984, p. xxiv), that is, the quest to construct an overarching explanation of the social world. According to Crotty (1998, p. 185), 'Instead [of] espousing clarity, certitude, wholeness and continuity, postmodernism commits itself to ambiguity, relativity, fragmentation, particularity and discontinuity'. From a postmodern perspective, grand social theories, such as Marxism or modernist forms of feminism, run the risk of ignoring local differences. This insight is especially important in alerting social workers to local experiences of power, identity and change processes. Consistent with their opposition to grand theories, post theorists also critique utopian social change projects. They argue that overarching social change projects carry within them a will to domination and so can reproduce the forms of domination they were intended to overcome (Lyotard, 1984). This criticism has substantial implications for social work practices linked to radical social change projects, such as some forms of anti-oppressive practice and consumer rights movements, discussed earlier in this book. At the very least, post theories urge us to be alert to the forms of domination and push to conformity that may lay concealed in progressive social change efforts.

Differences Among Post Theories

The term postmodernism is often used to describe the range of post theories, yet there are substantial differences among these theories. So far we have considered common themes in post theories. In this section, we will explore some differences among them; an understanding of these differences may be helpful to understanding the different ways social workers use these theories.

Postmodernism is concerned with theories of society, culture and history (Agger, 1991). Originating in the field of architecture, postmodernism has since extended into a range of social science and humanities disciplines (Weedon, 1997, p. 170). Postmodernists adopt a sceptical attitude to the truths of modernity, such as faith in rationality as the path to progress, on the grounds that these truths cannot help us understand, or respond to, the new cultural conditions of uncertainty and change (Leonard, 1997, p. 25; Lyotard, 1984, p. 5). Put simply, for postmodernists, the truths of modernity once made sense, but no longer do so (Butler, 1993).

Poststructuralism, by contrast, is primarily focused the influence of language on power, knowledge and identity (Agger, 1991). Poststructuralism derives, and deviates, from the work of Ferdinand de Saussure, a structural linguist (Weedon, 1997, p. 23). De Saussure showed that language is not merely a vehicle to reflect reality, but rather, language helps to create the things it describes (*ibid.*). Moving on from de Saussure's claims, post-structuralists argue that the relationship between language and the objects it describes is not fixed but shaped by the different meanings that discourses make available. For example, as we have discussed in the first half of the book, different discourses offer us competing ways of understanding concepts such as 'need' as well as the roles of social workers and service users. For poststructuralists, language is a key site of political struggle as discourses shape how core concepts such as 'rights' and 'needs' are understood within any context. This has enormous implications for modern social work practice, for as we have seen throughout this book, different discourses and theories for practice offer varying and sometimes conflicting ways of understanding and responding to client 'needs'.

Postcolonial theories are a third set of 'post' ideas relevant to social work practices. Postcolonialism is a broad discipline committed to understanding, and responding to, the ongoing legacy of European colonization. Leela Gandhi (1998, p. 27) defines postcolonialism as a discipline 'devoted to the academic task of revisiting, remembering and crucially, interrogating the colonial past ... Postcolonial theory commits itself to a complex project of historical and psychological recovery.' Postcolonial approaches are well established in contemporary humanities and social sciences, where they are used to analyse how the colonial legacy shapes contemporary understandings of, and responses to, a range of issues such as such as migration, race, gender, slavery and the representation of 'others'. Scholars in the fields of economics, sociology and development studies have used postcolonial perspectives to expose and critique the institutionalization of unequal economic and power relations between so-called advanced and developing nations (Midgley, 1998, p. 33).

Social work scholars have, as yet, shown little interest in postcolonial theory. This is regrettable as postcolonial perspectives may help us develop new forms of anti-racist practice grounded in an understanding of how the colonial legacy continues to be ingrained in modern social work practices, including even anti-racist approaches. Postcolonial scholars problematize fixed racial identities and attack the dualism between European and non-European identities. In her analysis of Asian and Black women's experiences as social workers, Lewis (2000) argues that social work scholars' continuing reliance on an opposition between European and non-European reinforces racialized social relations by ignoring substantial differences within identity groups such as 'Third World women', 'Europeans', 'Indigenous' people (see also Mohanty, discussed in Weedon, 1997, p. 179). Overall, this criticism strikes at the heart of the modern anti-racist social work (see Dominelli, 1988) in so far as this project accepts fixed identity categories such as 'European' and 'non-European' as the basis for analysis and social action. Instead, using postcolonial perspectives, social work scholar Gail Lewis (2000, p. 119) argues that 'race/ethnicity needs to be understood and analysed as a major, *but only one*, axis of differentiations organizing a contingent set of social relations' (italics added). For example, we need to understand how other categories such as disability and sexuality as well as local differences differentiate racial and ethnic identifications and experiences.

Key Concepts

In this section, we will consider four key concepts in post theories. These concepts are: discourse; subjectivity; power; and deconstruction. An understanding of these concepts is essential to comprehending social workers' use and development of postmodern practice perspectives.

Discourse

Discourse is central to postmodern, poststructural and postcolonial theories as it is used to refer to the language practices through which knowledge, truth, our sense of ourselves, and social relations are constructed. Throughout this book, I have used the term discourse to analyse how key concepts such as client needs and social work practices are constructed in health and welfare contexts and through different theories of practice. Thus the term is should be familiar to you by now, but we will briefly recap this concept here.

Discourse refers to the language practices through which we understand 'reality' and act upon it. Discourse constructs knowledge in practice, particularly what counts as true or sayable, and what is considered false or unsayable (Foucault, 1980b, p. 131). Discourses have 'real' or material effects in that they construct our understandings of key entities such as 'client needs' and 'social work practice'. From a postmodern viewpoint, words are not simply vehicles; they actually constitute things, including the social phenomena social workers deal with in their practice, like child abuse, ageing and domestic violence. This does not mean that experiences, such as domestic violence, are made up by language, but rather that we can only comprehend these experiences through language.

From a postmodern viewpoint, discourses profoundly shape service users' experiences of, and social workers' responses to, experiences such as mental illness and disabilities. This point is well illustrated by Crossley and Crossley (2001), who undertook a comparative analysis of two anthologies written by people living with mental illness in the 1950s and the 1990s. Their analysis showed that consumer rights discourses that emerged during the 1970s (see Chapter 4) created new opportunities for (some) people living with mental illness to assert authority based on their expertise as survivors, rather than as patients, of psychiatric institutions (*ibid.*, p. 1488). This transformed identity enabled some people living with mental illness opportunities to critique and, in some instances, opt out of biomedical approaches to psychiatric care.

Post theorists draw attention to the way in which discourses operate within specific sites of social work practices. Fook (2002, p. 90) points out that 'Because discourses are not fixed (that is, their meaning is relative to the situation and interpretation, and subject position), they may operate in different ways for different purposes at different times.' Focusing on the operations of discourse within specific practice contexts, we can see that even an apparently positive concept like consumer participation can be used to a range of ends, from promoting client involvement in statutory decision making through to facilitating the reduction of government involvement in the funding and provision of services (K. Healy, 1998). From a post-theory perspective, discourses shape our understandings of the rights, responsibilities, experiences of, and relationships between, service workers and services users. Moreover, social work agencies and social service agencies are often sites of competing discourses. For example, child welfare services are the site of competing interpretations of, for example, the rights and needs of parents and children. Aged care services are sites of contest concerning public and private care in old age and disability services are sites of contest between social responsibility and self-realization.

Practice Exercise

Discourse in practice

Reflecting on your context of practice, or a context of practice that interests you, identify and discuss:

(a) two discourses shaping the practice context (e.g. biomedicine, law, neo-classical economics, patients' rights and so on);

(b) the kinds of knowledge that are valued and whose knowledge is valued by these discourses;

(c) what these discourses present as the client's 'needs' in your context of practice.

Subjectivity

Post theorists use the term subjectivity, rather than identity, to refer to our sense of ourselves. They reject descriptions of 'identity' as fixed and unified; instead they insist that our identities are shaped by discourses and thus vary from context to context (Sawicki, 1991). Because different discourses offer competing systems of social reality, we may experience different aspects of our 'identity' as fragmented and contradictory (Healy, 2000, p. 46; Weedon, 1997, p. 33). For example, as a young social worker working in a statutory child protection service, I exercised power and authority associated with my statutory role, yet I also experienced powerlessness and vulnerability associated from my low status within the bureaucracy, my age, my gender and my (non-)parenting status. All these subjectivities affected how I experienced myself, and how I was seen by others, as well as the kinds of power and authority I was able to exercise. For instance, the professional assessments I was authorized and indeed required to undertake could be vetoed by others who were positioned more powerfully in these discursive fields of child protection, such as magistrates, doctors and institutional supervisors, even though these higher-status professionals may have had little or no direct contact with the families in question. Post theories suggest that these experiences of fragmentation and contradiction in our identities and our exercise of institutional power are an inevitable outcome of the clashes between different discourses that make up our practice contexts.

Just as we recognize the contradictions in the social work 'identity', from a poststructural perspective we must also acknowledge service users' multiple and often contradictory identifications For example, we may come to understand a 'violent offender' also as 'a victim of child abuse', 'an abusive parent', 'a loyal son', 'a person battling addiction' and so on. Indeed, in direct practice, practitioners often do recognize these multiple and often competing identifications and, ironically, this probably contributes to the popular and derogatory image of social workers as bleeding hearts.

Poststructural feminists challenge us to recognize ourselves and others as embodied beings. Poststructural feminists encourage us to recognize how bodily differences shape the way we inhabit different subjectivities (Healy, 2000, pp. 48–9). Consider the example of professional power. Critical social work theorists including Marxist, radical and feminist social work theorists have drawn our attention to the authoritarian dimensions of professional power in social work practice. This has been an important critical insight into social work practice and has led to increased awareness of the oppressive effects of power and authority in practice. In addition, poststructural feminists invite us to consider how bodily differences associated with age, height, skin colour, ethnicity and gender complicate one's identifications and thus one's capacity to exercise professional power (see Healy, 2000, ch. 7).

Practice Exercise

Poststructural reflection on self

With a partner, discuss how your subjectivities influence you in your role as a professional social worker. Consider the ways in which your subjectivities allow, or constrain, you in exercising professional authority in practice.

Critical social work commentators take particular exception to the post-theorist notion of open and fluid subjectivity proposed by post theorists (see Dominelli, 2002b). According to these commentators, the abandonment of fixed identities threatens progressive social movements which have relied on fixed and unified identifications such as 'women', 'people with disabilities' and so on (see *ibid.*, p. 32–6). Critical poststructural commentators counter this criticism on a number of grounds.

Postmodernists argue that the unified notion of self, central to many critical social theories and progressive social movements, requires us to embrace identifications that are the source of oppression in the first place. Judith Butler (1993, p. 48) argues:

> Surely there is caution offered here, that in the very struggle toward enfranchizement and democratization, we might adopt the very models of domination by which we are oppressed, not realizing that one way domination works is through the regulation and production of subjects.

For postmodern critical social workers, the challenge seems to be that of recognizing both how categories such as 'woman' or 'person with a disability' can explain our, or service users', experiences and form a basis for collaborative action, while also recognizing how these categories limit change activity. Instead, critical poststructural approaches assume that our identities are negotiated and provisional, rather than fixed. This can open up possibilities for recognizing differences within unified groups, such as 'women', 'European', 'people with disabilities', as well as opportunities to negotiate shared actions across groups (Butler, 1993; Corker and Shakespeare, 2002; Sawicki, 1991; Weedon, 1997). By recognizing and celebrating differences, post theories can support respectful collaboration across differences.

Power

Power is a central concern of critical post theorists, particularly Foucault and feminist poststructural authors such as Cixous and Kristeva (see Healy, 1999). Foucault explicitly rejects the 'juridico-discursive' model of power, which represents power as the possession of individuals and a force that is imposed by one set of subjects, such as the ruling class, on others (Sawicki, 1991, p. 52; Healy, 2000, p. 43). In contrast to critical sociological discourse and anti-oppressive theory, which focus on minimizing power differences, critical poststructuralists see power as an ever-present and productive feature of social relations. Further, poststructuralists contend that power is a product of discourse rather than something that is attached to specific identities, such as 'male' or 'professional'. Thus, from this view, if we want to understand power in any context, we need to analyse how discourses operate to construct identity, knowledge and power within that specific context.

According to Jana Sawicki (1991, p. 21), Foucault's approach to power rests on three axioms:

1. Power is exercised rather than possessed.

2. Power is not primarily repressive, but productive.

3. Power is analysed as coming from the bottom up.

Let's consider the implications of each of these principles for social workers.

Foucault invites us to shift our analysis from a focus on who possesses power to the consideration of how power is exercised from specific social locations and by specific people. Recognizing that power is exercised rather than possessed also allows us to acknowledge and expand possibilities for relatively powerless groups to exercise power. A number of social work authors have used the Foucauldian notion of power to show how empowering discourses lead workers to ignore the ways in which marginalized groups, such as Indigenous people, homeless young women and young mothers, exercise power even though they do not 'possess' it (see Crinall, 1999; Healy, 2000). These commentators argue that a poststructural perspective can contribute to empowering practice by encouraging workers to recognize and support the capacities of service users to exercise power, rather than to focus on their relative powerlessness from a structural perspective.

In contrast to the view of power as something that oppresses and constrains, Foucault urges us also to recognize the productivity of power. He argues that people submit to power because they gain something from their submission; in other words, a focus on power as oppressive ignores the positive dimensions of power. Foucault (1980b, p. 119) asserts that

> What makes power hold good, what makes it accepted, is simply the fact that it doesn't only weigh on us as a force that says no, but that it traverses and produces things, it induces pleasure, forms of knowledge, produces discourse.

In contrast to the focus on the oppressive social work power that has dominated modern critical social workers' accounts of social work practice (see Chapter 8), Foucault's work encourages us to recognize the productivity of this power as well. This point is well illustrated by a number of critical studies of the micro-politics of practice which have shown that some service users actively seek out social work services and gain something, such as improved capacities or sense of self, from the exercise of power in these practice contexts (see Healy, 2000; Wise, 1995).

Finally, in contrast to modern sociological discourse and anti-oppressive theories, Foucault urges us to analyse power from the local to the structural, rather than the other way around. Foucault (1980c, p. 99) argues that a focus on macro-processes of power is not particularly useful for understanding the micro-politics of power in local contexts. Rather than seeing power relations as merely an effect of macro-structures, such as capitalism or patriarchy, post theorists recognize the micro-contexts of social work practice as sites where power is also produced. This recognition of local production of power is particularly important in challenging the tendency towards structural determinism in some modern critical social work theories (see Chapter 8). It enables us to recognize the complex web of power relations within which service providers and service users are embedded and so guard against a tendency to see both as merely victims of social structures. For example, Featherstone and Fawcett (1994) have argued that, in child protection practice, a mother may be powerless in one context, say in relation to an abusive partner or the statutory authority, and yet powerful in others, such as in relation to her children. Thus, in one moment, a person may be 'both victim and victimizer and these positions themselves shift' (*ibid.*, p. 134).

Power in Practice

In relation to a field of practice that interest you, consider:

● the ways service users are constrained in the exercise of power;

● the extent and ways in which service users/patients/survivors exercise power (for example, by resisting conventional treatment, or seeking alternative treatments).

Deconstruction

Deconstruction is a term commonly used by postmodernists and is associated with the work of French literary theorist Jacques Derrida. The term is used to describe the process of identifying and undermining oppositions through which discourses represent things such as knowledge, identity and other social phenomena (Weedon, 1997, p. 159). Some of the oppositions found in social work discourse include:

● normal/abnormal

● true/false

● powerful/powerless

- worker/service user

- middle-class/working-class

- male/female

- expert/lay person

- able-bodied/disabled

- straight/gay or lesbian

You can probably identify other oppositions within your practice domain. Derrida (1991) criticizes these oppositions because they create a hierarchy between the two opposed terms – and, further, they hide differences within and between each of these terms. For example, a 'middle-class' person may once have been working-class and even within the category of middle-class there are significant variations.

Deconstruction is aimed at breaking apart dualisms to show the range of positions that lie within and beyond opposed entities. For example, using a deconstructive approach we would recognize that the states of 'powerful' and 'powerless' are two extremes on a continuum and that there are many positions of relative powerfulness and powerlessness in between. The process of deconstruction is endless, for the new forms of representation that deconstruction itself produces must themselves be subjected to deconstruction. In this sense, deconstruction involves ongoing interrogation of that which is excluded in the processes of representing anything. For example, people in the disability movement sometimes prefer the term 'differently abled' because the term 'disabled' only shows lack of ability, from a deconstructive approach we would also ask what the preferred term 'differently abled' also hides.

Post Theories and Social Work Practices

Over the past decade a burgeoning literature has emerged on the applications of post theories to social work. In a collection of practice-based writings, Napier and Fook (2000) present a range of practitioners' reflections on the use of post-theory ideas for enabling social workers to critically reflect on the construction of social workers' and clients' 'identities' and narratives in practice. Similarly, Taylor and White (2000) use discourse analytic tools to show how truths – such as claims about child abuse or mental health diagnosis – are constructed, rather than discovered, in practice.

Social workers in the modern critical traditions of social work (see Chapter 9) have been especially divided in their responses to post theories.

Some critical social work commentators suggest that post theories encourage an individualistic approach to practice, thus undermining options for collective action (see Dominelli, 2002b). Yet many other social workers within this tradition have demonstrated the uses of post theories for extending critical social work practices. Pease and Fook (1999) produced a collection of practice-based writings to show how critical social workers use post theories to extend and develop critical practice in policy, community development and casework. My own research has focused on using discourse analysis and deconstructive strategies to open the critical social work canon to a range of activisms in practice (see Healy, 2000). I am concerned that critical social work – radical, Marxist, feminist and anti-oppressive – has tended to privilege some forms and sites of activism and activist 'subjectivities', while marginalizing critical practice possibilities in other sites and by other 'subjectivities' – such as the middle-aged, middle-class social worker (Healy, 2000, p. 4). I am also interested in using poststructural theories to show the complexities of local power in practice to, in addition, the macro-analyses that dominate modern critical social work approaches to power.

Narrative Therapy: A Postmodern Practice Approach

Narrative therapy is a further, and possibly the most celebrated, illustration of the application of post-theory ideas to social work practices. The Australian social worker Michael White and his colleague, the New Zealand-based therapist David Epston, are widely recognized as the leading proponents of these ideas (see White and Epston, 1990). Workers associated with Dulwich Centre in Adelaide (Australia), a key centre for narrative therapy, have produced a wide body of work on the application of narrative ideas to a broad terrain of social service work, including group work and community development, and many fields of practice from mental health, family services and grief in Indigenous communities (see Wingard, 1998). Social work theorists have also applied these ideas to direct social work practice (see Parton and O'Byrne, 2001).

Narrative therapy centres on the idea that the narratives we, and others, construct about us actively shape our experiences, our sense of selves and our life options. According to this approach, service users' lives are constrained by the harmful narratives that they and others have generated about them (Fook, 2002, p. 137). Often these narratives have been produced in order to 'diagnose' and ultimately 'help' the person, but the effect is to imprison the person in a narrative that damages and constrains them. Narrative therapists contend that because narratives so powerfully shape our 'identities' and our life choices, these narratives should be the site of intervention. We turn now to key principles of this approach.

Practice Principle 1: Focus on the Narratives that Shape Service Users' Lives

In contrast to modernist forms of social service intervention, narrative therapy does not seek to uncover or construct a single truth about the causes of the service user's situation. Instead, narrative therapists seek to assess and transform the narratives that construct our lives. They seek to challenge the harmful narratives, that is, those that represent the service user in a negative and pathological frame, and instead aim to recognize and construct alternative narratives; that is, narratives that recognize and honour the person's capacities, including, for example, their capacity to take responsibility for violence (see Jenkins, 1990).

Narrative therapy requires the worker to adopt a curious and open, rather than truth-seeking, position towards the service user. An important feature of the initial engagement with the service user is that of exploring, with the service user, how they came to be 'recruited' into the dominant and harmful narrative about themselves. So, for example, rather than accepting the dominant narrative of Joan as schizophrenic, we might explore with Joan how this narrative was constructed, who constructed it, and how Joan herself has accepted or resisted this construction.

Practice Principle 2: Separate the Person from the Problem

Another principle of narrative therapy is that the person is not the problem, rather the 'problem is the problem'. In line with this principle, narrative therapists use the strategy of 'externalizing conversations' to separate the person from the problem. A feature of these conversations includes giving a name to the problem that is separate from the person. For example, we might rename an apparently uncontrollable anger as 'the dragon'. You may be thinking 'the dragon' is a little medieval! However, narrative therapists often use magical and unusual terminology as a way of unlocking the creative energies of the service user.

Let's say we are working with a young man, Peter, whose uncontrollable anger is leading to conflict and unhappiness at home and at school. Using the technique of externalizing conversation, we might ask 'When does the dragon visit?', 'What sorts of events are likely to waken the dragon?', 'When have you successfully fought the dragon?', 'What would need to happen to banish the dragon for good?' Through the use of externalizing

conversations, we can enable the service user to separate themselves from the problem, and to articulate the strategies they have already
used effectively to address the problems they face, and we can offer hope that
an alternative future is possible in which the problem does not control
them. Recognition of moments in which the service user has effectively
resisted the problem, sometimes referred to as 'news of difference', is especially important to the construction of alternative narratives about the self.

Practice Principle 3: Reconstruct the Dominant Story of the Self as One of Survival, Courage, Responsibility and Active Resistance

Narrative therapy aims to reconstruct the dominant narratives that shape
the service user's life from those that emphasize pathology to those that
highlight and support the service user's capacities. This focus is very similar
to the strengths perspective and, indeed, some proponents of the strengths
perspective draw on narrative practice techniques. This focus on the
narrative construction of a problem is not a Pollyanna position denying
the existence of, say, serious mental illness or violent behaviour, but rather
an approach that illuminates and builds the service user's capacity to live a
life of their choosing. For example, Alan Jenkins (1990) uses narrative
therapy approaches to invite men who are violent and abusive to take
responsibility for their actions. The three-step strategy, outlined by Jenkins
(1990, p. 62), involves:

- the worker declining 'invitations' by the man to attribute responsibilities
  for his actions to external factors, such as his partner's behaviour;

- inviting the man to challenge restraints on his acceptance of responsibility for his actions, such as sociocultural affirmations of male
  violence;

- acknowledging and highlighting evidence of the man's acceptance
  of responsibility for his actions, for example, drawing attention to
  moments when the man contained his violent behaviour and showed
  his capacities for respectful and non-violent responses to others.

Narrative therapists recognize that the narratives others also hold about the
service user similarly shape the service user's capacities to live a life of their
choosing. For this reason, narrative therapists often incorporate strategies
aimed at building a supportive and life-affirming community around the
service user. One way the service user's community can be recruited in the
new, life-affirming narrative is through the use of ceremonies that mark
the defeat of the pathological narrative and the emergence of alternative

narratives that affirm service users' capacities. For example, White and Denborough (1998) present a case study of a woman who invited her closest supporters to a ceremony at which they built a bonfire to destroy the psychiatric casefiles that contributed to the narrative of her life as a psychiatric patient.

Practice Exercise

Applying post theories in practice

Read through the following case study and identify how you could apply narrative therapy concepts and other post-theory ideas to analyse and respond to the situation.

Emily is a 55-year-old Indigenous woman who lives in a small rural township (population 700). Emily has diabetes mellitus (Type 2) – a life-threatening condition that is very common among Indigenous populations through the world. Because of her diabetes Emily is at risk of a number of serious health problems, including damage to her eyes, kidneys, nerves and blood vessels. Emily has regular contact with the regional mobile community health service and the nurses have closely monitored her blood pressure and cholesterol. Also, they have encouraged Emily to make a number of changes to her diet and to increase her exercise. To this point, Emily has been reluctant to adopt the lifestyle changes recommended by them. Nursing and medical staff are very concerned about a recent deterioration in Emily's health, including loss of sensation in her limbs and problems with her eyesight. There is some concern that Emily may require the amputation of part or all of her right foot because of very serious circulatory problems. The community health team has recommended to Emily that she be admitted to hospital for extensive testing and assessment of the circulation to her foot. Emily knows there is a chance that her foot may need to be amputated and that she could die if she does not receive medical intervention.

Last year the government decided to rationalize health services in the rural area and as a result the diabetes unit in the local hospital was closed and all patients were referred to the regional hospital. This means that the closest hospital with the facilities to undertake a full assessment of Emily's condition is in the regional city, a considerable distance from Emily's home town. The nurses have referred Emily to you to make arrangements for her transportation to the hospital. In your first interview with Emily, she reveals that she does not want to go to the regional hospital and would prefer to take her chances with her health. She tells you that she is tired of the community health staff 'pushing' her around. Emily also does not want to leave her three grandchildren, for whom she provides full-time care, in the care of other family members. She is concerned about the children's safety because of a

Uses and Limitations of Post Theories for Social Work Practices

Let's turn now to an analysis of post theories in social work. We will use examples from the Emily case study to discuss, in an applied way, the strengths and weaknesses of post theories for social work practices. A postmodern approach to practice encourages practitioners to recognize and explore a range of perspectives about the problem facing the service user. In relation to Emily, then, from a postmodern view, we would explore the multiple narratives shaping Emily's situation rather than seek to establish the truth of it. A focus on the narratives through which Emily and others construct her situation, including the professionals involved in this matter, would enable us to recognize its inherent complexities and ambiguities. From a postcolonial perspective we would analyse how race and ethnicity shape Emily's 'identity', experiences and options, yet we would recognize that 'racial/ethnic' subjectivity is only one of many identities which may be important to Emily's sense of self (see Lewis, 2000). From a postmodern perspective, we would also seek to understand how other discourses shape Emily's 'identity' and options. For example, in this case study, we can see that Emily is not only a person suffering from diabetes – which is her primary identity in the biomedical discourse – she is also 'an Indigenous woman', 'a mother', 'a grandmother', and she may also have many other subjectivities that are vital to her 'identity' and options for responding to the situation facing her. Exploring how Emily defines the problem, rather than assuming our own or others' definitions of it, is a vital step towards establishing a helping partnership with her.

Another significant advantage of postmodern theories is that they highlight the 'micro-politics' of practice. These theories draw attention to local contexts – including the institutional context – as key sites of analysis and action (K. Healy, 1998). This contrasts with liberal approaches to social work, such as task-centred practice, which have paid little attention to inequities between workers and service users. The post-theory approaches also differ from modern critical theories, including anti-oppressive practice, which have analysed local power relations as effects of structural processes (K. Healy, 1998).

From a postmodern perspective, we can recognize the oppressions faced by Emily while also acknowledging and supporting her capacity for agency (Crinall, 1999, p. 80). This could include recognizing the way in which Emily has resisted others' definitions of her crisis and by working with her to empower her to identify and work, individually and with others, towards the outcomes she seeks. This focus on the micro-politics of power also draws our attention to the political character of all social work practice (Crinall, 1999, p. 81). Consistent with Foucault's focus on analysing from the local to the structural, we can view our direct work, including our casework with Emily, as connected to, and influencing, broader struggles for Indigenous sovereignty, and we must recognize that our relations with her are also shaped by histories of European colonization of indigenous people.

From a postmodern approach, we can use discourse-analytic techniques to understand current institutional responses to Emily's situation and to foster alternative responses. In the Emily case study, we can see illustrations of at least two dominant discourses – biomedicine and neo-classical economics – discussed earlier in this book (see Chapter 2). We can use our understanding of these discourses to better understand the position of institutional stakeholders while, at the same time, creating space for other truths to be heard. For example, the nursing staff's response to Emily, which focuses on promoting physical health, is grounded in the biomedical discourse and as such highlights the medical basis of her condition and offers a biomedical response to it, including both preventive and tertiary medical interventions. We can recognize the nursing staff's position as *a* truth while at the same time we can show Emily that we respect *her* truth, such as her desire to place her caring responsibilities above her individual health outcomes. At the very least, we can use discourse analysis strategies to create an environment in which we are open to Emily's truths and, better still, we may help to facilitate an environment in which others, such as the nursing staff in this case, can hear these truths even while holding to their own. This is important for, as mentioned in the case study, Emily already feels 'pushed' around by health care staff. This more open environment in which the truth claims of all stakeholders are acknowledged can lay the foundations for collaborative decision making between Emily and health care providers.

Using discourse analysis strategies, we can also analyse and address the impact of neo-classical economics on shaping Emily's options. In the first instance we can acknowledge with Emily that her options for both health services and child care support are constrained by the rationalization of health and social care services. In this way, we may reduce Emily's possible sense of self-blame for her situation. Furthermore, we could work with Emily to see how we might contest this discourse – through, for example, linking Emily to consumer rights groups, particularly those agitating for improvements in Indigenous people's health.

Postmodernists also reject the notion that there is one desirable path for any individual or collective to follow and, instead, invite us to recognize and celebrate different paths and possibilities. In relation to the case study, this focus on differences would enable us to work with Emily to respect her decisions regarding Western health care and to consider other options, including those associated with traditional Indigenous medicine. Recognition of differences is also important to understanding that in some cultures, such as Indigenous culture, the well-being of the individual (in this case Emily) is not necessarily valued over collective responsibilities, such as Emily's responsibilities to her grandchildren.

Narrative strategies can be used to empower and energize service users by separating them from the perceived problem. This contrasts markedly with modernist forms of social work that have aimed to understand the service user's identity and issues and, in modern forms of critical social work, have encouraged individuals to embrace the oppressed identity (see Chapter 9). We could use narrative strategies to explore how Emily has already taken control of her health care and to help her investigate how she responds to the current 'crisis' in her health situation. Barbara Wingard (1998), an Indigenous person, uses the metaphor 'Sugar' to describe her own battle with diabetes. Drawing on Wingard's metaphor, we could work with Emily to explore how 'Sugar' has controlled her life and recognize moments where she has overcome 'Sugar'.

So far we have considered the uses of post theories for social work practices; now let's turn to the limitations of these perspectives. Again, we'll use the Emily case study to ground these criticisms in practice. The focus of postmodernism on language practices can lead us to ignore the material realities of oppression and the extent to which these oppressions are shaped by macro-social structures, particularly capitalism, patriarchy and imperialism (see Dominelli, 2002b; Ife, 1999). In relation to Emily, we can argue that her condition, and her options for responding to it, are shaped by her race/ethnicity, gender, class and age. These categories represent virulent social divisions that profoundly shape the life chances of disadvantaged people. For example, Indigenous people throughout the world experience rates of illness and death from diabetes Type 2 far in excess of the rates for non-Indigenous people. In most countries, health care services available to Indigenous people are substantially inferior to those available to non-Indigenous people. Thus a localized analysis and response to Emily's situation, as proposed by postmodernism, can lead us to neglect the broader contexts of Indigenous health and sub-standard health care for Indigenous people.

Many social workers question whether postmodern theories can provide a coherent framework for practice. The academic and often arcane language of most post-theory writing is profoundly alienating to many social workers. Agger (1991, p. 106) points out that most post-theory arguments are 'incredibly, extravagantly convoluted – to the point of dangerous absurdity'. But social workers' concern goes beyond issues of the inaccessibility of postmodern writings to concern about the relativism inherent in this perspective and thus the loss of a moral and political framework for action (Peile and McCouat, 1997). Professional social workers often develop and legitimate their practice by appealing to universal social values, particularly social justice. For example, in working with Emily many of the responses we've discussed so far are consistent with a social justice value stance. Some critical social workers have responded to concern about the loss of a clear value position by combining postmodern perspectives with other modernist frameworks such as human rights (Ife, 1999) or radical and feminist social work perspectives (see Fook, 2002; Healy, 2000; Leonard, 1997).

Critical social workers, in particular, argue that post theories can be used to support conservative policy agendas and practice approaches. While acknowledging the use of post theories for recognizing complexity and uncertainty, Ife (1999, p. 211) asserts that: 'a lingering doubt remains as to whether it [postmodernism] represents a "sell-out" to the very ideologies of individualism, greed and exploitation against which social workers have claimed to stand' (see also Dominelli, 2002a). In Emily's case study, for example, we can see many grounds for political protest, including the parlous state of Indigenous health in many countries throughout the world, the rationalization of health and welfare services that has reduced the health and social care options of so many service users, and the gendered character of violence as suggested between Emily's daughter and her partner. Post theories promote more critically self-reflective practice by demanding that we interrogate all our assumptions about identity, power and values, yet, in so doing, they also threaten to detract our attention and energies from much-needed broad-scale social change.

Conclusion

Over the past decade, the burgeoning literature on postmodern theories in social work practice and the growing popularity of narrative therapy have contributed to the legitimacy of these perspectives to the formal base of social work. In this chapter, we have discussed how social workers can and do apply post-theory concepts to practice. For example, social workers often find themselves in the difficult situation of making sense of multiple and competing truth claims (Taylor and White, 2000) and in our contact with service users we often encounter multiple subjectivities in ourselves and in others. Post theories can enrich our practice by providing a language for the complexities and ambiguities we face, yet, as we have discussed here, an uncritical embrace of post theories also threatens our capacity to develop coherent moral and political frameworks for practice.

Summary Questions

1. What are the common assumptions of post theories, such as post-modernism and poststructuralism?

2. How does the postmodern view of 'subjectivity' challenge the modern social work theories such as the strengths perspective and anti-oppressive practice?

3. Identify and discuss the practice principles of narrative therapy.

Reflection Exercise

Imagine you work in a community health centre and the doctor has referred Jenny, a 32-year-old woman, to you for counselling. The doctor has sent a referral letter in which he states that he believes that Jenny is suffering from postnatal depression associated with the difficult birth of her second child, three months ago. He explains that Jenny had an emergency Caesarean section and this had contributed to difficulties in her bonding with the child and to her depressed state. He also states that he believes Jenny is quite isolated having only recently moved to the local area in the last six months. The doctor has prescribed anti-depressants and thinks that Jenny could also be helped by counselling.

Discuss how you would use a postmodern approach to analyse Jenny's situation and to develop your practice approach with her. Role-play, with a colleague, your first meeting with Jenny.

Website

The Dulwich Centre Narrative Therapy Website: http://www.dulwichcentre.com.au
The Dulwich Centre is based in Adelaide, Australia and is an internationally

recognized leading centre in narrative therapy. The website includes papers introducing narrative therapy, notes from narrative therapy workshops, information on forthcoming workshops, and a guide to all the Dulwich Centre publications.

Recommended Reading

Foucault, M. *Power/Knowledge: Selected Interviews and Other Writings 1972–1977*, ed.
   C. Gordon (New York: Pantheon Books, 1980a).
This series of lectures, interviews and papers provides an accessible introduction to some of Foucault's most important ideas on power, subjectivity and change.

Healy, K. *Social Work Practices: Contemporary Perspectives on Change* (London: Sage,
   2000).
In this book, I discuss the historical development and application of post-theory ideas to social work with a strong emphasis on the implications for critical forms of social work practice.

Napier, L. and J. Fook, eds. *Breakthroughs in Practice: Theorising Critical Moments in
   Social Work* (London: Whiting and Birch, 2000).
In this collection of practice-based writings, practitioners and academics working within a broad range of settings, including income security, mental health, child protection and services related to death and dying, use post-theory ideas to reflect upon and develop their practice.

Weedon, C. *Feminist Practice and Poststructuralist Theory* (Oxford: Blackwell, 1997).
Chris Weedon provides a comprehensive and highly accessible introduction to poststructural theory in the context of feminist concerns. Highly recommended.

White, C. and D. Denborough (eds) *Introducing Narrative Therapy: A Collection of
   Practice-Based Writings* (Adelaide: Dulwich Centre Publications, 1998).
This beautiful collection of practice-based articles demonstrates a breadth of terrains for the application of narrative therapy ideas. I particularly recommend Barbara Wingard's article on grief in Indigenous communities.

White, M. and D. Epston. *Narrative Means to Therapeutic Ends* (New York: WW
   Norton, 1990).
This is widely regarded as a classic in narrative therapy by two of the 'founding fathers' of the school. If you are interested in using narrative approaches to practice, I strongly encourage you to read this text.

11

Creating Frameworks
for Practice

In Chapter 1, I introduced a model of social work as a dynamic activity. Throughout this book, this model has underpinned my analysis of the discourses and theories that inform social work practice. I have presented social work as a negotiated activity; in particular, our purpose and practices as social workers are negotiated through interactions between our institutional context, our 'formal' purpose, our professional base and our frameworks for practice. I have also argued that the potential for social workers to influence the contexts and formal knowledge base of the profession is, as yet, underdeveloped. One of my intentions in this book has been to enhance our capacities, as social workers, to actively use and influence the ideas that shape the institutional contexts of practice and the formal base of social work itself. In this chapter, I will consider how we can use this knowledge of the ideas underpinning the institutions and formal theories for practice to construct our framework for practice, which is the final component of the model introduced in Chapter 1.

Frameworks for Practice

In every practice encounter we are drawing on, but also constructing, our framework for practice. In Chapter 1, I introduced the term 'framework for practice' to refer to the combination of formal knowledge and skills and informal knowledge and skills developed by social workers in practice. This fusion includes formal theoretical and substantive knowledge as well as tacit, or difficult-to-articulate, knowledge that can be built up through repeated exposure to practice situations. Ideally, our frameworks develop over time, through practice, and become increasingly useful to us for constructing unique responses in each practice encounter (see Fook *et al.*, 2000).

The act of constructing our practice framework is creative in that we draw on ideas from multiple sources, such as institutional context and formal

216

theories, but we also transform these ideas through their application. For example, a social worker's application of the strengths perspective in one context, say with an older person with a mental health concern, is different from their use of this approach to support a young parent coping with the ongoing traumatic effects of childhood sexual abuse.

The processes through which we construct our practice frameworks are, to a large extent, unique to each social worker, but here I will summarize how the information in this book can be used to assist you to create your framework for practice. In the first part of the book, I outlined the ideas that underpin the institutional contexts of social service delivery. My intention was to show that social work is practised *in* context but it is not *of* context. To put it differently, the key concepts of social work practice, such as ideas about client needs and social work responses, are constructed through discourses and theories for practice, but they are not merely products of these discourses and theories. By understanding the ideas that underpin health and welfare institutions and our formal professional base, we enhance our capacity to actively use and, where necessary, to disrupt these ideas. For example, while our practice may be shaped and constrained by neo-classical economic discourse, we can also use our understanding of this discourse to challenge it on its own terms; that is, to show how particular service delivery processes are not only unjust but also cost-ineffective or, conversely, to argue against the use of a neo-classical framework for evaluating some service outcomes such as long-term community-building initiatives.

In this book, I have introduced five contemporary theories for social work practice. I presented the historical, geographical and disciplinary origins of these theories so as to enhance your capacity to actively use and transform these theories within your context of practice. Again, I have argued that we as social workers do not merely use theory but transform theory in our unique application of these ideas to address specific client needs within our practice contexts. Understanding the origins of these ideas is critical to their informed and creative use.

The creativity inherent in social workers' negotiation of their framework for practice is often unrecognized and unvalued. Over time the frameworks that we develop through a combination of knowledge, skills and experience become the 'common-sense' way of doing things and are rarely exposed to critical reflection except in the context of a critical event that leads us to reconsider the foundations of our practice. One way of developing our frameworks for practice is to open these 'common-sense' understandings of practice to critical scrutiny.

In this book I have used the discourse analysis approach to show how key entities such as client needs and social work practices are constructed in health and welfare services and in social work theories for practice. We can use this information to analyse how our practices are constructed in specific environments and how we might use or resist these constructions. Some questions that may guide you in developing your framework for practice within a specific institutional context are:

● How do the institutional discourses construct client 'need'?

● How do institutional discourses shape my role as a social worker?

● In what ways are these constructions consistent (or in tension) with my professional values?

● What opportunities do I have to resist or transform these constructions to be more consistent with issues of importance, such as the clients' understanding of need and my professional values and ethics?

Our framework for practice can also be enriched by the informed and creative use of formal theories for practice. In this book I have introduced the historical, geographical and disciplinary origins of our formal theory base in order to promote critical reflection on how you might apply and transform these theories for use within your specific contexts of practice. Critical questions that can guide your analysis, use and transformation of these theories include:

● What are the historical, geographical and institutional contexts in which this theory was developed? How relevant is this to my context(s) of practice and my purposes within it?

● How does this theory of practice construct the purpose and process of social work practice? What constructions of practice does this theory make possible, what possibilities does it marginalize?

Other components of our framework for practice include practice wisdom, practice skills and acquired knowledge, that is, knowledge and capacities that are primarily developed through action and critical reflection on action. As these kinds of practical attributes and knowledge are often revealed in action, it is useful to consider these elements via critical analysis of actual practice events. This analytic approach, which focuses on analysis in and on practice, draws on elements of the reflective tradition and reflexive approach which were discussed in Chapter 5. From the reflective tradition of Schön, we see knowledge as something that emerges in, and through reflection on, practice. From the reflexive approach of Taylor and White (2000), we understand social work practices to be constructed through discourse and through the viewpoints of different stakeholders; analysis of practice begins with the examination of how our different stakeholders construct their view of the situation of concern. Questions that can guide us in this analysis of knowledge in practice include:

- What elements of my practice experience are relevant to understanding this event?

- How do key stakeholders understand this situation and how does this fit with, enrich or confound my understanding of events?

- What substantive or context-based knowledge is critical for understanding this event? Do I have access to this knowledge? If not, how do I gain access to relevant knowledge?

- What capacities do I, and the service user, bring to respond to this environment?

- What resources and opportunities does my practice context, including the institutional environment, offer in responding to the situation?

Through critical analysis of how we use and develop knowledge in practice, our embedded framework for practice is revealed. Being able to articulate our framework for practice enhances our capacity to share and develop our approach with others, such as colleagues and service users. We are also in a position to understand the weaknesses of our framework for practice and this can provide directions for further development of our framework and future learning.

Formalizing Practitioner Contribution to Knowledge

I want finally to turn to the importance of social work practitioners using their framework for practice to influence the formal base of practice and the institutional contexts of our activity. In the dynamic model of social work practice introduced in Chapter 1, I emphasized that social workers actively create knowledge and theory in practice (see also Taylor and White, 2001). Most social workers engage in theory building in a tacit and informal way as our understandings are expressed in our direct practice and, at best, shared among immediate colleagues. Unfortunately, this tacit approach also does little to create a bridge between the formal theoretical base of the profession and the theoretical bases developed by practitioners.

Practice-based knowledge can potentially provide vital insights for the development of theories of practice, yet this potential remains underdeveloped. Institutional barriers provide one reason for the low levels of practitioner involvement in formal theory creation for the profession. During the 1990s a series of publications on practitioner–research partnerships pointed to the growing interest, at least within academic institutions, in involving practitioners in formal knowledge development (see McCartt-Hess and Mullen, 1995). Yet, according to Kirk and Reid (2002), in the longer run academic institutions, rather than service organizations, remain the primary site of practitioner–researcher partnerships, with most theory for practice continuing to be written by social workers located in academia. Thus the profession has missed opportunities for practice-based theory development and transformation. A significant challenge for the profession is that of promoting the benefits to social service institutions of investing in practitioner involvement in formal knowledge development processes.

Truly involving practitioners in the development of the formal professional base requires those of us formally charged with knowledge building for the profession, that is academic researchers and theorists, to be willing to open our ideas to practice-based scrutiny. Academic social workers must be willing to allow field-based workers to use their experiences of the messy and indeterminate nature of much social work practice to confound formal theories for practice. I want also to encourage practitioners, that is, those located in the direct delivery of social work services, to use the knowledge gained through practice, our frameworks for practice, to develop and disrupt the formal base of social work practice and the discourses that underpin service delivery processes. Again, collaborative efforts are needed to overcome the institutional and professional barriers to field-based social workers' participation in formal knowledge development. As a profession, we need collectively to challenge the underinvestment in social services research compared to other arenas of knowledge development. Trinder (2000, p. 144) observes that 'Personal social services research has always been the poor relation of health services research, with proportionately less funding.' Further research funding could be directed at enabling practitioners to participate in meaningful ways, through, for example, providing funding to release practitioners from their direct practice responsibilities to publish practice-based research. We need also to find ways to build the capacity of service providers and service users to present their work in scholarly forums. For example, the provision of seminars and mentoring processes to support practitioners and service users to conceptualize and prepare conference and journal papers is one way of realizing their contribution to a dynamic professional practice base.

Conclusion

Social work is a diverse and deeply contextual activity. As social workers, we actively construct our purpose and our professional framework for practice by using, sometimes resisting, and transforming aspects of our practice context and our formal professional base. Social workers face many barriers to formally influencing both our contexts of practice and the formal base of the profession. In this book we have examined the ideas under-pinning the institutional contexts and formal theories for social work practice in the hope that not only might we better understand them, but that we might also participate in transforming them.

Bibliography

Adams, R., L. Dominelli and M. Payne (eds). *Social Work: Themes, Issues and Critical Debates*, 2nd edn (Basingstoke: Palgrave, 2002).

Agger, B. 'Critical Theory, Poststructuralism, Postmodernism: Their Sociological Relevance', *Annual Review of Sociology*, **17** (1991), 105–31.

Aldridge, S. *The Thread of Life: The Story of Genes and Genetic Engineering* (Cambridge: Cambridge University Press, 1996).

Alston, M. and J. McKinnon. *Social Work: Fields of Practice*, 2nd edn (Melbourne: Oxford University Press, 2005).

Anleu, S. *Law and Social Change* (London: Sage, 2000).

Australian Institute of Health and Welfare. *Australia's Health 2002* (Canberra: AIHW, 2002).

Bailey, R. and M. Brake. *Radical Social Work* (London: Edward Arnold, 1975).

Ball, C. *Law for Social Workers*, 3rd edn (Aldershot: Arena, 1996).

Banks, S. *Ethics and Values in Social Work*, 2nd edn (Basingstoke: Macmillan, 2001).

Barnes, C. 'Institutional Discrimination Against Disabled People and the Campaign for Anti-Discrimination Legislation', in D. Taylor (ed.) *Critical Social Policy: A Reader* (London: Sage, 1996), pp. 95–112.

Bartlett, H. *The Common Base of Social Work Practice* (Washington: National Association of Social Workers, 1970).

Bloom, S. 'Social Work and the Behavioural Sciences: Past History, Future Prospects', *Social Work in Health*, **31**(3) (2000), 25–37.

Boas, P. and J. Crawley. *Explorations in Teaching Generic Social Work Theory* (Bundoora: Preston Institute of Technology Press, 1975).

Bolland, K. and C. Atherton. 'Chaos Theory: An Alternative Approach to Social Work Practice and Research', *Families in Society*, **80**(4) 1999, 367–73.

Borden, W. 'The relational paradigm in contemporary psychoanalysis: Toward a psychodynamically informed social work perspective', *The Social Service Review*, **74**(3) (2000), 352–79.

Bourdieu, P. 'The Force of Law: Toward a Sociology of the Juridical Field', *Hastings Law Journal*, **38**(5) (1987), 805–54.

Brady, S. 'The Sterilization of Children with Intellectual Disabilities: Defective Law, Unlawful Activity and the Need for a Service Oriented Approach', *Australian Journal of Social Issues*, **33**(2) (1998), 155–77.

Braye, S. and M. Preston-Shoot. *Practising Social Work Law*, 2nd edn (Basingstoke: Macmillan, 1997).

Brayne, H., G. Martin and H. Carr. *Law for Social Workers*, 7th edn (Oxford: Oxford University Press, 2001).

Brewster, B. and J. Whiteford. *Sociology and Social Work: New Perspectives for Practitioners* (Hatfield: Organisation of Sociologists in Polytechnics and Cognate Institutions, 1976).

Bricker-Jenkins, M., N.K. Hooyman and N. Gottlieb. *Feminist Social Work Practice in Clinical Settings* (Newbury Park: Sage, 1991).

Bronfenbrenner, U. *The Ecology of Human Development: Experiments by Nature and Design* (Cambridge, Mass: Harvard University Press, 1979).

Burke, B. and P. Harrison. 'Anti-Oppressive Practice', in R. Adams, L. Dominelli and M. Payne (eds) *Social Work: Themes, Issues and Critical Debates*, 2nd edn (Basingstoke: Palgrave, 2002), pp. 227–36.

Butler, J. *Bodies That Matter: On the Discursive Limits of 'Sex'* (New York: Routledge, 1993).

Campbell, J. and M. Oliver. *Disability Politics: Understanding Our Past, Changing Our Future* (London: Routledge, 1996).

Canda, E. 'Conceptualizing Spirituality for Social Work: Insights from Diverse Perspectives', *Social Thought*, **14**(1) (1988), 30–46.

Capra, F. *The Web of Life* (New York: Anchor and Doubleday, 1996).

Carlson, G. and J. Wilson. 'A Model of Substitute Decision-Making', *Australian Social Work*, **51**(3) (1998), 17–23.

Carmichael, A. and L. Brown. 'The Future Challenge for Direct Payments', *Disability and Society*, **17**(7) (2002), 797–808.

Carniol, B. 'Structural Social Work: Maurice Moreau's Challenge to Social Work Practice', *Journal of Progressive Human Services*, **3**(1) (1992), 1–20.

Carrington, K. *Offending Girls: Sex, Youth and Justice* (St Leonards, New South Wales: Allen and Unwin, 1993).

Clark, C. *Social Work Ethics: Politics, Principles, and Practice* (Basingstoke: Macmillan, 2000).

Clear, M. (ed.) *Promises, Promises: Disability and Terms of Inclusion* (Sydney: Federation Press, 2000).

Coleman, J. and B. Leiter. 'Legal Positivism' in D. Patterson (ed.). *A Companion to the Philosophy of Law and Legal Theory* (Malden: Blackwell Publishers Ltd, 1999).

Corker, M. and T. Shakespeare (eds) *Disability/Postmodernity: Embodying Disability Theory* (London: Continuum, 2002).

Corrigan, P. and P. Leonard, *Social Work Practice Under Capitalism: A Marxist Approach* (London: Macmillan, 1978).

Cowger, C. 'Clientism and Clientification: Impediments to Strengths Based Social Work Practice', *Journal of Sociology and Social Welfare*, **25**(1) (1998), 25–37.

Cree, V. *Sociology for Social Workers and Probation Officers* (London: Routledge, 2000).

Crinall, K. 'Challenging Victimisation in Practice with Young Women', in B. Pease and J. Fook (eds) *Transforming Social Work Practice: Critical Postmodern Perspectives* (Sydney: Allen and Unwin, 1999), pp. 70–83.

Crompton, M. *Children, Spirituality, Religion and Social Work* (Aldershot: Ashgate, 1998).

Crossley, M. and N. Crossley. '"Patient" Voices, Social Movements and the Habitus: How Psychiatric Survivors "Speak Out"', *Social Science and Medicine*, **52** (2001), 1477–89.

Crotty, M. *The Foundations of Social Research: Meaning and Perspective in the Research Process* (St Leonards, New South Wales: Allen and Unwin, 1998).

D'Abbs, P. *Who helps? Support Networks and Social Policy in Australia – Monograph No. 12* (Melbourne: Australian Institute of Family Studies, 1991).

Daly, J., M. Gullemin and S. Hill. 'Introduction: The Need for Critical Compromise', in J. Daly, M. Gullemin and S. Hill (eds) *Technologies and Health: Critical Compromises* (Melbourne: Oxford University Press, 2001), pp. xii–xx.

Dalrymple, J. and B. Burke. *Anti-oppressive Practice: Social Care and the Law* (Buckingham: Open University Press, 1995).

Darley, V. 'Emergent Phenomena and Complexity.' Fri. 14 Oct. 12:38:41 EDT 1994. Division of Applied Sciences, Harvard University. Accessed 15 December 2003. ⟨http://www.santafe.edu/~vince/emergence_alife/emergence_alife.html⟩.

Darlington, Y. and R. Bland. 'Strategies for Encouraging and Maintaining Hope Amongst People Living with Serious Mental Illness', *Australian Social Work*, **52**(3) (1999), 17–23.

Davis, A. and J. George. *States of Health: Health and Illness in Australia*, 2nd edn (Pymble, New South Wales: Harper Educational, 1993).

Day, P. *Sociology in Social Work Practice* (Basingstoke: Macmillan, 1987).

De Shazer, S. *Keys to Solution in Brief Therapy* (New York: W.W. Norton and Company, 1985).

Decker, J. and J. Redhorse. 'The Principles of General Systems Theory Applied to the Medical Model', *Journal of Sociology and Social Welfare*, **6**(2) (1979), 144–53.

Derrida, J. 'Différance', in P. Kamuf (ed.) *A Derrida Reader: Between the Blinds* (New York: Columbia University Press, 1991), pp. 59–79.

Doel, M. 'Task-Centred Work', in R. Adams, L. Dominelli and M. Payne (eds) *Social Work: Themes, Issues and Critical Debates* (Basingstoke: Macmillan, 1998).

Doel, M. and P. Marsh. *Task-centred Social Work* (Aldershot: Ashgate, 1992).

Dominelli, L. *Anti-racist Social Work: A Challenge for White Practitioners and Educators* (Basingstoke: Macmillan, 1988).

Dominelli, L. 'De-Professionalizing Social Work: Anti-Oppressive Practices, Competencies and Postmodernism', *British Journal of Social Work*, **26** (1996), 153–75.

Dominelli, L. *Sociology for Social Work* (Basingstoke: Macmillan, 1997).

Dominelli, L. 'Anti-Oppressive Practice in Context', in R. Adams, L. Dominelli and M. Payne (eds) *Social Work: Themes, Issues and Critical Debates*, 2nd edn (Basingstoke: Palgrave, 2002a), pp. 3–19.

Dominelli, L. *Feminist Social Work: Theory and Practice* (Basingstoke: Palgrave, 2002b).

Dominelli, L. and A. Hoogvelt. 'Globalization and Technocratization of Social Work', *Critical Social Policy*, **16** (1996), 45–62.

Dominelli, L. and E. McLeod. *Feminist Social Work* (Basingstoke: Macmillan, 1989).

Donzelot, J. *The Policing of Families* (Baltimore: Johns Hopkins University Press, 1997).

Dung, T. 'Understanding Asian families: A Vietnamese perspective', *Children Today*, **13**(2) (1984), 10–12.

Edwards, L. *How to Argue with an Economist: Reopening Political Debate in Australia* (Cambridge: Cambridge University Press, 2002).

Edwards, P. 'Spiritual Themes in Social Work Counselling: Facilitating the Search for Meaning', *Australian Social Work*, **55**(1) (2002), 78–87.

Epstein, L. and L. Brown. *Brief Treatment and a New Look at the Task-Centered Approach*, 4th edn (Boston, MA: Allyn and Bacon, 2002).

Fay, B. *Critical Social Science: Liberation and its Limits* (Ithaca: Cornell University Press, 1987).

Featherstone, B. and B. Fawcett. 'Feminism and Child Abuse: Opening up Some Possibilities?', *Critical Social Policy*, **14**(3) (1994), 61–80.

Fish, R., J. Weakland and L. Segal. *The Tactics of Change: Doing Therapy Briefly* (San Francisco: Jossey-Bass, 1983).

Fook, J. *Radical Casework: A Theory of Practice* (Sydney: Allen and Unwin, 1993).

Fook, J. *Social Work: Critical Theory and Practice* (London: Sage, 2002).

Fook, J., M. Ryan and L. Hawkins. *Professional Expertise: Practice, Theory and Education for Working in Uncertainty* (London: Whiting and Birch, 2000).

Ford, P. and K. Postle. 'Task-centred Practice and Care Management' in P. Stepney and D. Ford (eds) *Social Work Models, Methods and Theories: A Framework for Practice* (Dorset: Russell House Publishing Ltd.), pp. 52–64.

Foucault, M. *The Birth of the Clinic* (London: Tavistock, 1973).

Foucault, M. *Power/Knowledge: Selected Interviews and Other Writings 1972–1977*, ed. C. Gordon (New York: Pantheon Books, 1980a).

Foucault, M. 'Truth and Power', in C. Gordon (ed.) *Power/Knowledge: Selected Interviews and Other Writings 1972–1977* (New York: Pantheon Books, 1980b), pp. 109–33.

Foucault, M. 'Two Lectures', in C. Gordon (ed.) *Power/ Knowledge: Selected Interviews and Other Writings 1972–1977* (New York: Pantheon Books, 1980c), pp. 78–108.

Foucault, M. *The History of Sexuality, Vol. 1*. Trans. R. Hurley (London: Pelican Books, 1981a).

Foucault, M. 'The Order of Discourse', in R. Young (ed.) *Untying the Text: A Poststructuralist Reader* (London: Routledge and Kegan Paul, 1981b), pp. 48–78.

Foucault, M. *Discipline and Punish: The Birth of the Prison*. Trans. A. Sheridan (London: Penguin, 1991).

Foucault, M. *Madness and Civilization: A History of Insanity in the Age of Reason*. Trans. R. Howard (London: Routledge, 1997).

Friedman, M. *Capitalism and Freedom* (Chicago: University of Chicago Press, 1982).

Friedman, M. and R. Friedman. *Free to Choose: A Personal Statement* (Melbourne: Macmillan, 1980).

Galper, J. *Social Work Practice: A Radical Perspective* (New Jersey: Prentice-Hall, 1980).

Gandhi, L. *Postcolonial Theory: A Critical Introduction* (St Leonards, New South Wales: Allen and Unwin, 1998).

Garrett, A. 'The Worker–Client Relationship', in H. Parad (ed.) *Ego Psychology and Dynamic Casework: Papers from the Smith College School for Social Work* (New York: Family Service Association of America, 1958), pp. 53–72.

George, J. and A. Davis. *States of Health: Health and Illness in Australia*, 3rd edn (Melbourne: Addison, Wesley and Longman, 1998).

Germain, C. and A. Gitterman. *The Life Model of Social Work Practice: Advances in Theory and Practice*, 2nd edn (New York: Columbia University Press, 1996).

Gibelman, M. *What Social Workers Do* (Washington: National Association of Social Workers Press, 1995).

Gibelman, M. and H. Demone. 'The Commercialization of Health and Human Services: Natural Phenomenon or Cause for Concern', *Families in Society: Journal of Contemporary Human Services*, **83**(4) (2002), 387–97.

Goffman, E. *Asylums: Essays on the Social Situation of Mental Patients and Other Inmates* (Harmondsworth: Penguin, 1991).

Golan, N. 'Crisis Theory', in F. Turner (ed.) *Social Work Treatment: Interlocking Theoretical Approaches* (New York: The Free Press, 1986).

Golan, N. *Treatment in Crisis Situations* (New York: Free Press, 1978).

Golfus, B. and D.E. Simpson. 'When Billy Broke His Head: Life After Brain Damage'. National Disability Awareness Project, USA, 1994. Video Cassette.

Goldstein, H. *Social Work Practice: A Unitary Approach* (Columbia, South Carolina: University of South Carolina Press, 1973).

Gordon, W. 'Basic Constructs for an Integrative and Generative Conception of Social Work', in G. Hearn (ed.) *The General Systems Approach: Contributions Toward a Holistic Conception of Social Work* (New York: Council on Social Work Education, 1969), pp. 5–11.

Gorman, K. 'Cognitive Behaviourism and the Holy Grail: The Quest for a Universal Means of Managing Offender Risk', *Probation Journal*, **48**(1) (2001), 3–9.

Green, G. and A. Haines. *Asset Building and Community Development* (London: Sage, 2002).

Gutiérrez, L., R. Parsons and E. Cox (eds) *Empowerment in Social Work Practice: A Sourcebook* (Pacific Grove: Brooks/Cole Publishing, 1998).

Haley, J. *Strategies of Psychotherapy* (New York: Grune and Stratton, 1963).

Hamilton, G. *Theory and Practice of Social Case Work*, 2nd edn (Columbia University Press, New York, 1951).

Hamilton, G. 'A theory of personality: Freud's contribution to social work', in H. Parad (ed.) *Ego Psychology and Dynamic Casework: Papers from the Smith College School for Social Work* (New York: Family Service Association of America, 1958), pp. 11–37.

Hanmer, J. and D. Statham. *Women and Social Work: Towards a Woman Centred Practice* (Basingstoke: Macmillan Education, 1999).

Harris, M., P. Halfpenny and C. Rochester. 'A Social Policy Role for Faith-Based Organizations? Lessons From the UK Jewish Voluntary Sector', *Journal of Social Policy*, **32**(1) (2003), 93–112.

Healy, J. *Welfare Options: Delivering Social Services* (St Leonards, New South Wales: Allen and Unwin, 1998).

Healy, K. 'Participation and Child Protection: The Importance of Context', *British Journal of Social Work*, **28** (1998), 897–914.

Healy, K. 'Power and Activist Social Work', in B. Pease and J. Fook (eds) *Transforming Social Work Practice: Critical Postmodern Perspectives* (St Leonards, New South Wales: Allen and Unwin, 1999).

Healy, K. *Social Work Practices: Contemporary Perspectives on Change* (London: Sage, 2000).

Healy, K. 'Social Work in Australia', in G. Hutchinson, L. Lund, R. Lyngstad and S. Oltedal (eds) *Social Work in Five Countries: A Report* (Bodo: University of Bodo, 2001), pp. 15–43.

Healy, K. 'Managing Human Services in a Market Environment: What Role for Social Workers?', *British Journal of Social Work*, **32** (2002), 527–40.

Healy, K. and A. Hampshire. 'Social Capital: A Useful Concept for Social Work?', *Australian Social Work*, **55**(3) (2002), 227–38.

Healy, K. and G. Meagher. 'Practitioner Perspectives on Performance Assessment in Family Support Services', *Children Australia*, **26**(4) (2001), 22–8.

Healy, K. and G. Meagher. 'The Reprofessionalization of Social Work: Collaborative Approaches for Achieving Professional Recognition', *British Journal of Social Work*, **34** (2004), 157–74.

Healy, K. and K. Walsh, 'Making Participatory Processes Visible: Practice Issues in the Development of a Peer Support Network', *Australian Social Work*, **50**(3) (1997), 45–52.

Healy, K. and Young Mothers for Young Women. 'Valuing Young Families: Child Protection and Family Support Strategies with Young Mothers', *Children Australia*, **21**(2) (1996), 23–30.

Hearn, G. 'Progress Toward a Holistic Conception of Social Work', in G. Hearn (ed.) *The General Systems Approach: Contributions Toward a Holistic Conception of Social Work* (New York: Council on Social Work Education, 1969), pp. 63–70.

Howe, D. *An Introduction to Social Work Theory: Making Sense in Practice* (Aldershot, England: Arena, 1987).

Hudson, C.G. 'The Edge of Chaos: A New Paradigm for Social Work?', *Journal of Social Work Education*, **36**(2) (2000), 215–30.

Human Rights and Equal Opportunity Commission. 'The Human Rights and Equal Opportunity Commission Act 1986: Its Application to the Religious Freedom and the Right to Non-Discrimination in Employment'. Human Rights and Equal Opportunity Commission, 15 December 2003. ‹http://www.hreoc.gov.au/human_rights/religion›

Humphrey, J. 'Disabled People and the Politics of Difference', *Disability and Society*, **14**(2) (1999), 173–88.

Hunter, M., I. O'Dea and N. Britten. 'Decision-Making and Hormone Replacement Therapy: A Qualitative Analysis', *Social Science and Medicine*, **45**(10) (1997), 1465–603.

Hutchinson-Reis, M. ' "And For Those of Us Who Are Black?" Black Politics in Social Work', in M. Langan and M. Lee (eds) *Radical Social Work Today* (London: Unwin Hyman, 1989), pp. 165–77.

Hutchinson, G., L. Lund, R. Lyngstad and S. Oltedal (eds). *Social Work in Five Countries: A Report* (Bodo: University of Bodo, 2001).

Hutchison, W. 'The Role of Religious Auspiced Agencies in the Postmodern Era', in R. Meinert, J. Pardeck and J. Murphy (eds) *Postmodernism, Religion and the Future of Social Work* (New York: The Haworth Press, 1998), pp. 55–69.

Hyde, M. and D. Power. 'Informed Parental Consent for the Cochlear Ear Implantation of Young Deaf Children: Social and Other Considerations in the Use of the Bionic Ear', *Australian Journal of Social Issues*, **35**(2) (2000), 117–20.

Ife, J. 'Postmodern, Critical Theory and Social Work', in B. Pease and J. Fook (eds) *Transforming Social Work Practice: Critical Postmodern Perspectives* (St Leonards, New South Wales: Allen and Unwin, 1999), pp. 211–23.

Industry Commission. *Charitable Organisations in Australia* (Melbourne: Australian Government Publishing Service), Report 45.

Jenkins, A. *Invitations to Responsibility: The Therapeutic Engagement of Men who are Violent and Abusive* (Adelaide: Dulwich Centre Publications, 1990).

Jenkins, J. and R. Barrett. 'Introduction', in J. Jenkins and R. Barrett (eds) *Schizophrenia, Culture, and Subjectivity: The Edge of Experience* (Cambridge: Cambridge University Press, 2004).

Johnson, P. *Feminism as Radical Humanism* (St. Leonards, New South Wales: Allen and Unwin, 1994).

Kanel, K. *A Guide to Crisis Intervention* (Pacific Grove, CA: Brooks/Cole, 2003).

Kanter, J. 'Reevaluation of Task-Centred Social Work Practice', *Clinical Social Work Journal*, **11**(3) (1983), 228–44.

Kaplan, C. 'An Early Example of Brief Strengths Based Practice: Bertha Reynolds at the National Maritime Union', *Smith College Studies in Social Work*, **72**(3) (2002), 403–16.

Kemp, S., J. Whittaker and E. Tracy. *Person in Environment Practice: The Social Ecology of Interpersonal Helping.* (New York: Aldine de Gryter, 1997).

Kenen, R. 'The At-Risk Health Status and Technology: A Diagnostic Invitation and the Gift of Knowing', *Social Science and Medicine*, **42**(11) (1996), 1533–45.

Killen, K. (1996). 'How far have we come in dealing with the emotional challenge of abuse and neglect?', *Child Abuse and Neglect*, **20**, 791–5.

Kirk, S. and W. Reid. *Science and Social Work: A Critical Appraisal* (New York: Columbia University Press, 2002).

Kissman, K. and L. Maurer. 'East Meets West: Therapeutic Aspects of Spirituality in Health, Mental Health and Addiction Recovery', *International Social Work*, **45**(1) (2002), 35–43.

Kretzmann, J. and J. McKnight. *Building Communities from the Inside Out* (Chicago: Center for Urban Affairs and Policy Research, 1993).

Lees, R. *Politics and Social Work* (London: Routledge and Kegan Paul London, 1972).

Leighninger, R. 'Systems Theory', *Journal of Sociology and Social Welfare*, **5** (1978), 446–66.

Leonard, P. *Sociology in Social Work* (London: Routledge and Kegan Paul, 1966).

Leonard, P. 'Towards a Paradigm for Radical Practice', in R. Bailey and M. Brake (eds) *Radical Social Work* (London: Edward Arnold, 1975).

Leonard, P. *Postmodern Welfare: Reconstructing An Emancipatory Project* (London: Sage, 1997).

Levine, E. 'Church, State and Social Welfare: Purchase of Service and the Sectarian Agency', in M. Gibelman and H. Demone (eds) *The Privatization of Human Services: Policy and Practice Issues* (New York: Springer, 1998).

Lewis, G. *'Race', Gender, Social Welfare: Encounters in a Postcolonial Society* (Cambridge: Polity Press, 2000).

Lewis, H. 'Ethical Assessment', *Social Casework*, **65**(4) (1984), 203–11.

Lindsay, R. *Recognising Spirituality: The Interface between Faith and Social Work* (Nedlands, Western Australia: University of Western Australia Press, 2002).

Lupton, D. 'A Postmodern Public Health?', *Australian and New Zealand Journal of Public Health*, **22**(1) (1998), 3–5.

Lyall, D. 'Spiritual Institutions?', in H. Orchard (ed.) *Spirituality in Health Care Contexts* (London: Jessica Kingsley Publishers, 2001), pp. 47–56.

Lyotard, J. *The Postmodern Condition: A Report on Knowledge.* Trans. G. Bennington and B. Massumi (Minneapolis: University of Minnesota Press, 1984).

Lyons, M. *Third Sector: The Contribution of Nonprofit and Cooperative Enterprise in Australia* (St. Leonards, New South Wales: Allen and Unwin, 2001).

Maidment, J. and R. Egan (eds). *Practice Skills in Social Work and Welfare: More than Just Common Sense* (Crows Nest: Allen and Unwin, 2004).

Mainzer, K. *Thinking in Complexity: The Complex Dynamics of Matter, Mind, and Mankind* (Berlin: Springer, 1996).

Martin, J. 'Historical Development of Critical Social Work Practice', in J. Allan, B. Pease and L. Briskman (eds) *Critical Social Work: An Introduction to Theories and Practice* (Crows Nest, Sydney: Allen and Unwin, 2003), pp. 17–31.

Mattaini, M. and C. Meyer. 'The Ecosystems Perspective: Implications for Practice', in M. Mattaini, C. Lowery and C. Meyer (eds) *The Foundations of Social Work Practice: A Graduate Text* (Washington, DC: National Association of Social Workers Press, 2002), pp. 3–24.

McCartt-Hess, P. and E. Mullen. *Practitioner–Researcher Partnerships: Building Knowledge From, In, and For Practice* (Washington, DC: National Association of Social Workers Press, 1995).

McGrath, P. 'Chemotherapy, Bioethics and Social Work: Forging the Link', *Australian Social Work*, **50**(4) (1997), 53–60.

McLeod, E. and P. Bywaters. *Social Work, Health, and Equality* (London: Routledge, 2000).

McMillen, J.C. 'Better for it: How People Benefit from Adversity', *Social Work*, **44**(5) (1999), 455–68.

Meagher, G. and K. Healy. 'Caring, Controlling, Contracting, and Counting: Governments and Non-Profits in Community Services', *Australian Journal of Public Administration*, **62**(3) (2003), 40–51.

Messner, M. *The Politics of Masculinities: Men in Movements* (Thousand Oaks, CA: Sage, 1997).

Meyer, C. *Social Work Practice* (New York: The Free Press, 1976).

Meyer, C. *Assessment in Social Work Practice* (New York: Columbia University Press, 1993).

Middleman, R.R. and G. Goldberg. *Social Service Delivery: A Structural Approach to Social Work Practice* (New York: Columbia University Press, 1974).

Midgley, J. 'Colonialism and Welfare: A Post-Colonial Commentary', *Journal of Progressive Human Services*, **9**(2) (1998), 31–50.

Mishler, E. 'Critical Perspectives on the Biomedical Model', in P. Brown (eds) *Perspectives in Medical Sociology* (Belmont, CA: Wadsworth, 1989).

Moreau, M. 'Empowerment Through Advocacy and Consciousness-Raising: Implications of a Structural Approach', *Journal of Sociology and Social Welfare*, **17**(2) (1990), 53–67.

Mullaly, B. *Challenging Oppression: A Critical Social Work Approach* (Ontario: Oxford University Press, 2002).

Mullaly, R. *Structural Social Work: Ideology, Theory, and Practice* (Toronto: McClelland and Stewart, 1993).

Mune, M. 'Exploring the Utility of the General Systems Approach', in F. Pavlin, J. Crawley and P. Boas (eds) *Perspectives in Australian Social Work* (Bundoora, Victoria: PIT Publishing, 1979), pp. 61–77.

Munro, E. 'Avoidable and Unavoidable Mistakes in Child Protection Work', *British Journal of Social Work*, **26**(6) (1996), 793–808.

Munro, E. *Understanding Social Work: An Empirical Approach* (London: The Athlone Press, 1998).

Napier, L. and J. Fook (eds) *Breakthroughs in Practice: Theorising Critical Moments in Social Work* (London: Whiting and Birch, 2000).

O'Brien, M. and S. Penna. *Theorising Welfare: Enlightenment and Modern Society* (London: Sage, 1998).

O'Connell, B. *Solution-Focused Therapy* (London: Sage, 1998).

Oliver, M. 'Disability Issues in the Postmodern World', in L. Barton (ed.) *Disability Politics and the Struggle for Change* (London: David Fulton Publishers, 2001), pp. 149–55.

Opie, A. *Beyond Good Intentions: Support Work with Older People* (Wellington, New Zealand: Institute of Policy Studies, 1995).

Orchard, H. (ed.) *Spirituality in Health Care Contexts* (London: Jessica Kingsley Publishers, 2001).

Parad, H. *Crisis Intervention: Selected Readings* (New York: Family Service Association of America, 1965).

Parad, H. and L. Parad. 'A Study of Crisis-Oriented Planned Short-Term Treatment: Part 1', *Social Casework*, **49**(1968), 346–55.

Parker, N. 'Speaking About Human Rights', in R. Lawrence (ed.) *Norma Parker's Record of Service* (Sydney: The Australian Association of Social Work in association with the Department of Social Work at Sydney University and the Department of Social Work at the University of New South Wales, 1969).

Parsons, R., L. Gutiérrez and E. Cox. 'A Model for Empowerment Practice', in L. Gutiérrez, R. Parsons and E. Cox (eds) *Empowerment in Social Work Practice: A Sourcebook* (Pacific Grove: Brooks/Cole Publishing Company, 1998).

Parton, N. ' "Problematics of Government", (Post) Modernity and Social Work', *British Journal of Social Work*, **24** (1994), 9–32.

Parton, N. 'Some Thoughts on the Relationship Between Theory and Practice in and for Social Work', *British Journal of Social Work*, **30** (2000), 449–63.

Parton, N. 'Rethinking Professional Practice: The Contributions of Social Constructionism and the Feminist "Ethics of Care" ', *British Journal of Social Work*, **33** (2003), 1–16.

Parton, N. and P. O'Byrne. *Constructive Social Work: Towards a New Practice* (Basingstoke: Macmillan, 2001).

Payne, M. *Modern Social Work Theory*, 2nd edn (Basingstoke: Macmillan, 1997).

Pearman, J. *Social Science and Social Work: Applications of Social Science in the Helping Professions* (New Jersey: The Scarecrow Press, 1973).

Pearman, J. and B. Stewart. 'The Social and Behavioural Science Input to Social Work Practice', in J. Pearman (ed.) *Social Science and Social Work: Applications of Social Science in the Helping Professions* (New Jersey: The Scarecrow Press, 1973), pp. 9–22.

Pease, B. and J. Fook (eds). *Transforming Social Work Practice: Postmodern Critical Perspectives* (St. Leonards, New South Wales: Allen and Unwin, 1999).

Peile, C. *The Creative Paradigm: Insight, Synthesis and Knowledge Development* (Aldershot, England, Avebury, 1994).

Peile, C. 'Research Paradigms in Social Work: From Stalemate to Creative Synthesis', *The Social Service Review*, **62** (1988), 1–19.

Peile, C. and M. McCouat. 'The Rise of Relativism: The Future of Theory and Knowledge Development in Social Work', *British Journal of Social Work*, **27** (1997), 343–60.

Pelton, L. 'Child Abuse and Neglect: The Myth of Classlessness', *American Journal of Orthopsychiatry*, **48**(4) (1978), 608–17.

Perlman, H. *Social Casework: A Problem-Solving Process* (Chicago: The University of Chicago Press, 1957).

Perry, B. 'Childhood Experience and the Expression of Genetic Potential: What Childhood Neglect Tells Us about Nature and Nuture', *Brain and Mind*, **13**(1) (2002), 79–100.

Pincus, A. and A. Minahan. *Social Work Practice: Model and Method* (Madison: University of Wisconsin, 1973).

Puddifoot, J. 'Some Problems and Possibilities in the Study of Dynamical Social Processes', *Journal for the Theory of Social Behaviour*, **30**(1) (2000), 79–95.

Queensland Ombudsman, *Report of the Queensland Ombudsman: An Inquiry into the Adequacy of Actions of Certain Government Agencies in Relation to the Safety and Well-being of the Late Baby Kate who Died Aged 10 weeks* (Brisbane: Queensland Ombudsman's Office, 2003), 29 January, 2004. ⟨http://www.ombudsman.qld.gov.au/publications⟩

Quinn, P. *Understanding Disability: A Lifespan Approach* (Thousand Oaks, CA: Sage, 1998).

Rapp, C. *The Strengths Model: Case Management with People Suffering from Severe and Persistent Mental Illness* (New York: Oxford University Press, 1998).

Rapp, R. 'The Strengths Perspective and Persons with Substance Abuse Problems', in D. Saleebey (ed.) *The Strengths Perspective in Social Work Practice* (New York: Longman, 1997).

Reid, W. 'Task-Centered Treatment and Trends in Clinical Social Work', in W. Reid and L. Eptsein (eds) *Task-Centered Practice* (New York: Columbia University Press, 1977).

Reid, W. *Task-Strategies: An Empirical Approach to Clinical Social Work* (New York: Columbia University Press, 1992).

Reid, W. 'The Empirical Practice Movement', *Social Service Review*, **68** (1994), 165–84.

Reid, W. and L. Epstein. *Task-Centered Casework* (New York: Columbia University Press, 1972).

Reid, W. and A. Shyne. *Brief and extended casework* (New York: Columbia University Press, 1969).

Reisch, M. and J. Andrews. *The Road Not Taken: A History of Radical Social Work in the United States* (Philadelphia: Brunner–Routledge, 2001).

Reynolds, B. *Social Work and Social Living: Exploration in Philosophy and Practice* (New York: Citadel Press, 1951).

Richmond, M. *Social Diagnosis* (New York: Russell Sage Foundation, 1917).

Rojek, C., G. Peacock and S. Collins. *Social Work and Received Ideas* (London: Routledge, 1988).

Rose, N. *Governing the Soul: The Shaping of the Private Self* (London: Free Association Books, 1999).

Rosenman, L., I. O'Connor and K. Healy. 'Social Work', in The Academy of Social Sciences in Australia (ed.) *Challenges for the Social Sciences in Australia* (Canberra: Australian Government Publishing Service, 1998), pp. 215–21.

Saleebey, D. 'The Strengths Perspective in Social Work Practice: Extensions and Cautions', *Social Work*, **41** (1996), 296–305.

Saleebey, D. (ed.) 'Introduction: Power in the People', in *The Strengths Perspective in Social Work Practice*, 2nd edn (New York: Longman, 1997), pp. 3–19.

Saleebey, D. (ed.) *The Strengths Perspective in Social Work Practice*, 3rd edn (Boston, MA: Allyn and Bacon, 2002).

Sandberg, P. 'Genetic Information and Life Insurance: A Proposal for an Ethical European Policy', *Social Science and Medicine*, **40**(11) (1995), 1549–59.

Sandler, T. *Economic Concepts for the Social Sciences* (Cambridge: Cambridge University Press, 2001).

Sawicki, J. *Disciplining Foucault: Feminism, Power and the Body* (New York: Routledge, 1991).

Schön, D. *The Reflective Practitioner* (New York: Basic Books, 1983).

Schön, D. 'Reflective Inquiry in Social Work Practice', in P. McCartt-Hess and E. Mullen (eds) *Practitioner–Researcher Partnerships: Building Knowledge From, In, and For Practice* (Washington, DC: National Association of Social Workers Press, 1995), pp. 31–55.

Scott, D. 'Creating Social Capital: The Distinctive Role of the Non-Government Agency', *Children Australia*, **24**(1) (1999), 4–7.

Semidei, J., L.F. Radel and C. Nolan. 'Substance Abuse and Child Welfare: Clear Linkages and Promising Responses', *Child Welfare*, **LXXX**(2) (2001), 109–27.

Shah, H. ' "It's Up to You Sisters": Black Women and Radical Social Work', in M. Langan and M. Lee (eds) *Radical Social Work Today* (London: Unwin Hyman, 1989), pp. 178–91.

Shakespeare, T. 'Rights, Risks and Responsibilities: New Genetics and Disabled People', in S. Williams, L. Birke and G. Bendelow (eds) *Debating Biology: Sociological Reflections on Health, Medicine and Society* (London: Routledge, 2003), pp. 198–209.

Shanahan, D. 'Churches Allowed to Discriminate'. *The Australian*, 6 October 2000, p. 7.

Sheldon, B. 'Cognitive Behavioural Methods in Social Care: Looking at the Evidence', in P. Stepney and D. Ford (eds) *Social Work Models, Methods and Theories* (Dorset: Russell House Publishing, 2000), pp. 65–83.

Shoemaker, L. 'Early Conflicts in Social Work Education', *Social Service Review*, **72**(2) (1998), 182–92.

Simpkin, M. *Trapped Within Welfare: Surviving Social Work* (London: Macmillan, 1979).

Smith, C. 'Trust and Confidence: Possibilities for Social Work in 'High Modernity', *British Journal of Social work*, **31**(2) (2001), 287–305.

Smith, D. and M. Vanstone. 'Probation and Social Justice', *British Journal of Social Work*, **32**(6) (2002), 815–30.

Stein, H.D. 'Social science in social work practice and education', in H. Parad (ed.) *Ego Psychology and Dynamic Casework: Papers from the Smith College School for Social Work* (New York: Family Service Association of America, 1958), pp. 226–40.

Stein, H. 'Social Science and Social Work Education', in N. Aronoff (ed.) *Challenge and Change in Social Work Education: Toward a World View, Selected Papers by Herman D. Stein* (Virginia: Council on Social Work Education, 2003), pp. 101–18.

Stillwell, F. 'Neoclassical Economics: A Long Cul-de-Sac', in F. Stillwell and G. Argyrous (eds) *Economics as a Social Science: Readings in Political Economy* (Sydney: Pluto Press, 1996).

Stoez, D. 'Renaissance', *Families in Society*, **81**(6) (2000), 621–628

Sullivan, M. *Sociology and Social Welfare* (London: Unwin Hyman, 1987).

Summers, N. *Fundamentals for Practice with High-Risk Populations* (Pacific Grove, CA: Thompson Brooks/Cole, 2003).

Swain, P. 'A Critical Alliance? Some Concluding Thoughts', in P. Swain (ed.) *In the Shadow of the Law: The Legal Context of Social Work Practice* (Annandale, Sydney: The Federation Press, 2002a), pp. 266–8.

Swain, P. 'Confidentiality, Record-Keeping and Social Work Practice', in P. Swain (ed.) *In the Shadow of the Law: The Legal Context of Social Work Practice* (Annandale, Sydney: The Federation Press, 2002b), pp. 28–49.

Swain, P. 'Why Social Work and Law?', in P. Swain (ed.) *In the Shadow of the Law: The Legal Context of Social Work Practice* (Annandale, Sydney: The Federation Press, 2002c), pp. 2–6.

Taylor, C. and S. White. *Practising Reflexivity in Health and Welfare: Making Knowledge* (Buckingham: Open University Press, 2000).

Taylor, S. 'A Case of Genetic Discrimination: Social Work Advocacy Within a New Context', *Australian Social Work*, **51**(1) (1998), 51–7.

Taylor, S. 'The New Quest for Genetic Knowledge: The Need for Critique and Compromise in Predictive Technologies', in J. Daly, M. Gullemin and S. Hill (eds) *Technologies and Health: Critical Compromises* (Melbourne: Oxford University Press, 2001), pp. 2–15.

Thompson, N. *Theory and Practice in Health and Social Welfare* (Buckingham: Open University Press, 1995).

Thompson, N. *Anti-discriminatory Practice* (Basingstoke: Macmillan, 1997).

Thompson, N. *Promoting Equality: Challenging Discrimination and Oppression* (Basingstoke: Palgrave Macmillan, 2003).

Thornton, M. 'Neo-Liberalism, Discrimination and the Politics of Ressentiment', in M. Jones and L. Basser Marks (eds) *Explorations on Law and Disability in Australia* (Annandale, Sydney: The Federal Press, 2000), pp. 8–27.

Throssell, H. 'Social Work Overview', in H. Throssell (ed.) *Social Work: Radical Essays* (Brisbane, Queensland: Queensland University Press, 1975), pp. 3–25.

Trinder, L. 'Evidence-Based Practice in Social Work and Probation', in L. Trinder and S. Reynolds (eds) *Evidence-Based Practice: A Critical Appraisal* (Oxford: Blackwell Science, 2000), pp. 138–62.

Tripcony, P. 'Too Obvious to See: Aboriginal Spirituality and Cosmology'. 1996 National Conference of the Australian Association of Religious Education, 15 December 2003. ‹http://www.oodgeroo.qut.edu.au/staff/research_papers›

Trotter, C. *Working with Involuntary Clients: A Guide to Practice* (St. Leonards, New South Wales: Allen and Unwin, 1999).

Turnell, A. and S. Edwards. *Signs of Safety: A Solution and Safety Oriented Approach to Child Protection Casework* (New York: Norton, 1999).

Turner, B. *Medical Power, Social Knowledge* (London: Sage, 1995).

Vallacher, R. and A. Nowak. 'The Emergence of Dynamical Social Psychology', *Psychological Enquiry*, 8(2) (1997), 73–99.

Van Wormer, K. *Counselling Female Offenders and Victims: A Strengths-Restorative Approach* (New York: Springer Publishers, 2001).

Van Wormer, K. and R. Davis. *Addiction Treatment: A Strengths Perspective* (Pacific Grove, CA: Brooks/Cole, 2003).

Von Bertalanffy, L. *General Systems Theory: Foundations, Development, Applications* (New York: George Braziller, 1968).

Wakefield, J. 'Does Social Work Need the Eco-Systems Perspective? Part 1: Is the Perspective Clinically Useful?', *The Social Service Review*, 70(1) (1996a), 1–32.

Wakefield, J. 'Does Social Work Need the Eco-Systems Perspective? Part 2: Does the Perspective Save Social Work from Incoherence?', *The Social Service Review*, 70(2) (1996b), 183–213.

Warren, K., C. Franklin and C. Streeter. 'New Directions in Systems Theory: Chaos and Complexity', *Social Work*, 43(4) (1998), 357–72.

Weakland, J., R. Fisch, P. Watzlawick and A. Bodin. 'Brief Therapy: Focused Problem Resolution', *Family Process*, 13 (1974), 141–68.

Weedon, C. *Feminist Practice and Poststructuralist Theory* (Oxford: Blackwell, 1997).

Weeks, W. (ed.) *Women Working Together: Lessons From Feminist Women's Services* (Melbourne: Longman Cheshire, 1994).

Weick, A., C. Rapp, P. Sullivan and W. Kisthardt. 'A Strengths Perspective for Social Work Practice', *Social Work*, July (1989), 350–54.

White, C. and D. Denborough (eds) *Introducing Narrative Therapy: A Collection of Practice-Based Writings* (Adelaide: Dulwich Centre Publications, 1998).

White, M. and D. Epston. *Narrative Means to Therapeutic Ends* (New York: WW Norton, 1990).

Williams, S. *Medicine and the Body* (London: Sage, 2003).

Wilson, E. 'Feminism and Social Work', in R. Bailey and M. Brake (eds) *Radical Social Work and Practice* (London: Edward Arnold, 1980), pp. 26–42.

Wingard, B. 'Introducing "Sugar"', in C. White and D. Denborough (eds) *Introducing Narrative Therapy: A Collection of Practice Based Writings* (Adelaide: Dulwich Centre, 1998).

Wise, S. 'Becoming a Feminist Social Worker', in L. Stanley (ed.) *Feminist Praxis: Research, Theory and Epistemology in Feminist Sociology* (London: Routledge, 1990).

Wise, S. 'Feminist Ethics in Practice', in R. Hugman and D. Smith (eds) *Ethical Issues in Social Work* (London: Routledge, 1995), pp. 104–19.

Woods, M.E. and F. Hollis. *Casework: A Psychosocial Therapy*, 4th edn (New York: McGraw-Hill, 1990).

Younghusband, E. *Social Work in Britain: 1950–1975, A Follow-Up Study* (London: Allen and Unwin, 1978).

Index

Addams, J. 175

Anleu, S. 41

anti-oppressive practice 14, 103, 197; background 172; case study 181–3; challenges of 189; in context 172–3; and contribution of local change processes 188–9; core assumptions of 179–81; critical assessment of service users' experiences 184; critical reflections 183, 188–91; definition of 179; emergence of 178; empowering service users 185–6; growing popularity of 189; and high-risk decision-making 189; and impact of institutional context 191; interaction of oppressions 180–1; intervention strategies 181; limitations of 189–90; and minimal intervention 187–8, 189–90; multiple forms of oppression 179–80; political role of social work 180; and power relations 190–1; and promotion of dialogue 190; and reliance on oppositional stance 190; and social divisions/disempowerment 180; and value of social justice 188; and working in partnership 186–7, *see also* modern critical social work

anti-racist social work 176, 177

asset-based community development 165

Atherton, C. 144–5

Ball, C. 35

Banks, S. 7

Bertalanffy, L. von 134

biomedical discourse 18, 73; biological reductionism of 25; and contribution to social oppression 26; criticism of 19, 25–7; definition of 20–1; equity/confidentiality implications of 23; and focus/nature of assessment 22; and

holistic approach 25–6; and improvements in management/treatment of illness 24; and increased medicalization 26; interest in 20; key ideas 21–2; power/influence of 20, 22; practical effects of 22; and predictive genetic information 22–3; and shaping of practice 22–3; and social justice 26–7; specificity of view 21; truth status of 22; understanding of 19; uses, issues, problems 24–7

biomedicine 8, 12

Bolland, K. 144–5

Bourdieu, P. 36

Bowlby, J. 50

Brayne, H. *et al.* 36, 37, 38

Brief Therapy Centre 156

Brown, L. 114, 115, 116, 124, 125

Burke, B. 179, 187, 189

Butler, J. 2002

Caplan, G. 125

Carniol, B. 178

Charity Organisation Society (COS) 98

Cixous, H. 195, 202

cognitive behavioural therapy (CBT) 54

collaborative approach 161–2; creative solution seeking 163; interpersonal relationships 162–3; physical environment 162

community 69, 71; change built on capacities/assets 165–6; change from inside 165; change oriented towards sustainable growth 166; change as relationship driven 166; creation of 164–5; need for 73–4

complex systems theories, application of 144–5, 145; background 142–3; change as usual feature of 143; definition of 143; deterministic chaos